...FOR DUMMIES

COMPUTER
BOOK SERIES
FROM IDG

Great Software For Kids & Parents™

Cheat Sheet

About the Family Computer

Computer maker _____

Model _____

Processor _____

Clock speed (MHz) _____

RAM (MB) _____

Available hard disk space (MB) _____

Monitor _____

CD-ROM drive speed _____

Operating system (version) _____

Six Steps to Shopping Smarts

1. **Do your homework.**

   • Choose the software "food groups" that you want to add to your library.

   • Zero in on specific titles by reading this book and talking with your kids' teachers, the school technology coordinator, and friends. Compare their opinions with reviews in magazines and newspapers or on the World Wide Web.

2. **List the *exact* capabilities of your computer.**

   • Make sure you have the list handy when you shop or order.

3. **Try before you buy.**

   • Order demo disks that let you preview a software company's programs.

   • Look at demos available on software publishers' World Wide Web sites.

   • Look for retailers with "try-out" computer systems that let you test software.

   • Visit a computer show or a children's museum to see programs first-hand before you shop.

4. **Ask questions while you test, for example:**

   • Does the software create a really unique learning experience for my kids?

   • Will my kids get to actively participate? Or will they mostly watch, point, and click?

   • Does all the multimedia really enhance learning? Or are there cool effects just for technology's sake?

5. **Compare the fine print on the package to your computer's capabilities.**

6. **Learn the store's return policy.**

   • For example, choose retailers who let you return CD-ROMs that don't live up to your expectations.

The Dummies Guide to Family Computing™

Great Software For Kids & Parents™

...For Dummies
COMPUTER BOOK SERIES FROM IDG

Cheat Sheet

Basic Skills to Teach Your Kids

1. How to point, double click, and navigate within kids' programs
2. How to turn on and shut down the computer
3. How to use the features of their special desktop and launch their programs from the main screen
4. How to open and close a program
5. How to name and save their games, written files, or artwork
6. How to use the pull-down menus, icons, and commands
7. How to handle CD-ROMs and floppy disks
8. How to adjust the volume
9. How to use the microphone
10. How to restart the system

Hallmarks of Good Software

- Provides fun learning experiences
- Invites active participation, exploration, and discovery
- Offers an opportunity for kids to put their new-found knowledge to work
- Includes great design and use of multimedia (multimedia that *really* adds value to the learning experience)
- Is appealing and easy to use
- Has high replay value (brings kids back again and again)
- Brings something unique to your child's experience or something that only the computer can provide

Basic Rules for Kids

Forget food, and don't drink. Crumbs always wind up where they don't belong, and drinks eventually spill.

Beware of magnets. They can mess up data on floppy disks and wreck your computer screen.

Make a mess somewhere else. Pencil-sharpener shavings, paper clips, crayons, glue sticks, and the like have their place — but not near computers!

Handle CD-ROMs with care. They're tough but not indestructible. Be careful as you remove and replace CD-ROMs in their cases. Gently open and close the computer's CD-ROM tray.

Save your work frequently. We can't say that enough!

Stick to your own programs. Although *do* explore when an adult says some exploration and experimentation is okay.

Get parental okay *each and every* time you go online. Do this even if you're only downloading e-mail — and honor the time limits for online use.

***Never* give out personal information.** This includes things such as gender, full name, phone number, or address.

Keep passwords secret. Don't write them down. Parents should also change passwords from time to time.

Don't register for anything — for example, a Web site, a contest, a survey. First check with a parent.

The Dummies Guide to Family Computing™

GREAT SOFTWARE FOR KIDS & PARENTS™

by Cathy Miranker
and Alison Elliott

Foreword by Oliver Strimpel
Executive Director, The Computer Museum

IDG BOOKS WORLDWIDE™

IDG Books Worldwide, Inc.
An International Data Group Company

Foster City, CA ♦ Chicago, IL ♦ Indianapolis, IN ♦ Southlake, TX

Great Software For Kids & Parents™

Published by
IDG Books Worldwide, Inc.
An International Data Group Company
919 E. Hillsdale Blvd.
Suite 400
Foster City, CA 94404
http://www.idgbooks.com (IDG Books Worldwide Web site)
http://www.dummies.com (Dummies Press Web site)

Library of Congress Catalog Card No.: 96-079268

ISBN: 0-7645-0099-6

Printed in the United States of America

10 9 8 7 6 5 4 3 2

1B/SQ/QT/ZW/IN

Distributed in the United States by IDG Books Worldwide, Inc.

Distributed by Macmillan Canada for Canada; by Transworld Publishers Limited in the United Kingdom and Europe; by WoodsLane Pty. Ltd. for Australia; by WoodsLane Enterprises Ltd. for New Zealand; by Longman Singapore Publishers Ltd. for Singapore, Malaysia, Thailand, and Indonesia; by Simron Pty. Ltd. for South Africa; by Toppan Company Ltd. for Japan; by Distribuidora Cuspide for Argentina; by Livraria Cultura for Brazil; by Ediciencia S.A. for Ecuador; by Addison-Wesley Publishing Company for Korea; by Ediciones ZETA S.C.R. Ltda. for Peru; by WS Computer Publishing Company, Inc., for the Philippines; by Unalis Corporation for Taiwan; by Contemporanea de Ediciones for Venezuela. Authorized Sales Agent: Anthony Rudkin Associates for the Middle East and North Africa.

For general information on IDG Books Worldwide's books in the U.S., please call our Consumer Customer Service department at 800-762-2974. For reseller information, including discounts and premium sales, please call our Reseller Customer Service department at 800-434-3422.

For information on where to purchase IDG Books Worldwide's books outside the U.S., please contact our International Sales department at 415-655-3023 or fax 415-655-3299.

For information on foreign language translations, please contact our Foreign & Subsidiary Rights department at 415-655-3021 or fax 415-655-3281.

For sales inquiries and special prices for bulk quantities, please contact our Sales department at 415-655-3200 or write to the address above.

For information on using IDG Books Worldwide's books in the classroom or for ordering examination copies, please contact our Educational Sales department at 800-434-2086 or fax 817-251-8174.

For press review copies, author interviews, or other publicity information, please contact our Public Relations department at 415-655-3000 or fax 415-655-3299.

For authorization to photocopy items for corporate, personal, or educational use, please contact Copyright Clearance Center, 222 Rosewood Drive, Danvers, MA 01923, or fax 508-750-4470.

 is a trademark under exclusive license to IDG Books Worldwide, Inc., from International Data Group, Inc.

About the Authors

Cathy Miranker and **Alison Elliott** are "moms with a mission": They intend to make sure their kids (and yours) have nothing but "smart fun" with the family computer.

Cathy and Alison began to evaluate and review kids' software several years ago, when they went looking for truly great software for their kids. At the time, they discovered that there were no good independent sources of impartial information about kids' software for parents. In partnership with The Computer Museum in Boston, they first ventured into print with *The Computer Museum Guide to the Best Software for Kids.* They continue to assist the museum with their software expertise. Among other things, their activities include selecting the software for the popular The Best Software for Kids Gallery exhibit at The Computer Museum.

Cathy and Alison bring their collective experience in the areas of education, journalism, the computer industry, and, of course, parenting to their work with kids' software.

Like a great many people who work with computers, neither Cathy nor Alison started out as a computer professional! In her first career — and both authors have had several! — Alison was a teacher on the East Coast, responsible for inspiring 6th, 7th, and 8th graders to learn — and love — history and English. After heading West, Alison went to work at Apple, marketing the Apple II computer. She's worked in Silicon Valley ever since, developing and marketing software for education and business.

Alison's latest professional incarnation — author and kids' software guru — allows her to combine her understanding of software and her experience of how kids learn. She lives in the San Francisco Bay area with her husband Steve, daughters Katie and Sarah, assorted family pets, and five computers.

Writing about kids' software is career No. 3 for Cathy. She started out on the East Coast as an editor and reporter, migrated West, and wrote a weekly newspaper column about the computer industry before switching gears. Career No. 2 saw Cathy working as a wordsmith for the marketing groups at start-up computer companies in Silicon Valley.

Cathy sees her work with kids' software as a natural extension of her experience as a critical observer and an exacting writer. She lives in the San Francisco Bay area with her husband Glen, daughters Emily and Molly, one dog, two hamsters, and five computers.

ABOUT IDG BOOKS WORLDWIDE

Welcome to the world of IDG Books Worldwide.

IDG Books Worldwide, Inc., is a subsidiary of International Data Group, the world's largest publisher of computer-related information and the leading global provider of information services on information technology. IDG was founded more than 25 years ago and now employs more than 8,500 people worldwide. IDG publishes more than 275 computer publications in over 75 countries (see listing below). More than 60 million people read one or more IDG publications each month.

Launched in 1990, IDG Books Worldwide is today the #1 publisher of best-selling computer books in the United States. We are proud to have received eight awards from the Computer Press Association in recognition of editorial excellence and three from *Computer Currents'* First Annual Readers' Choice Awards. Our best-selling *...For Dummies*® series has more than 30 million copies in print with translations in 30 languages. IDG Books Worldwide, through a joint venture with IDG's Hi-Tech Beijing, became the first U.S. publisher to publish a computer book in the People's Republic of China. In record time, IDG Books Worldwide has become the first choice for millions of readers around the world who want to learn how to better manage their businesses.

Our mission is simple: Every one of our books is designed to bring extra value and skill-building instructions to the reader. Our books are written by experts who understand and care about our readers. The knowledge base of our editorial staff comes from years of experience in publishing, education, and journalism — experience we use to produce books for the '90s. In short, we care about books, so we attract the best people. We devote special attention to details such as audience, interior design, use of icons, and illustrations. And because we use an efficient process of authoring, editing, and desktop publishing our books electronically, we can spend more time ensuring superior content and spend less time on the technicalities of making books.

You can count on our commitment to deliver high-quality books at competitive prices on topics you want to read about. At IDG Books Worldwide, we continue in the IDG tradition of delivering quality for more than 25 years. You'll find no better book on a subject than one from IDG Books Worldwide.

John Kilcullen
President and CEO
IDG Books Worldwide, Inc.

*Eighth Annual
Computer Press
Awards ≥1992*

*Ninth Annual
Computer Press
Awards ≥1993*

*Tenth Annual
Computer Press
Awards ≥1994*

*Eleventh Annual
Computer Press
Awards ≥1995*

Dedication

To our families — our husbands Glen and Steve and our girls Emily, Molly, Katie, and Sarah — and to our friends at The Computer Museum.

Authors' Acknowledgments

This message is for the most wonderful families in the world — our husbands and daughters, our extended family at The Computer Museum, the "test" families who helped evaluate every software program in this book, and our editorial family at IDG Books.

As this book was going to press, our kids weren't thinking kind thoughts about it! "The book" was to blame when we were late picking them up at school; when we missed the soccer game, the dance performance, and the piano recital; and when we opted out of many evenings and weekends of family fun.

But, girls: It was your curiosity about computers that got us started in the first place! And we want to thank you for being as understanding as kids can be about our devotion to this project, for being the "guinea pigs" who helped test hundreds and hundreds of CD-ROMs, and for inspiring us with your enthusiasm.

Our husbands had their curmudgeonly moments, too! But we can't imagine a more wonderful pair than Glen and Steve. Your insights, your technical know-how, and your involvement with the kids have been invaluable to us.

Credit for creative ideas and wordsmithing also goes to Cathy's parents. And thanks for all that extra babysitting!

After working with The Computer Museum for the past four years, we regard the people there as our extended, East Coast family. It was Gwen Bell, the museum's founding president, who got us started on our first book about children's software. She helped us tap into the expertise of Museum staff and board members and spurred our subsequent ventures. Since then, we've been privileged to work with the museum's staff to develop the popular The Best Software for Kids Gallery exhibit and to extend our work to the World Wide Web. Our thanks to: Oliver Strimpel, John Marchiony, Gail Jennes, Carol Welsh, Mary McCann, Betsy Riggs, Gail Breslow, Christopher Grotke, Lise LePage, Larry Weber, Mitchel Resnick, David Greschler, Diane Franklin, Brian Lee, Owen Mysliwy, Jane Hussey, and other Museum colleagues. And special thanks to Sari Boren for providing the technical review of this book.

Far too numerous to mention by name — sorry, guys! — are all the parents, kids, and teachers who tested software for us and shared their insights with us. Our test families went far beyond a simple "thumbs up" or "thumbs down" reaction, helping us understand which software "clicked" for their kids, which didn't, and why.

Finally, our thanks to all the people at IDG, who understood the need for this book and got it into print fast. Our special thanks to Diane Steele, who had the vision for this series; Seta Frantz who guided us through the ...*For Dummies* process; our project editor Melba Hopper with her eagle eye; Chris Collins who was always there when we needed him; Kristin Cocks who was there when Chris wasn't; Shelley Lea for his photo wizardry, Joyce Pepple who sweated the details; Kevin Spencer and Mary Bednarek who made the CD-ROM a reality; and Judi Taylor who helped get us noticed.

And to Margot Maley, our agent: Thanks for believing in us!

Publisher's Acknowledgments

We're proud of this book; please send us your comments about it by using the Reader Response Card at the back of the book or by e-mailing us at feedback/dummies@idgbooks.com. Some of the people who helped bring this book to market include the following:

Acquisitions, Development, & Editorial

Project Editor: Melba D. Hopper

Acquisitions Editor: Tammy Goldfeld

Product Development Manager: Mary Bednarek

Permissions Editor: Joyce Pepple

Technical Reviewer: Sari Boren, Kevin Spencer

General Reviewers: Elizabeth D. Thorne, Debra H. Bush

Editorial Manager: Seta K. Frantz

Editorial Assistants: Chris H. Collins, Constance Carlisle

Production

Project Coordinator: Debbie Stailey

Layout and Graphics: Brett Black, Linda M. Boyer, Elizabeth Cárdenas-Nelson, J. Tyler Connor, Maridee V. Ennis, Angela F. Hunckler, Drew R. Moore, Brent Savage, Kate Snell

Proofreaders: Betty Kish, Rachel Garvey, Nancy Price, Dwight Ramsey, Robert Springer, Carrie Voorhis, Karen York

Indexer: Steve Rath

General and Administrative

IDG Books Worldwide, Inc.: John Kilcullen, CEO; Steven Berkowitz, President and Publisher

IDG Books Technology Publishing: Brenda McLaughlin, Senior Vice President and Group Publisher

Dummies Technology Press and Dummies Editorial: Diane Graves Steele, Vice President and Associate Publisher; Judith A. Taylor, Brand Manager; Kristin A. Cocks, Editorial Director

Dummies Trade Press: Kathleen A. Welton, Vice President and Publisher; Stacy S. Collins, Brand Manager

IDG Books Production for Dummies Press: Beth Jenkins, Production Director; Cindy L. Phipps, Supervisor of Project Coordination, Production Proofreading, and Indexing; Kathie S. Schutte, Supervisor of Page Layout; Shelley Lea, Supervisor of Graphics and Design; Debbie J. Gates, Production Systems Specialist; Tony Augsburger, Supervisor of Reprints and Bluelines; Leslie Popplewell, Media Archive Coordinator

Dummies Packaging and Book Design: Patti Sandez, Packaging Specialist; Lance Kayser, Packaging Assistant; Kavish+Kavish, Cover Design

◆

The publisher would like to give special thanks to Patrick J. McGovern, without whom this book would not have been possible.

◆

Contents at a Glance

Cartoons at a Glance

By Rich Tennant • Fax: 508-546-7747 • E-mail: the5wave@tiac.net

page 11

page 33

page 57

page 123

page 155

page 291

page 253

Table of Contents

Foreword

Here at The Computer Museum, we're always on the lookout for new ways to inspire people about technology. Over the years, we've developed hundreds of interactive exhibits that give kids and parents hands-on insight into the possibilities — and pleasures — of computing. Visitors can set our collection of robots in motion and watch the antics of computer-powered toys. Walking past our "antique" computers, they can see how enormous computers (and the components inside them) once were and how quickly they shrank. Families can try out virtual-reality machines. Kids can create computer-controlled laser light shows. Virtual visitors to our cyberspace location can work together on an electronic puzzle.

For sheer fun, nothing beats The Walk-Through Computer 2000. It's a gigantic scale-model of a personal computer, and it really works. Kids love scrambling over its enormous keyboard and rolling a trackball the size of a car. By reversing reality and making people seem small and components seem big, the Walk-Through dispels the notion that computers are an unapproachable domain.

Because computers are only as good as the software they run, we also have the Best Software for Kids Gallery for kids and parents to explore. This exhibit features a constantly changing collection of the best kids' titles available. The Gallery radiates cheerfulness and energy (not to mention noise, both from the software and the kids who try it out!). It's our way of giving kids from all walks of life hands-on computing time and of offering busy parents helpful yet bite-sized (or should I say byte-sized?) information about choosing programs that can inspire their kids to create, explore, and learn by doing.

Why am I telling you this? Of course, I'd love you to visit the Kids' Software Gallery (and all our exhibits) in person or pay us a cyberspace visit. But you already have access to the same expertise we tapped in creating this exhibit!

That's because the authors of *Great Software For Kids & Parents* — Cathy Miranker and Alison Elliott — were our co-curators. They selected the software for our exhibit. They wrote the evaluations that parents can read while their kids play. They shared insights from real families who tested the programs. And they provided guidelines for museum-goers to follow as they try to gauge a program's value for themselves. And what Cathy and Alison helped us achieve in our exhibit space, they're now doing for you in print.

Great Software For Kids & Parents is a lively, one-stop educational resource that makes it easy for parents — and teachers — to zero in on software that inspires kids to create and learn. It's filled with profiles of CD-ROMs that feature inventive, hands-on opportunities for learning. It's filled with tips, advice, and guidelines. It's filled with ideas for activities that will help your kids get more mileage out of their software. And it's filled with cyberspace suggestions, too, for finding fun learning adventures on the World Wide Web.

With *Great Software For Kids & Parents* as your guide, I think you'll find it's as easy to select great software for your kids as it is to choose clothing that fits.

As you try the programs recommended in the pages that follow, please keep us in mind. Send us e-mail at guide@tcm.org. We'd love to share your software opinions with visitors to the Kids' Software Gallery. Think of us as a long-distance resource for putting parents who care about software in touch with each other, in touch with Museum experts, and in touch with software gurus like Cathy and Alison.

Oliver Strimpel
Executive Director
The Computer Museum

Introduction

● ●

*E*very family has a different story about how and when the computer came into their lives. In our case, it arrived because of work. But no matter how a computer gets into kids' lives, its effect on them seems universal. Toddlers climb right up onto your lap and try to "compute," too. Preschoolers tug your elbow and chant "Me, too! Me, too!" Kids in the early grades demand a turn. And preteens and teens may even demand one of their own.

We were delighted by our kids' interest, their confidence, and their instant competence (compared to ours). And we were excited by the prospect of hunting up software for them At first, that is. Then we got a glimpse of the darker side of kids' software.

Like the time we saw that avid, absorbed look on our kids' faces when they somehow got their hands on an action game. Or the time they got the glazed-over look that comes from watching too much TV. Or the time they played a "learning" game for hours — but couldn't answer a single question about what they'd learned!

That's when we knew what we *didn't want* from our family computer:

  ✔ We didn't want it to turn into a high-priced video-game player.

  ✔ We didn't want it to be an electronic baby-sitter.

  ✔ We didn't want it to be a desktop TV.

We just *knew* kids' software could be better than that. So we set out to discover just how great it could be.

Our first stop was the country's No. 1 resource for kids and computing: The Computer Museum in Boston. It's a cross between a fun house and a living lab for interactive learning, with years of insight into how computers inspire kids to ask questions, explore, experiment, and have fun. Working with Museum experts, we began to define the ingredients of great kids' software:

  ✔ Creates inventive, hands-on opportunities for fun learning

  ✔ Offers kids something special, something that takes advantage of the computer's unique capabilities

> ✔ Encourages kids (and parents) to make connections between their computer-inspired discoveries and real life
>
> ✔ Fits in with our kids' lives without eclipsing the books and toys, games and adventures, and traditional pastimes that we value

And then, with those qualities in mind, the search was on! We tested more than 1,000 titles against those standards. And then we tested the best again — with kids ages 2-12, with parents like you, and with teachers, too.

The result: software titles, computing activities, and online adventures that inspire both fun and brain gain, that encourage kids to think creatively and learn independently.

What This Book Does

Our aim in these pages is to share our discoveries with parents and teachers of children 2-12. (But if you have older kids, too, don't despair. You can find lots of programs in these pages to challenge them, with suggested age ranges like 10-16, 11 & up, 7-13, 12 & up. And don't forget "all ages" software that can be used by everyone in the family.)

More than that, we concentrate on helping *you* become experts in your own right — so you can evaluate constantly emerging titles for yourself. But our advice about how to do the important things — like the following — will put you firmly in control for a long time to come:

> ✔ Evaluate software for yourself
>
> ✔ Build your own family software library
>
> ✔ Connect your kids' computer fun to their classroom activities
>
> ✔ Make computing a source of family fun

What's Where in This Book

Great Software For Kids & Parents has eight parts that tell you everything (we hope!) that you need to know to create great computing experiences for your kids. You can read them from beginning to end or in any order you like. Here are the parts of the book and what they contain.

Part I: Getting Started

As its title suggests, this part is chock full of the information, advice, and to-do lists you need to get kids started with their software.

Chapter 1, "Get Your Kids Computing — the Very First Day," is a great place to start if you're really new to family computing. It gives you a quick-start approach to getting those eager kids up and running — with the right kinds of software. You also find some good basic ground rules for your kids and handy checklists for you, which all make taking the next steps in family computing a snap.

In **Chapter 2, "Building a Family Software Library,"** we help you map out a plan for building a software library that's right for you and your kids. We cover the *kinds of software titles* that are good for kids at different ages. We get very specific about which *particular titles* are the right ones for your kids. And we offer great tips on shopping for the best software.

Part II: Launching Little Kids

Part II is little-kid territory. It covers all your software needs for kids 2-5.

It may come as a surprise, but even for kids as young as 2, you can find different categories of software! We tell you about the four types that are worthy of your consideration in **Chapter 3, "Playing to Learn."** You find learning-by-doing software, problem-solving adventures, creativity tools, and school-readiness programs. You also find ideas for weaving the family computer into the other activities you do to get your kids ready for school.

Part III: Building the Basics

With its focus on 3 'R software, Part III covers the best starter software for kids in the early grades.

Chapter 4, "Using the Computer to Help Raise Readers," covers the first of the 3 'Rs: reading. We see the learning-to-read process as part inspiration, part perspiration. And we identify software titles that correspond to both parts! Interactive stories can help you spark your kids' interest in books and ease their transition from listener to reader. We also cover skill-building reading games that encourage kids to practice the fundamentals, from beginning ABCs to phonics to spelling.

In **Chapter 5, "Using the Computer to Help Kids As Writers,"** you find computer programs that encourage every stage of your kids' development as writers. The programs range from storytelling software that lets little kids express themselves — before they can reliably wield a pencil — all the way to products with special appeal for the preteen crowd.

Chapter 6, "Using the Computer to Help Kids Master Math," is all about using the computer to help your kids grow up math literate — even if you're not! We're pleased to say that software developers are devoting lots of creative attention to math these days. You find titles that offer a playful, hands-on introduction to math concepts, math-facts drills, and thinking challenges that help kids gain confidence as problem solvers.

Part IV: Homework! Oh, Homework!

Part IV shows you and your kids how to use the computer to take the sting out of take-home assignments.

Aimed at families with older kids, **Chapter 7, "Writing It Down!,"** takes a look at using the computer for writing homework assignments. It covers different kinds of writing and typing programs, profiles several titles worth adding to your software library, and suggests new ways to tackle traditional assignments, such as book reports, by using writing software.

When you're ready to assemble a home reference library where kids can look up answers and find homework facts, turn to **Chapter 8, "Looking It Up!"** It covers the in's and out's of electronic research. It offers step-by-step pointers for showing kids the kind of information different CD-ROM and online resources offer. It also gives you pointers for demonstrating electronic look-it-up techniques.

Part V: Explorations for Inquiring Kids

This part is about the "places" the computer can take kids — and kids at heart.

Chapter 9, "Using the Computer for Explorations around the World," covers using the computer to help your kids grow up with geography smarts. We find that computer-based geography experiences tend to fall into three categories, and this chapter offers a look at all three: geography games, CD-ROM references, and Web encounters with distant places and people. You also find lots of suggestions for integrating software with off-the-computer activities.

Chapter 10, "Using the Computer for Explorations Back in Time," abounds in ideas for making history accessible and appealing for your kids. We tell you about historical "simulations" that thrust kids into someone else's shoes so they can experience the hopes, hardships, and challenges of historical figures. We also cover Web resources and reference CD-ROMs that shine at making history facts and figures easy to research.

We hope that **Chapter 11, "Doing Science On-Screen,"** convinces you that science really can happen on the computer! The software in this chapter gives kids a real feel for doing and enjoying science. They get to think *and* act like scientists, posing questions and discovering answers for themselves. We also offer plenty of ideas for connecting on-screen science to the real thing!

The software in **Chapter 12, "Stimulating the Brain — with Simulation Software,"** lets kids do things they could never, ever do in real life. These programs are called *simulations*. Think of them as incredibly sophisticated "let's pretend" games, aimed at kids in the double-digit ages. But don't be fooled by the word *game*. Simulations are great for giving kids mental exercise and insight into real-life situations.

Chapter 13, "Using the Computer to Learn Foreign Languages," suggests ways you can immerse kids in the sights and sounds of foreign countries via the computer. We talk about software that can tutor kids in a new language, test them, and tempt them to explore new words, people, and places, and then test their learning. You also find some great Web adventures with foreign languages.

Part VI: Creative Pursuits

Throughout this book, we encourage parents to use their kids' software. It's fun, it's educational, and it gives you a new connection with your children. But the programs in Part VI may be the ones you like best!

Chapter 14, "Cool Tools for Cool Kids," introduces cutting-edge creativity software that entices kids to explore new ways of working with words, images, and sounds. Because they yield such intriguing results, these "cool tools" are great for enterprising computer users and older kids who are eager for sophisticated artistic challenges.

Chapter 15, "Painting, Publishing, and Perusing Art," looks at painting, animation, and publishing programs, along with the wealth of creative activities these programs inspire for kids. We also tell you about CD-ROMs and Web sites where families can explore artwork from different eras and cultures.

Part VII: The Part of Tens

Crammed with lists and computing tips, the **Part of Tens** is a grab bag of helpful (but miscellaneous) goodies. So if you like lists, head straight to this part.

Chapter 16, "Ten (well, nine) Lists of Our Favorite Kids' Software," is a series of extremely useful lists of our favorite software for different ages and different purposes. There are lists for 2- to 3-year-olds, 4- to 5-year-olds, 6- to 7-year-olds, 8- to 9-year-olds, and 10- to 14-year-olds. You also find our most essential list — "The Ten Must-Have Titles for Every Family."

Chapter 17, "Creating Screen Captures for Off-the-Computer Activities," is a very how-to oriented chapter. It steps you through the process of *capturing* and printing scenes from your kids' programs. And it suggests some fun and instructive things to do with those screen captures.

Chapter 18, "Using the Computer to Help Raise Great Girls," features intriguing Web sites of special interest to girls who are on the brink of adolescence. In this chapter, you find some great resources (some for moms, some for daughters) for grappling with tough growing-up issues.

If there are boys in your life, we'd like to hear from you. Please let us know at `feedback/dummies@idgbooks.com` about boys' only sites and advice sites for parents of boys. We'd love to know about them.

Part VIII: Appendixes

You find more helpful lists in the three appendixes that are part of this book.

If you're interested in a particular product, turn to **Appendix A.** It's an alphabetical listing of all the titles we mention in the book.

Appendix B lists all the software publishers whose products are profiled in this book. Plus it gives you helpful contact information like phone numbers and Web addresses.

Finally, **Appendix C** tells you about using the CD-ROM that comes with this book. You can use the CD-ROM to take a closer look at some of our favorite software.

Conventions Used in This Book

We do a lot of little tricks with typography and design in this book to make important information jump right out at you. Here they are.

"In This Chapter" lists: Let's start at the very beginning, with the lists at the start of every chapter. They represent a kind of table of contents in miniature. They tell you the topics we cover; the software we profile at length; and the age range for which they are best suited.

Age range: By the way, whenever we profile a program, we also put the age range right next to the title. In pretty big print, too! That way, you can easily spot titles that match your kids' ages as you flip through the pages of this book.

Software round-ups: We also provide short descriptions of other programs related to our main software profiles. They're easy to spot, too; just look for text within the shaded "electronic" screens.

Italics: We put the names of software series (like the *Mighty Math* series) and the titles of individual programs (like *Orly's Draw-A-Story*) in italics. We also use italics for emphasis, for new terms, and for foreign words or phrases.

Capitalization: We capitalize the first letters in the names of activities within a software program, for example, the Make-A-Movie activity in *Sammy's Science House*. A capitalized word (or words) in quote marks usually refers to a section within a chapter of this book, such as the "Wordplay" section of Chapter 5.

Numbered lists: We provide numbered lists when we suggest that you follow steps in a specific order.

Bulleted lists: Often we provide bulleted lists. We use these lists for things that you can do in any order or for special descriptive information.

Web addresses: When we describe activities or sites of interest on the World Wide Web, we include the address or Uniform Resource Locator (URL) in a special typeface often like this: `http://www.tcm.net`.

Don't be surprised if your browser can't find a Web address you type. It's not your fault, and it's probably not our fault either! Blame it on the World Wide Web itself: Web addresses (and sites themselves) can be pretty fickle. Try looking for a "missing" site with a search engine. And try shortening the address by deleting everything after the `.com` (or `.org` or `.edu`).

Note: By the way, all the Web sites that we talk about in our WebVentures are online at the Dummies Web site's *Great Software For Kids & Parents* at `http://www.dummies.com/bonus/great_sw/`. On that page, you can click on links that will take you directly to the various WebVenture sites discussed in this book.

Software lingo: We use several terms interchangeably in this book: Software, programs, and titles. Sometimes we call them applications and products, too. After all, a rose is a rose is a rose, right?

Note: In most cases, there is *no* information about format (floppy disk or CD-ROM) or platform (Macintosh or Windows). That's because — unless otherwise stated — all programs profiled in this book are available on CD-ROM for Windows 3.1, Windows 95, and Macintosh systems.

Icons Used in This Book

Great Software For Kids & Parents also uses special graphical elements to get your attention. We call them *icons*. Here's what they look like and what they mean:

Indicates really important lists of procedures or ideas for you to remember.

Emphasizes ideas for using software at home to complement classroom learning.

Alerts you to together-time activities that will help kids, siblings, and parents get more mileage out of children's software — on the computer and away from it, too.

Indicates that the CD-ROM at the back of this book contains a demo version of the software.

Flags practical advice about particular software programs or about issues of importance to parents.

Marks your gateway to online fun and learning. It's always followed by great, family-tested suggestions for learning adventures on the World Wide Web.

Feedback!

The whole point of this book is to help you make great use of the family computer. So please let us know how you're doing! You can reach us by *snail mail* at:

IDG Books Worldwide Inc.
7260 Shadeland Station, Suite 100
Indianapolis, IN 46256

Or you can e-mail us at feedback/dummies@idgbooks.com. And remember to check out the *...For Dummies* Website at http://www.dummies.com.

Part I
Getting Started

The 5th Wave   **By Rich Tennant**

"SHE JUST FOUND OUT SHE'D RATHER BE A JET PILOT THAN A FAIRY PRINCESS, BUT SHE DOESN'T WANT TO GIVE UP THE WARDROBE."

In this part . . .

Some people start something new by jumping right in and just doing it. Others start by doing some preparation. Either way works fine when the something new is kids' software. And we've structured this book to suit parents of both persuasions: the just-do-it types *and* the get-prepared types.

If you're the just-do-it type, you can jump into this book any old where. Turn to any part, any chapter, and you find ideas and tips that help your family get more mileage out of the software you already have. You also find software profiles that guide your choices for what to add next.

If you're the get-prepared and take-it-step-by-step type, these first two chapters are for you. If you're very new to family computing, try Chapter 1 first. (Logical, isn't it?) This chapter offers a "quick start" approach to getting eager kids up and running with the right kinds of software. If you're not so new to family computing, you might skip to Chapter 2 and learn how to map out a plan for building a software library that's right for you and your kids.

Some of you just-do-it types may want to flip through Chapters 1 and 2 to find some good basic ground rules for your kids. We provide lists that make it easy to remember the essentials for smart shopping, plus great tips on what kinds of software are good for kids at different ages.

Chapter 1

Get Your Kids Computing — the Very First Day

● ●

In This Chapter

▶ Going with what you've got — bundled software

▶ Making your first purchases — for ages 2–12

▶ Computing smart right from the start — basic rules and skills

● ●

This chapter is for all you folks who are really, really new to family computing. Just how new? Try answering these questions to gauge your "newness" quotient:

✔ Is your floor still littered with Styrofoam packing material, cardboard boxes, manuals, and registration cards?

✔ Have you and the kids discovered *all* the bundled bonuses that came preloaded on your system?

✔ Have the kids gotten cookie crumbs in the keyboard yet?

✔ Are they already pestering you for more software?

If you answered *yes . . . no . . . no . . . no,* then this chapter is for you. If your answers were *no . . . yes . . . yes . . . yes,* then you can probably skip ahead to Chapter 2.

If your family fits our tongue-in-cheek "newness" profile, it's a good bet that your kids have been dancing up and down with impatience from the moment you got the system up and running.

The right thing to do, of course, would be to spell out some rules. Like no food or drinks, take turns, stay away from grown-up stuff. But this is reality. So we'll get to the right thing a little later and do the expedient thing instead: Just let 'em at it!

The easiest way to get your kids started with the family computer is simply to go with what you've got — the preinstalled software that came with your computer. The advantage: no advance planning required. The disadvantage: The free software may not be exactly what you'd like for your kids. But you can always make a quick trip back to the store to supplement the bundled software.

Starting with Something Bundled

Your new computer probably came with a bunch of bundled software titles. *Bundled* refers to software (in this book, sometimes called an application, a program, a product, or a title) that comes with your computer, either installed on your hard drive or free on separate CD-ROMs. In fact, depending on the system you bought, you may already have anywhere from a half-dozen to more than two dozen applications! All you've got to do is locate one for the kids, launch it, and let the kids have their fill.

When the computer is *really* new to your household, there's no point in talking about time limits to over-eager kids. As long as they're sharing the experience in some way or taking turns, let them use a new program as long as they want. Once the edge is off their excitement, they'll be more open to the rules you have in store for them.

Table 1-1 lists the software that's bundled with two different family computers, typical systems that you might find in catalogues or stores. Both systems include nearly two dozen applications. The software in Column 1 comes bundled with a Windows 95 system; the software in Column 2 comes bundled with a Macintosh computer. (These bundles are examples only; computer makers constantly change the software they bundle with their systems.)

Which title first?

If you're the owner of a system with a bundle like one of these, then right off the bat, you've got more than 20 titles to check out. And nearly half of them (in both the Windows 95 and Macintosh lists) are good for kids!

If you can get some time with your system *before* turning the kids loose, explore *Launch Pad* (Berkeley Systems) and *At Ease* (Apple) first. With these programs, you can specify which software you want your kids to use and create a personalized desktop for each child. The *desktop* is a special area that displays pictures of the kids' software. At the desktop, kids can launch their titles with a single click or access fun stuff like calendars and address books. And it keeps them away from everything else — grown-up applications, your checkbook, the Internet connection, you name it. (Another good desktop utility is *KidDesk* from Edmark, shown in Figure 1-1.)

Table 1-1	Software Bundles for Two Typical Family PCs
Windows 95 Bundle	**Macintosh Bundle**
ABC's Wide World of Animals	3D Atlas
Battle Beast	Adobe Photo Deluxe
BodyWorks	America Online
Compton's Interactive Encyclopedia	The American Heritage Children's Dictionary
Creative Writer	The American Heritage Dictionary
Cyberia	Amazing Writing Machine
Internet Access Kit	At Ease
Jack Nicklaus Golf	Blockbuster Guide to Movies & Video
Jumpstart Kindergarten	ClarisWorks
Launch Pad	ClickArt Collection/ClipArt Treasure Pak
Lotus SmartSuite	Club KidSoft CD
Magic Theatre	Descent
MechWarrior	DOGZ Adoption Kit
Microsoft Encarta	Grolier Multimedia Encyclopedia
Microsoft Works	Internet Connection Kit
Music Mentor	Mayo Clinic Family Health
Netscape Navigator	NOW TouchBase & DateBook Pro
Online service software	Our Times
Quicken SE	Quicken SE
Rand McNally Tripmaker	SurfWatch
Sports Illustrated for Kids	Thinkin' Things Collection 2
Wall $treet Money	Web Workshop

For older kids, you can simply demonstrate how to find and launch programs from the Macintosh desktop or from the Windows Start menu.

But your kids are probably begging to play, right? Don't worry, you can safely defer desktop setup for a little while. Just launch a title for your kids, and stick around — to answer questions, help them navigate, and make sure they keep to the kid stuff. And plan to set up their desktops after they're in bed.

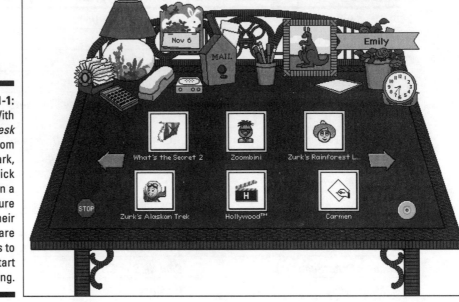

Figure 1-1:
With
KidDesk
from
Edmark,
kids click
once on a
little picture
of their
software
titles to
start
playing.

Your best bet for picking the very first title to launch for your kids is to play with the bundled kids' titles when your children are not around — when they're in bed or at school. That way, you'll have a sense of which titles they'll like and which ones you consider most appropriate for first-time users.

Playing with your kids' software is also a great ice-breaker if you're new to computing. Kids' software is easy to use. It's fun to play. It's good recreation after the often-onerous process of setting up a new computer. And with a quick late-night session or two, you'll be able to answer any questions your kids have as they explore their new programs.

Most likely, however, your computer-crazed offspring won't give you that luxury! So take a quick look at the material that came with the computer for the suggested age ranges of the bundled software. Then launch a title that's right for your kids' ages.

Using the sample bundles in Table 1-1 as examples, *JumpStart Kindergarten* is a good choice for toddlers. Kids 7 and up can play solo with *Amazing Writing Machine* (which, despite its name, contains lots of art activities) or an animation title like *Magic Theatre*. Kids over 7 will have a good time with *Thinkin' Things Collection 2* or *ABC's Wide World of Animals*.

First encounters with many other bundled titles should be a family activity. Not that there's anything inappropriate about the software. It's just that most kids need some adult guidance when they first venture into an electronic encyclopedia (*Encarta, Grolier's, Compton's*), a geography resource like *3D Atlas,* a science reference like *BodyWorks,* a Works package (*Microsoft Works* or *ClarisWorks*) or a sophisticated creativity tool (*Adobe Photo Deluxe* or *Web Workshop*).

Beyond the bundle

Some of the titles bundled with your computer, particularly encyclopedias or Works packages, will be long-term hits with kids and grown-ups alike. Others are right only for certain ages. Kids may outgrow some programs quickly, or it may be months (or years) before they're old enough for others. And your bundle may not include some software that you consider important. Neither the Windows 95 nor the Macintosh bundle includes interactive storybooks or math programs, which are both high on our list of must-have titles.

After your kids use the bundled software long enough for you to figure what's not quite right or what's missing, you'll probably be ready to make another purchase. But only one or two. After all, you (and your bank account) may still be suffering from the sticker shock that strikes all computer buyers!

Always go slow with software purchases. And not just because they're costly! If your kids have too many choices, they may be tempted to zip from one title to another without slowing down, exploring all the possibilities, and becoming absorbed. Good software has a lot to offer. But only persistent, inquiring kids will find it all — with your encouragement.

Making Your First Purchases: The Quick-Start Method

If you can add only a single software program, choose one that children of different ages (and that includes grown-ups) can share. Table 1-2 suggests a few titles, all of them profiled in later chapters:

Table 1-2	First Purchases for Kids to Share	
Title	*Age range*	*Category*
Kid Pix Studio	Ages 3-12	Art & animation
Math Workshop	Ages 5-12	Math
Imagination Express	Ages 5-12	Storytelling
Explorapedia	Ages 6-10	Nature
Strategy Games of the World	Ages 7-13	Strategic gameplay
The Lost Mind of Dr. Brain	Ages 9 & up	Logic puzzles

By the way, every single CD-ROM we profile in this book is available for both Macintosh and Windows 95 systems, unless otherwise noted. So you don't need to worry about whether it will run on your system — 99 percent of the time it will.

Keeping everybody happy

Let's say you can add one program *per child*. On the plus side, you eliminate sibling squabbles! On the minus side, you have some homework to do. Making choices among software is what Chapter 2 is all about. But since this is the get-them-computing-fast chapter, we've got a quick-start approach for you. Simply base your choice on the age of each child and what's missing from your bundled software. Here are some pointers for four different age ranges. For more suggestions, check Part VII of this book for lists of our favorite software for different ages and needs.

Little-kid choices

If your bundled software doesn't include an interactive storybook, that's a great first choice. Interactive stories make an ideal introduction to the computer. Because they're so easy to use, they make it a snap for little kids to learn the point-and-click process of using a mouse. Equally important, they add a fun new twist to the "tell me a story" experience that every child loves. (See Chapter 3 for specific titles.)

On the other hand, an art program is an essential outlet for creative expression. Any child who can click-and-drag can have the tremendous satisfaction of making an on-screen picture. And even more pleasing, perhaps, is blowing it to smithereens with the click of the mouse! (See Chapter 15 for specific titles.)

What if you can really get only *one* additional title? Should it be a storybook or art program? We'd opt for the art program. The reason: An art program lets kids use the computer as a tool to explore, experiment, and create something personal. Storybooks make a sweet beginning, but art is a lifelong, imaginative adventure.

You'll find good little-kid art activities in *Kid Pix Studio, Playskool Puzzles,* and *Paint, Write & Play!,* also profiled in Chapter 3.

What's good for ages 5–7

School skills are a big priority for this age group. And there's more software devoted to the 3 'Rs than anything else!

Look for titles that dovetail with the approach in your kids' classrooms. Or try programs that cover similar material in a different fashion. The more ways kids encounter concepts, skills, and facts, the better they learn them. (Look for specific titles in Part III of this book.)

If you don't find a math program in your software bundle, you'll want one in that category right away. Check Chapter 6 for lots of suggestions. But if you want to head to the store *right now,* look at the *Mighty Math* series from Edmark or *Math Munchers Deluxe* from MECC.

Buying for the 8- to 10-year-old

Good software for the 8- to 10-year-old crowd challenges kids to explore, experiment, and express themselves. They're ready for adventures back in time or around the world, on-screen experiments, logic games, and more sophisticated creative pursuits. (Check Part V of this book for suggested titles.)

Consider *Where in the World Is Carmen Sandiego?* if your bundle doesn't have a geography title. Or if history is the missing link, your kids will love *Oregon Trail II.*

Adults can have as much fun as kids with titles like these. Better yet, you can play them together. And that's something you *should* do — as often as you can. Treat your computer as a resource for family activities, and you're less likely to see it misused as an electronic baby-sitter, an overpriced video-game system, or a multimedia quiz-master.

Ages 11 & up

Kids in the double-digit ages enjoy titles with spunk and complexity. (And at homework time, your kids will appreciate electronic references, too.) A *simulation* (a program that mimics real-life scenarios, with kids in charge) is a must-have (see Chapters 10 and 12). So are programs that foster creative expression (see Chapters 5, 14, and 15).

Here are some quick-start suggestions: *Hollywood High* from Theatrix Interactive, for its creative fun; and *SimCity 2000* from Maxis, for its strategic challenges.

Computing Smart — from the Start

OK, now that your kids are happily computing (either with a bundled title or a specially purchased program), it's time to cover all the basics and rules we skipped over earlier in the chapter. Some of the information that follows covers computer smarts, some covers kids' behavior, and some covers online safety. Everything we're about to tell you is just common sense. But since when do kids exercise common sense without a dozen or so reminders!

Basic skills

Your kids are probably already ahead of the game when it comes to computer skills! They pick up a lot of the basics simply by playing their software. Ask them to show you everything they know — from turning on the system, to shutting down, and everything in between. That way, you can spot the gaps in their knowledge and fill them in — and the sooner the better.

Here's a list of ten how-to's kids should learn early on, presented roughly in the order kids need to know them. But feel free to do things differently or cover more computer skills with your kids; what kids need to know at different ages differs in every family. (Check the Cheat Sheet at the front of this book for a handy tear-out version of these basic skills.)

___ How to point, double click, and navigate within kids' programs

___ How to turn on/shut down the computer

___ How to use the features of their special desktop and launch their programs from its main screen

___ How to open and close a program

___ How to name and save their games, written files, or artwork

___ How to use the pull-down menus, icons, and commands

___ How to handle CD-ROMs and floppy disks

___ How to adjust the volume

___ How to use the microphone

___ How to restart the system

Before you get to show kids how to save their work, you need to do a bit of computer housekeeping. Create a folder or directory for each child, using their names as folder names. Put the folders where kids can find them (the My Computer area in a Windows 95 system, perhaps, or a family file drawer on a Macintosh). And now your kids have a place for their saved files.

Before you show kids how to restart the computer, decide whether you want kids restarting the system at all. We like our kids to come and get us if one of their games or a school application "hangs" the system. That way, we can ask them exactly what was happening when the program stopped working. And if it happens again, we can do some troubleshooting or report the problem to the software publisher.

Basic rules

The first six of the following ground rules cover computer etiquette and apply to all children (and adults, for that matter). The last four cover online safety; introduce them when you feel your kids are responsible enough for some World Wide Web activities. (At the very beginning of this book, you find these rules summarized on the Cheat Sheet, which you can tear out and post right near the computer.)

- ✔ **Forget food, and don't drink.** Crumbs always wind up where they don't belong, and drinks eventually spill.

- ✔ **Beware of magnets.** They can mess up data on floppy disks and wreck your computer screen.

- ✔ **Make a mess somewhere else.** Pencil-sharpener shavings, paper clips, crayons, glue sticks, and the like have their place — but not near computers!

- ✔ **Handle CD-ROMs with care.** They're tough but not indestructible. Remove them carefully and remember to return them to their proper cases. Gently open and close the computer's CD-ROM tray.

- ✔ **Save your work frequently.** We can't say that enough!

- ✔ **Stick to your own programs.** Although when an adult says it's OK, do explore and experiment.

- ✔ **Get parental OK *each and every* time you go online.** Do this even if you're just downloading e-mail — and honor family time limits for online use.

- ✔ ***Never* give out personal information.** This includes things such as gender, full name, phone number, and address.

✔ **Keep passwords secret.** Don't write them down; memorize them. It's a good idea to change passwords periodically, too.

✔ **Don't register for anything without first checking with a parent.** This includes things such as a Web site, a contest, or a survey.

More rules — especially for your family

You'll probably want to devise some rules of your own, tailored to your kids and the computing crises that come up (or that you'd like to forestall) in your household. Here are some issues to consider:

✔ When may kids use the computer?

✔ For how long?

✔ Who gets it first?

✔ Should older kids be allowed to participate in online chats?

✔ What's a reasonable time limit for online use?

Letting kids online

Your computer system probably gives you six different ways to go online! And that means more stuff to learn, more decisions to make. But just because the capability is there doesn't mean you have to use it. In fact, if your kids are under age 10, we suggest that you forget about going online with them for the time being.

Again, get used to what you've got first. Concentrate instead on exploring the kids' programs that you have, making the most of them, using them as a source of family fun, and extending them with off-the-computer activities. Begin planning a family software library and gradually adding to it (see Chapter 2). An agenda like that will keep you and your kids busy for a good long time!

When you think your kids are ready to venture online, do it together. That way, you can guide their experience and help them learn how to be responsible participants in this new community.

For family surfing suggestions in this book, look for WebVenture icons. Used throughout this book (except in the Little Kids section), WebVenture icons point you to good sites for online learning and fun — for parents and kids together.

For more general advice about kids online, you may want to check out *The World Wide Web For Kids & Parents, TakeCharge Computing For Teens & Parents, or The World Wide Web For Teachers,* all published by IDG Books Worldwide, Inc.

Time for More Software?

Absolutely, positively *do not* buy any more kids' software! Well, not exactly. Just don't go shopping until you do the following:

- ✔ Explore what you already have.
- ✔ Map out a plan for what to get next.
- ✔ Fill out the system checklist that appears in the following sidebar.

Pick up any CD-ROM package (for kids or adults), and you see some fine print on the back or the side. This fine print is the system requirements. It states the minimum specifications your computer must meet in order for the software to work. We highly advise that you have your computer specifications firmly in mind (or better yet, on paper) before you go shopping. So why not get it over with right now?

Note: You also find a fill-in-the-blank list in the Cheat Sheet at the very beginning of this book. Tear it out and take it shopping with you!

Now that you've taken care of the details, you may want to turn to the big picture in Chapter 2: mapping out a plan and putting together a software library that's right for your family.

About the family computer

Computer maker _____

Model _____

Processor _____

Clock speed (MHz) _____

RAM (MB) _____

Available hard disk space (MB) _____

Monitor _____

CD-ROM drive speed _____

Operating system (version) _____

Chapter 2

Building a Family Software Library

*Y*ou know those menus where you choose one dish from column A and two from column B, and no matter what you pick, you wind up with a tasty meal? If only choosing software for kids were so easy!

Well, this chapter won't make choosing quite *that easy*. But it will help — by giving you a well-defined plan of action for building a software library. With a plan in hand, here's what *won't happen* to you:

✔ You won't get flustered when you see 20 math titles side-by-side at the store — and grab the wrong one!

✔ You won't buy a title you already own but had forgotten about!

✔ You won't buy a title only to have your kids exhaust its so-called "riches" just two weeks later!

✔ You won't be a pushover when the kids start saying, "Gimme this one, gimme this one" at the store!

✔ You won't buy a title and then discover the kids won't "get it" for another three years!

Think of building a software library as a three-step process:

✔ **Understand the kinds of software titles that are good for kids.** Hundreds and hundreds of kids' titles are out there. (We also call them programs, applications, products, and software.) But once you understand that kids really need *only five categories* of software, your task suddenly becomes a lot more manageable.

✔ **Figure out which specific titles are the right ones for your kids.** As a conscientious parent, you already know a lot about your kids — their interests, developmental abilities, school needs, learning styles. Just keep those characteristics in mind as you do your homework, and you'll find that making good choices is easier than you might think.

✔ **Go get 'em.** We can't spare you the chore of shopping. But this chapter gives you lots of ideas for smarter shopping.

Now let's take a closer look at each part of the library-building process.

Understanding the Building Blocks

Back to the meal metaphor, if you don't mind. You try to prepare well-balanced meals, right? Meals that serve the essential food groups growing kids need. Assembling a good software library follows a similar logic. This library needs to provide a varied mix of products for children at different ages. The U.S. government says there are five food groups. And what do you know? We say there are five software groups, too.

The five software "food" groups

Choose software from these groups — early learning, creative pursuits, academic skill builders, exploration and enrichment, and homework helpers — and you'll be building a well-rounded library and sparking your kids to learn while having fun.

Early learning

Remember that little kids learn through play. So your best bets for preschoolers are titles abounding in playful, imaginative activities, and specifically designed for kids too young to read and write. Simply by following visual clues and spoken directions, little kids can play a game, hear a story, or explore the ABCs, numbers, colors, shapes, and more. Look for software that fosters discovery: Programs that let kids play and discover at their own pace make the best introduction to early-learning concepts. And keep it simple: Software that bombards young children with too much animation, music, or video can be overwhelming. (See Part II in this book for great choices in the early-learning software "food group.")

Choose software you can play with your kids. Personalized playtime means a lot to them. And your interest and involvement are more important, in fact, than the lessons in the software.

If a program looks too much like TV or a movie, think twice before buying it. Your computer is only as good as the software it runs. And if you give kids cartoon software, they'll have a TV kind of experience.

Creative pursuits

Kids get years of fun from freehand art, painting, animation, creative writing, printing, and multimedia programs. But just because the emphasis is on fun, don't underestimate a program's educational value. Creativity titles lay the groundwork for lots of learning. They provide subtle encouragement for kids to experiment and explore, to envision and express what's in their mind's eye, and to recognize the need for skills and information that will, in turn, let them produce richer creations. (See Part VI in this book for great choices in the creative-pursuits software "food group.")

Look for products that give kids inventive, new ways to express themselves. Why pay $30 for on-screen coloring books or electronic dot-to-dots when your kids can get the same pleasures from an inexpensive dime-store activity book?

Be an appreciative audience for the artwork, stories, and productions your kids create. Show how much you care. For example, turn colorful animations into screen savers, send e-mail stories to friends and relatives, or thumbtack their pictures on your office walls.

Academic skill builders

This category of software is the equivalent of the bread-and-pasta group in the food pyramid: the biggest building block for growing kids. In the early grades, your kids may spend much of their computer time with basic-skill titles. But basic doesn't mean boring. Most skill-builders give a contemporary, kid-pleasing twist to practicing the traditional 3 'Rs. And the best ones inspire kids to become eager readers, mathematical thinkers, and enthusiastic writers. (See Part III in this book for great choices in the skill-builder software "food group.")

The computer alone can't transform your kids into successful students. Use software (sparingly) to spark their enthusiasm and encourage practice. But don't park the kids at the computer for hours on end. Make sure you provide them with plenty of opportunities to read, write, and use math in "real life."

Find out how (and when) your kids' school teaches the 3 'Rs. Talk with the teachers about your kids' capabilities and learning styles. Then keep that information in mind as you look at software.

Exploration and enrichment

Exploration software — thanks to photographic images, informative animation, video clips, realistic sounds, and kid-friendly text and narrative — takes kids to places they can't ordinarily go and makes them feel as if they're really there. Good titles go beyond multimedia wizardry: They hook kids with a quest, a mystery, or an adventure that gets them all fired up about delving into history, geography, and science. And the best programs go even further, offering children a hands-on opportunity to *experiment* with their on-screen surroundings. (See Part III in this book for great choices in the explorations software "food group.")

Go easy on click-and-watch titles: They may look pretty, and they may make it easy to find information, but they often don't encourage kids to think hard and use their newly discovered knowledge creatively.

Don't underestimate geography, history, or science adventures for reading practice. When kids get involved in a great game, they really push themselves to master skills (like reading) that will help them play better.

Homework helpers

When your kids reach the higher elementary and middle school grades, it's time to look into programs for researching and writing homework assignments. You won't need many CD-ROM references at first; an encyclopedia and an atlas may suffice. Chances are, the most essential of those resources are bundled with your computer system. Consider additional titles when your kids get passionate about particular topics. (See Part IV in this book for great choices in the homework-helpers software "food group.")

Don't wait till your kids are 10 to explore CD-ROM references. You can use them with younger kids the same way you use complicated books with fascinating pictures: Just skip the words and talk about what you see. Besides enjoying "together" time with you, your kids will realize that there's a gold mine awaiting discovery on those big-kid CD-ROMs.

If you show them the ropes, kids 10 and up will be eager students of the family word-processing, calendar, address book, or spreadsheet software. And then you might not have to buy anything special at all!

What about the top of the pyramid?

Can you picture the food pyramid? The bread and pasta group is at the bottom, vegetables and fruit are above the grains, and the milk and meat groups come next. That's five. But what about the top? Is something else up there? Yes. And it's a group that doesn't count "officially": fats and sweets, of course.

Games are the software equivalent of fats and sweets. And we didn't count them as an official category, either. Why? Well, kids think of *all* the programs in those five software "food" groups as games. After all, they're fun. They're entertaining. Some feature competitive play with two or more players. Others encourage collaborative play. Many involve a lot of strategy. And that fits most definitions of games that we know.

But there are many popular games that you won't find anywhere in *Great Software For Kids & Parents* — for example, CD-ROM video games (too violent, no food for thought), sports games (fast action, not much food for thought), and games that are beyond the 2-12 age range covered by this book.

But because 2- to 12-year-olds do play some pretty cool games that are intended for older kids, we give you some good choices at the end of Chapter 16.

What's Right for Your Kids?

Back to the food pyramid again. Besides telling you which foods you need to eat, it tells you how many servings you need from each group. But sorry to say, that's where the analogy breaks down. We wish some formula existed for determining how many titles from each category make a great software library. But there isn't such a formula!

Balancing the diet

The kinds of additions you make to the family software library will depend on the ages of your kids and the priorities you have for their education. Let's consider the choices, age by age:

- ✔ **For kids under school age:** The answer is pretty easy. Stick to early-learning titles and an easy-to-use creativity program.

- ✔ **For 5- to 7-year-olds:** Because school skills are a big priority, the balance of your new software purchases may tip toward skill builders for a few years. But the mix should also include creativity and exploration titles; both categories foster learning experiences that are as important as basic skills.

- ✔ **For 8- to 10-year-olds:** Most additions to your library should come from the exploration category. Programs in this category challenge kids to put the basics they've been mastering to work. And these programs dovetail with the lessons in geography, history, and science that kids encounter through 5th grade. This is also the time to begin using CD-ROM references you already own and evaluating new titles that might help with schoolwork.

✔ **For kids 11 and up:** New creativity titles can inspire preteens to approach assignments with enthusiasm. And more CD-ROM references and exploration software can help them keep up with the subjects they're studying.

How many?

Building a software library for your children is a lot like buying books, toys, or games. The collection grows the way your kids do, sometimes in spurts, sometimes little by little.

In general, it's best to start small and add titles slowly. The reason: With fewer titles, kids are more likely to turn their software inside out, uncover everything they can find, learn everything the software has to teach. Provide too many titles, and they spend too little time with each program.

Sample "meal plans"

Which specific titles should be on the menu for kids? You find a wealth of lists in Chapter 16, representing balanced "meals" for different age groups. Each list has a great mix of titles that kids can grow with.

Be sure to look at a program's recommended age range when you're deciding on software. And buy it when your kids are at the *lower end* of the age range. That way, they'll get the longest use from the title.

Separating the wheat from the chaff

In identifying good software programs for this book, we've had the good luck to be guided by The Computer Museum. This institution, with exhibits in Boston and its historical collection in Silicon Valley, is in the business of introducing kids and families to computers. And with 170 hands-on interactive exhibits, The Computer Museum is a terrific laboratory for what makes a great multimedia learning experience. Here is a list of qualities that The Computer Museum experts expect from great kids' software, and they're the qualities you should look for, too:

✔ **Fun learning experience:** Does the software invite active participation, exploration, and discovery? Does it provide an opportunity for kids to put their new-found knowledge to work?

✔ **Great design and use of multimedia:** Is the software easy and appealing to use? Does its use of multimedia really add value to the learning experience?

> ✔ **High replay value:** Do kids come back again and again? Or do they lose interest once the novelty wears off?
>
> ✔ **A new dimension:** Does it bring something unique to the child's experience? Something that only the computer can provide?

Keep these criteria in mind (or in hand, since you'll also find them on the tear-off Cheat Sheet at the front of the book) as you prepare to go shopping.

Shopping Smart

Successful software shopping is in large part good advance planning and persnickety testing, as you can see from this to-do list. Actually, there are two lists.

Getting ready to shop

Here are some tasks to check off before you go shopping:

___ *Do your homework.*

Choose the software "food groups" that you want to add to your library. Zero in on specific titles by reading this book. Talk with your kids' teachers, the school technology coordinator, and friends; compare their opinions with reviews in magazines, newspapers, or the World Wide Web.

___ *Try before you buy.*

Order demo disks that let you preview a software company's programs. Look at demos available on the software publishers' World Wide Web sites. Visit a computer show or a children's museum to see programs first-hand before you go shopping.

___ *Write down the exact capabilities of your computer.*

Be sure to take this information to the store with you (check for this handy fill-out list on the Cheat Sheet, too). Or keep it in hand if you order by phone.

Shopping for software

Then at the store, we suggest these for your list:

___ *Again, try before you buy!*

Look for retailers with "try-out" computer systems that let you test software.

___ *And, again, do your homework!*

Compare the fine print on the package with your computer's capabilities. Learn the store's return policy; choose retailers who let you return CD-ROMs that don't live up to your expectations.

___ *Ask questions while you test.*

Does this software create a really unique learning experience for my kids?

Will my kids get to actively participate, or will they mostly watch, point, and click?

Do all the multimedia really enhance learning? Or are they just cool effects for technology's sake?

But what about the kids?

Notice anything weird in those two lists you just read? Kids are conspicuously absent from the shopping process.

Of course, we think the kids should be involved. But not when you're actually doing the deed. You won't be able to think straight if someone's tugging your sleeve, asking for a toy, some candy, or a CD-ROM that's *not* on your approved list.

Consider making two forays every time you shop for new software. Once with the whole gang, so the kids can try out titles. And once solo, so you make the final decision.

As we mention in Chapter 1, try to install the new software when your kids are not around. That way, you won't hear their disappointed moans and groans if the installation proves tricky or the CD-ROM is defective and has to be returned.

If at all possible, get familiar with new software *before* you show it to your children. That way, you can offer help if they need it and encourage them to explore areas they may overlook.

Register your software. It's sometimes essential to do this before you can get technical assistance, should you need it. And you'll wind up on the mailing list for special offers, new product offerings, and the like.

Part II
Launching Little Kids

The 5th Wave   By Rich Tennant

©RICHTENNANT

"I COULDN'T SAY ANYTHING—THEY WERE IN HERE WITH THAT PROGRAM WE BOUGHT THEM THAT ENCOURAGES ARTISTIC EXPRESSION."

In this part . . .

*I*f you're reading this, we assume you are the proud parent (grandparent, relative, friend, maybe teacher) of someone under six. And we assume that you've been asking yourself some questions: Should a child still in diapers use a computer? Should we trust our rambunctious 3-year-old with the family's new multimedia system? If kids can't read or write yet, can they learn anything on the computer?

The answer is yes! Kids have a natural fascination with computers. Unlike some parents, they're rarely intimidated by them. They just seem to "get it." And we encourage you to let them get to it!

To help, we filled Part II with practical advice and useful tips. We offer family-tested recommendations. We tell you about the best kinds of software for young children. And we help you weave the family computer into the other things you do to get your kids ready for school.

Chapter 3

Playing to Learn

• •

In This Chapter

▶ Learning comes naturally to kids — and so do computers!

▶ Getting kids started

▶ Choosing the best software for little kids

▶ Learning-by-doing software
    The *House* series (ages 2–6)

▶ Playing problem-solving adventures
    The *Junior Adventures* series (ages 3–8)

▶ Spinning stories
    Paint, Write & Play! (ages 4–7)
    Build-A-Book with Roberto (ages 2–4)

▶ Developing ready-for-school skills
    The *Jumpstart* series (ages 2–6)

▶ Making your own learning games for kids

• •

Kids arrive in this world filled with wonder, curiosity, and an instinct to learn. For little kids, learning is a no-brainer — as effortless as breathing or playing. It's how they make sense of the world.

In their early years, kids learn from the people, ideas, and things they encounter each day — especially while playing. That's why the best software for little kids "feels" like play. As children click around, they explore new environments, investigate relationships, and test assumptions. The software never tells kids that they did something wrong. Instead, it gently prompts them to try again. Great software makes little kids feel empowered and competent. And kids who believe they can succeed are more willing to trust their abilities, are more open to new challenges, and are more likely to perform well in school.

Starting Kids Out

Kids are eager to try anything they see you doing. If you cook, they want be up on the kitchen counter helping. If you garden, they want to dig. If you use a computer, they want to bang the keyboard, too.

Your word processor can be an intriguing plaything for a curious toddler. Two and one-half-year-old Katie loved to watch while her Mom composed this book at her computer. So, of course, Katie wanted to type, too. As a result, Mom launched the word processor, set the type size really large, and asked Katie to choose a color. With enormous delight, Katie banged on the keyboard and watched letters, numbers, and punctuation marks fill the screen. (And don't worry, it's unlikely that little hands will really hurt your keyboard.)

When your child shows a sustained interest in the computer, it's time for a program specially designed for young kids. First install the software and make sure it works on your system. Then explore it together. Let kids press their fingers to the screen to show where they want to "go." Once they master the mouse, let them take the lead. Don't try to explore everything in one sitting; your toddler will be happy to visit the same programs over and over for months to come.

Mastering the mouse

With adult's software, you click a menu choice like Print or Undo to direct the computer. With early-learning software, kids make things happen by clicking pictures. So kids don't need to know much about the keyboard. But they do need to control the mouse.

Mouse action — positioning the cursor at the right spot, holding the cursor steady, and pressing the button — requires a good deal of hand/eye coordination. Most kids get the hang of it sometime between the ages of 2 and 4, although you can expect a lot of variation, as with all developmental skills. If your child keeps becoming frustrated, consider a special kid-sized mouse or a track ball. Both do the same job as the mouse but are easier for small hands to control.

What's good for little kids?

Store shelves are filled with programs for kids ages 3-6. Some of these programs are great. Many are not. So where do you start? Here's an easy two-step approach to help you cut through all the software clutter and choose the best programs to get your kids started.

First look for software that creates the right kind of learning environment for young kids. Don't be overly swayed by familiar movie characters or TV pals. Instead, take a deeper look at how your child interacts with the software. Keep the following five questions in mind as you evaluate a program.

___ *Are kids in charge?*

On the computer, kids should be in control. Look for programs that give your kids lots of freedom to decide where to go, when to go there, and what to do when they get there.

___ *Can kids easily move around the program on their own?*

Kids need software they can use without getting "lost" or frustrated. Too many on-screen choices can be confusing. Choose programs that let kids move from one activity to another by clicking simple icons.

___ *Do kids do more than click and watch?*

Research shows that kids learn more by doing than by watching and listening. So don't let your computer turn into another TV or VCR. Stay away from software with long animation sequences or video clips where kids have nothing to do but watch.

___ *Are kids smiling?*

A good dose of silliness boosts a program's fun factor. And fun helps capture kids' attention and spurs their desire to use a program over and over.

___ *Do you like it?*

Look for software you can use with your child. Your interest and involvement is as important as the lessons in the software. Choose titles you like — because you'll be seeing and hearing them a lot!

Variety is the spice of life, and that goes for little kids too. So make sure you add some variety to your child's computer experience. Even for little kids, you can find different types of software, each with its special pleasures and benefits. In this chapter, we tell you more about these categories — and our favorite software programs in each. You'll read about the following:

- *Learning-by-doing software* that invites kids to explore, to build, and to make things

- *Problem-solving adventures* that challenge little kids to reason and think

- *Creativity programs* that let kids express their ideas and feelings in new ways

- *School-readiness software* that lets kids practice a wide range of early learning skills

As you purchase software through your child's preschool years, be sure to try a program or two from each category. Your kids will have more fun, and you'll know they're off to a great start.

To get the most from your investment in kids' software, it's best to buy at the lower end of a program's age range. For example, if the package suggests that a program is appropriate for kids from ages 3-6, buy the program for your 3- or 4-year-old, but not your 6-year-old. Two to three years from now, your kids will still enjoy many of the same programs they played when they were three. A number of programs, in fact, build in multiple levels of challenge so that the software can grow with your child.

Learning-By-Doing Software

Ever notice how little kids like to get their hands into everything? They touch and throw, push and pull, pile up and knock down. They build forts, dig holes, paint in bold strokes, and spin in endless circles. And while they're immersed in all this physical activity, their brains are busy, too, measuring, analyzing, theorizing, testing, and building their knowledge through experience.

Little kids need these same kinds of active, learning-by-doing experiences on the computer, too. And they'll find them in the early learning programs from Edmark.

The Edmark House series (ages 2–6)

How about a play date where your child gets to assemble machines in a workshop, write a book, build a bug, or decorate cookies? That's the kind of fun they have when they visit *Bailey's Book House* or *Sammy's Science House,* or any one of the five *House* titles in the Edmark Early Learning series.

The Edmark programs may not look all that different from other early learning programs you've seen. They've got the same talking animals, colorful animation, lively music, and assorted collection of learning games. So what makes the Edmark titles stand out? Edmark has an instinct for creating software that piques kids' curiosity and challenges them to extend their thinking. We like the fact that each Edmark program focuses on a single subject like math, science, reading, storymaking, or geography. Kids can explore concepts in depth. (We hate to see kids cruise at breakneck speed through a software program without a thought — the way they graze through meals.)

We like the two modes of play in every Edmark activity because they perfectly suit the developmental needs of little kids for both open-ended play and a little bit of structure. With *Explore and Discover,* kids can play and experiment at their own pace. With *Question and Answer,* kids are challenged to find the best answer — again, at their own pace. We especially like the layers of complexity subtly woven throughout every title. The result? Programs of exceptional depth, gentle humor, and rich challenges. Programs that kids play with for years.

The Edmark *House* programs are so good you may want to invest in more than one. Here are some of the stand-out activities in each of the titles in this series.

Millie's Math House (ages 2–6)

For the youngest kids, our favorite Edmark title is *Millie's Math House.* We've never met a child who didn't love Millie and her pals.

At Millie's house, kids explore seven activities that introduce beginning math concepts like quantity, number recognition, counting, shapes, patterns, sizes, and comparisons. Our favorite activity is dressing Little, Middle, and Big, the world's most engaging peanut figures. (You can check them out for yourself in Figure 3-1.) Your child's task: to help find the right pair of shoes for Little, Middle, and Big. Goofy as it looks — and sounds — kids can't get enough of this game. When kids match the right shoes to the right character, the high-tops or party shoes instantly appear on the character's feet. But don't be surprised if your child purposely selects the wrong shoes. Kids love to see Little pucker up her face and hear her squeaky protest "Oh no! Too big!" as she practically disappears into Big's oversized cowboy boots.

Little kids explore and interpret the world by touching, tasting, looking, listening, and more, and all the *House* titles present opportunities for kids to learn through their senses. (OK, they can't really taste what's in the computer. But the software characters can.) Take the Cookie Factory game in *Millie's Math House,* for example, where children help Harley and Froggy decorate cookies with red jelly beans. Kids *see* a numeral on the cookie machine; they *click* on the jelly beans to count them (touching them in a virtual way); and they *hear* the numbers counted aloud as they click.

Don't be surprised if your child plays an activity over and over again. Chances are, it's not mindless repetition. Little kids need lots of practice to learn new things. And kids appreciate the fact that computers, unlike parents, have infinite patience with their need to test their skills and understanding with repetition.

Figure 3-1:
In *Millie's Math House,* kids play with the concept of size by choosing shoes for Little, Middle, and Big.

Bailey's Book House (ages 2–6)

Bailey's Book House lets kids get creative with the building blocks of reading: letters, sounds, rhymes, words, and sentences. The best activities in *Bailey's* are ones that let kids make something to take away from the computer. In Make-A-Card, for example, little kids can design their own cards by clicking on pictures they like and simple words to go with them. Out of the printer come party invitations, Mother's Day cards, or special notes to grandparents. With *Bailey's,* kids can also make their own books. As they scroll through a series of pictures, like the one in Figure 3-2, kids choose a character, a setting, and an event and watch them grow into a simple four-page story. They can play the story back on the computer (narrated with a real voice). Or they can print it and staple the pages together to make their very own book.

Sammy's Science House (ages 3–6)

Sammy's five activities inspire kids to think like scientists. In Weather Machine, kids observe different weather conditions and also get to tinker with the elements to create a rainy day or a snow storm. In Sammy's Workshop, shown in Figure 3-3, kids explore the relationship of parts to a whole by assembling a camera, a rocket ship, or a locomotive. In Make-a-Movie, kids figure out the logical sequence for natural phenomena, such as a sunset and an eclipse. When they drag the stages of an event into the right order, they can play it as a movie — forward (of course) or backward (even better).

Figure 3-2:
In *Bailey's Book House,* kids can create their own stories and listen as the computer reads them.

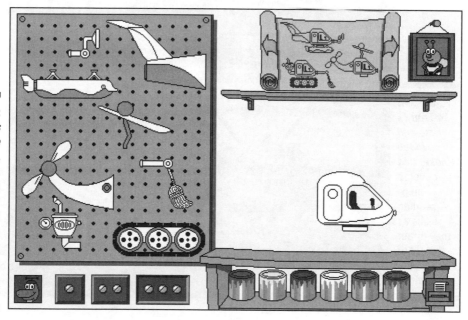

Figure 3-3:
In *Sammy's Science House,* construction projects range from simple (a clock, a windmill) to complex (a helicopter, a robot).

Trudy's Time and Place House (ages 3–6)

In *Trudy's Time and Place House,* abstract concepts like direction and time become concrete and accessible for young kids. In Calendar Clock, kids manipulate the measures of time — seconds, minutes, hours, days, or months — and watch the changes that result. Day turns into night, winter into spring, the sun sets, a snowman melts. The Time Twins — Analog Ann and Digital Dan — help kids visualize the relationship between different representations of time. (See Appendix C for information about software on the *Great Software For Kids & Parents* CD-ROM.)

Our favorite activities in *Trudy's* let kids manipulate the basic elements of maps. Earth Scout helps kids understand the relationship between what they see on the globe and what they see on a flat map. In Symbol Sandbox, kids place map symbols on a grid and watch the real thing — a city, a mountain, a river — rise in the sandbox. Jellybean Hunt, shown in Figure 3-4, challenges kids to direct an ant along the horizontal and vertical stripes of a tablecloth to reach the jellybeans spread across a picnic table.

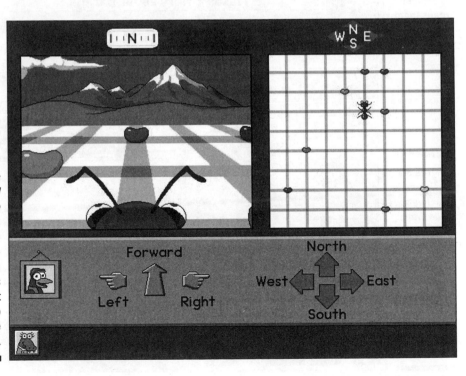

Figure 3-4:
In *Trudy's Time and Place House,* kids develop map-reading skills as they direct the ant to the jellybeans.

If your child is not ready for telling time, don't push it. Remember that kids have an internal developmental clock (if you'll forgive the pun) that governs their readiness to learn. They need to develop a *sense* of time — understanding today, tomorrow, and yesterday; morning, noon, and night; school days versus weekends — before they're interested in actually telling time. When they are ready, remember The Time Twins in *Trudy's Time and Place House.* Even though the rest of the program may seem babyish, the clock activity may strike exactly the right note for kids in the 2nd or 3rd grade.

Stanley's Sticker Stories (ages 3–6)

All the animals in Edmark's Early Learning neighborhood get together in *Stanley's Sticker Stories.* Kids can create stories about Millie and Bailey, Edmo and Houdini, Sammy and Trudy, and all their favorite Edmark characters and assemble alphabet and counting books. You can find a lot of storymaking programs for little kids, but we especially like *Stanley's* for its colorful, uncluttered graphics, its simplicity, and its sense of what tickles little kids' fancies.

What's a kid who can't read or write doing making stories? Even though their fingers can't yet form letters, kids love to tell their stories with pictures. You can encourage self-expression by asking your kids what their pictures are saying. Be the scribe when your children dictate a story. And choose age-appropriate software that lets them assemble pictures and words, click-and-point fashion, on their own.

A printer is a *must-have* with most little kids' programs. It lets you extend your kids' fun and learning after they leave the computer. Print the stories your kids create in *Stanley's Sticker Stories* or *Bailey's Book House,* and the stories become books to read in the car or before bed. Kids not only feel a great sense of ownership, but they're also highly motivated to read the stories they write. (It doesn't matter if they can't read yet. Pretending is important, too.) Kids also enjoy writing in the little field book they find in *Sammy's Science House.* If you print the book, they can take it on excursions into the backyard, the park, or beyond. It's just right for kids who are inveterate collectors of stuff.

Problem-Solving Adventures

All too often, we find that children's software programs are little more than electronic versions of familiar pastimes. Not that there's anything wrong with coloring books, a game of concentration, or connect-the-dots. But do your kids really need a Pentium processor to play them? We think you'd do better to look for software that uses the power of the computer to create a unique experience, something kids can't get any place else.

Problem-solving adventures do just that, and the *Junior Adventures* series from Humongous Entertainment does an especially good job.

The Junior Adventures series (ages 3–8)

Junior Adventures programs look as good as Saturday morning cartoons — but there's a lot more to them. Part game, part storybook, part treasure hunt, the *Junior Adventures* series also challenge kids to think.

While most early-learning programs focus on basics, such as numbers, letters, colors, and shapes, *Junior Adventures* programs focus on reasoning and logical thinking. They encourage kids to make choices and predictions, discover cause and effect relationships, formulate hypotheses, and test their ideas. And we're talking about kids as young as 3!

In every adventure, kids team up with an appealing character like Putt-Putt, the little purple car, or Freddi, a talking fish, to complete a quest. In fact, one of the best things about the *Junior Adventures* series is their unique characters. It's a refreshing change from the barrage of recycled movie and television characters that seem to dominate our children's lives (on lunch boxes, sleeping bags, CD-ROMs, and more).

Kids get deeply involved in these programs. And even after they've figured out a solution, the freedom of choice and the satisfaction of completing each task bring kids back to play again and again.

Start the youngest kids out with the *Putt-Putt* series. But don't be surprised if older kids want to play along. *Junior Adventures* games are great choices for collaborative computer play. Even squabbling siblings will work together to reach the end of the story.

Putt-Putt Saves the Zoo (ages 3–8)

It's opening day for the new Cartown Zoo, but some of the baby animals are missing. Putt-Putt offers to help the zookeeper find the missing animals and take them home. But that's easier said than done: Kenya the lion cub is stranded on a ledge above a rushing waterfall, and Baby Jambo the elephant is held captive by a small but ferocious mouse. With a click of their computer's mouse, kids drive Putt-Putt through the zoo. (You can see him chugging merrily along the road in Figure 3-5.) Along the way, they can click and find lots of hidden animations and discover clues and tools that they can store in Putt-Putt's glove compartment. Encourage kids to pick up anything they find. They may not know what to do with that log or shovel at first, but eventually they'll discover it's a useful tool for rescuing a lost lion cub.

Figure 3-5:
In *Putt-Putt Saves the Zoo,* kids direct Putt-Putt where to go and what to do.

Go ahead, cook dinner! We've seen the wriggliest 4-year-olds become totally engrossed in a *Putt-Putt* adventure for more than an hour at a time. But be forewarned: Even with such persistence, Humongous *Adventures* may take little kids more than one sitting to complete. When they need to stop (for dinner, for bed), select the *S* key on the keyboard to save a game in progress, and follow the directions on the screen.

What does a *Putt-Putt* adventure have to do with learning? Predicting outcomes, remembering directions, spotting objects, and figuring out the sequence of events — all these skills are important for reading comprehension and mathematical reasoning. And it doesn't hurt if your kids practice at every opportunity, including while they play adventure games.

Other Putt-Putt adventures

Putt-Putt Joins the Parade (ages 3-8) was the original title in this series, so its graphics look a bit dated. But the story is still a winner. Putt-Putt wants to join the Cartown Pet Parade, but first he needs to find a pet and get his car washed. It's up to your kids to help Putt-Putt locate the things he needs; they have to earn money for a car wash and make their way around obstacles, such as a cow in the road. In *Putt-Putt Goes to the Moon* (ages 3-8), an accident at the fireworks factory sends Putt-Putt to the moon. Kids direct Putt-Putt around the lunar landscape and help him find the missing parts of the rocket ship so that he can get back home. Putt-Putt also stars in *Putt-Putt and Pep's Balloon-O-Rama* and *Putt-Putt and Pep's Dog on a Stick,* two collections of junior arcade-style games for kids ages 3-8.

The Freddi Fish Adventures

Freddi Fish is a plucky heroine who helps foil Boss and Spongehead, a pair of sharks who make mischief in the underwater world where Freddi lives. In Freddi's first adventure, *Freddi Fish and the Case of the Missing Kelp Seeds* (ages 3-8), kids help Freddi and her sidekick Luther follow a series of clues to solve the mystery of Grandma Grouper's kelp seeds.

In *Freddi Fish 2 and the Case of the Haunted Schoolhouse* (ages 3-8), a mysterious ghost haunts Mrs. Croaker's schoolhouse and steals toys from the students. "There's no such things as ghosts," declares Freddi, and she hatches a plan to trap the marauders. Kids direct her search through an intriguing underwater land (pictured in Figure 3-6) for the cork, the rope, and the other objects she needs to build her ghost-busting trap.

Figure 3-6:
Kids help
Freddi and
Luther solve
the mystery
in *Freddi
Fish 2 and
the Case of
the Haunted
Schoolhouse.*

The Pajama Sam Adventures

When his Mom turns off the light, Sam's just a kid who's afraid of the dark. But armed with his trusty flashlight, Sam transforms himself into Pajama Sam, the world's youngest superhero, ready to confront his fears in Figure 3-7. In his first adventure, *No Need to Hide When It's Dark Outside* (ages 3-8), Sam sets off for the Land of Darkness to find out where Darkness lives. When his superhero gear is impounded by the Customs Trees, Sam must travel through this strange world to recover his mask, flashlight, and lunch box. As kids help Sam, they encounter talking trees, dancing furniture, and a series of puzzles and challenges. With added complexity, more locations to explore, and predicaments to overcome, *Pajama Sam* appeals to kids who've already mastered the *Putt-Putt* and *Freddi Fish Adventures*.

What should you be doing while your preschooler plays on the computer? Take your cue from your kids. Trust their instincts, and let them set the pace. After all, it's their game and their style of playing — and learning — that counts. Chances are, they'll want you around at first. But resist the urge to interfere. When parents hurry kids at the computer or push them into activities that don't interest them, kids wind up frustrated.

Figure 3-7:
To help Pajama Sam make his way through the Land of Darkness, kids must think creatively, experiment with different solutions, and be persistent!

As your kids gain competence with the mouse, they'll want to spend more independent time at the computer. But don't disappear. Ask them to show you how to play their favorite game. Talk to them about what they like and what seems hard for them to do. If you think your kids may be ready to move on to a more challenging level, explore new levels together first. They may need your cheerleading to take the next step.

More Adventure Games for Little Kids

The Humongous adventures aren't the only thinking games for young kids. Here are three other adventure-style programs your kids will enjoy:

✔ *Mr. Potato Head Saves Veggie Valley:* Remember Mr. Potato Head? Now he has his own computer game. Kids join the famous spud and his daughter Sweet Potato to help them bring water to drought-stricken Veggie Valley. The seven activities along the way range from silly stuff (for example, creating disguises and chewing quickly at a pie-eating contest) to beginning math to problem-solving. (Hasbro, Ages 3-7)

✔ *Gregory & the Hot Air Balloon:* Gregory Chuckwood desperately wants a ride in Mr. Underwood's hot air balloon, until one day, by mistake, he takes off in the balloon solo. Kids help Gregory find the things he needs to get back home. For kids who enjoy stories on-screen, this program includes three animated stories that kids can read along with the computer. (Broderbund, Ages 3-7)

✔ *Darby the Dragon:* When Darby the flying dragon made a wish, it came true. Now his little sister has shrunk, and Darby must figure out how to make her big again. Kids wander through magical lands in search of special objects to help undo the magic. (Broderbund, Ages 5-9)

Spinning Stories

Once toddlers are old enough to enjoy making a mess with fingerpaints, they're old enough for creativity software. Our favorite creativity titles are much more than no-mess alternatives to crayons, chalk, paints, and markers. These programs encourage kids to stretch their imaginations, express themselves, build self-confidence, and develop social skills. In fact, in a research study on preschool children and computers, the biggest gains in intelligence and self-esteem came when kids used art and storywriting software that let them extend and enrich their own ideas. The two titles we profile in this section help nurture a child's imagination in very different ways.

Paint, Write & Play! (ages 4–7)

Paint, Write & Play! (from the Learning Company) is right on the mark for little kids. It is comprised of three areas: the travel agency, where kids can play with ideas; the art studio, where kids find paint tools and stamps for creating pictures; and the publishing house, where kids go to work with words.

Your little ones will be happy just mousing around the travel agency's ten locales, which range from the familiar (a beach, a farm, the three bears' house) to the more exotic (the Arctic, a desert, the African savanna). As their cursor passes over objects in the scenes, kids see the objects' names written on-screen and hear the names aloud. And all those words automatically appear in a personal word list (along with a little picture) that you and your kids can print and read together.

Other kids prefer to begin in the art studio, where they can work freehand (unlike *Stanley's Sticker Stories*) or create pictures from backgrounds and stamps. The simple art tools in *Paint, Write & Play!* are just right for little kids, who may be overwhelmed by extensive choices in more sophisticated art programs. In a nice touch, the stamps are all line drawings that kids can color. And many are images kids encountered in the travel agency (a wildebeest, an orca, a falcon, a hammerhead shark), along with the more usual collection of pets, vehicles, and everyday objects.

 Kids' pictures almost always inspire a story (like the 5-year-old's tale pictured in Figure 3-8), and that's where you come in. Ask your preschooler what's going on in the picture and take dictation. In *Paint, Write & Play!*, you find simple options for printing a book — complete with front and back covers, title page, author's dedication, and page numbers.

 Writing or dictating stories helps kids get ready to read. As they watch their ideas take form as words on a page and hear them read aloud, kids make the connections between speaking and writing and reading. They also encounter storywriting basics such as settings, characters, and actions. And they sense the classic patterns — beginning, middle, and ending — that make stories so satisfying.

Figure 3-8:
In *Paint, Write & Play!*, little kids can play with words and pictures, create stories, and print their own books.

The writing tools in *Paint, Write & Play!* are easy enough for kindergartners and 1st graders to use on their own. Visiting the travel agency first is a good way to get ideas and assemble a list of related words. That list "follows" kids back to the publishing house. And when they click a word, it automatically jumps onto the story page. Kids can use the ABC buttons to find other word lists. Under each letter (shown in upper- and lowercase), they find a dozen words or more, all starting with that letter. Most words are paired with a little picture, too, making it easy for kids to begin recognizing those words on sight.

Use the word pictures in *Paint, Write & Play!* to create personal messages and rebus puzzles for your youngster to read. What's a *rebus?* It's text in which pictures or symbols substitute for words and syllables. Because they're based on the idea that symbols stand for words, rebuses are an excellent introduction to the alphabet and reading. Don't worry if your rebus message sounds silly. The point is to help your kids feel confident about reading on their own.

Build-A-Book with Roberto (ages 2–4)

Build-A-Book with Roberto (from Theatrix Interactive) is a perfect preschool product because of its unique focus: friends and feelings. If your preschooler's at that stage when you're constantly saying "Don't hit . . . use your words" or needs your help putting words to feelings, consider *Build-A-Book.*

The hero, Roberto, is a hippo with a classic kids' problem. Hovering at the edge of the pool, he desperately wants to join the other hippos in a game of hippo ball. But when Roberto asks "Can I play with you?" his "friends" tell him to get lost. What's a hippo to do?

Kids help Roberto decide how to make his way into the game. Animated thought-balloons, like those pictured in Figure 3-9, pop up over Roberto's head every time he gets an idea, and kids choose one. Sometimes the possibilities are emotional ("I could get angry" or "I could pout"). Sometimes they're imaginative ("I could amaze them" or "I could give them popsicles"). Sometimes they're outrageous ("I could pump all the water out of the pool"). When kids click their choice, the story resumes, and they watch the consequences. Sometimes Roberto's strategy works. Sometimes it fails miserably, and then Roberto conjures up some more ideas, and kids make another choice.

Figure 3-9:
Kids create a new story each time they play by choosing which action Roberto will try to join in the hippos' game.

Playing with Roberto is great for preschoolers who are just becoming aware of how their behavior affects others. Kids get to experiment with different emotions and watch how others react. When Roberto throws a temper tantrum, for example, he scares the other hippos right out of the pool. And when he pouts, the others simply ignore him.

At any point, kids can choose to watch or print the stories they create. They can also experiment with emotions as they play with masks and puppets in the program's art room. By clicking Roberto's face, kids can watch his emotions change from angry to silly to surprised. Print the face, and you have a mask perfectly sized for a small child. Kids can color the mask on the computer or print it and color it by hand. In the same way, kids can create Roberto puppets that skip happily or scowl angrily, depending on their choice. The Parents' Guide on the CD-ROM has some great tips about assembling Roberto books, masks, and puppets so kids can create Roberto stories off the computer, too.

Build-A-Book with Roberto is a great choice for the youngest computer users. Its simple, uncluttered screen is easy for small children to navigate, and Roberto's silly song-and-dance routines are a wonderful reward for just a click of the mouse. While kids play, talk to them about what they're seeing on the screen. Your questions and observations will deepen their understanding and help them relate Roberto's behavior to their own.

Getting-Ready-for-School Skills

Educators agree that very young children don't gain much from formal instruction in academic skills. So save the drill software until your kids are older. On the other hand, preschool kids are surprisingly able learners, and they can readily pick up many kindergarten skills from early-learning software before heading off to school.

What's the benefit of this exposure? Well, every little bit helps. Kids build on what they know. If they are already familiar with a word, task, or concept when they encounter it at school, they'll feel more confident about what they're doing.

If your kids are in preschool, you're probably hearing a lot about kindergarten readiness. Here's a checklist of kids' readiness skills to bear in mind when you consider software, toys, and books for your kids:

___ Identifies feelings (happy, sad, angry, and so on)

___ Plays cooperatively — or competitively — as appropriate

___ Focuses for at least 10 minutes on a single task

___ Tolerates a reasonable amount of frustration without tears or anger

___ Listens to a story for at least 15 minutes

___ Shows responsibility for playthings and books

___ Recognizes shapes, colors, and sizes

___ Makes comparisons (similar and different)

___ Knows letters and numbers, simple counting

___ Sorts and classifies

___ Understands spatial relationships (top, middle, bottom, up, down, and so on)

___ Expresses quantity and size (less, more, small, large, and so on)

___ Recognizes calendar concepts (days of the week, months, holidays)

Every program in this chapter can help prepare children for school. But if you're especially concerned about your child's school readiness, you may want to consider a software program expressly designed to introduce school skills. For practicing basic skills, you can't go wrong with a *JumpStart* program from Knowledge Adventure.

The JumpStart series (ages 2–6)

There's a *JumpStart* program for every year, from the toddler stage through 2nd grade. Kids enjoy these programs because they offer so much to do. Parents like them because they cover a broad range of skills. But there is a trade-off: In a *JumpStart* program, kids get a little practice in lots of areas, but they don't get to explore anything in real depth.

In *JumpStart Preschool* (ages 2-5), pictured in Figure 3-10, kids get a dose of early math and reading skills when they visit 11 different play areas. Kids can paint by number, match letters in a concentration game, and create connect-the-dot pictures by sequencing numbers and letters. The program also entertains kids with musical lessons like nursery rhymes and the *ABC* song.

JumpStart Kindergarten (ages 4-6) is filled with skill-oriented games, puzzles, and songs. In the garden, kids practice sequencing by completing the plant patterns. In the puzzle games, they match numbers, letters (upper- and lowercase), opposites, and more. With stacking dolls, kids practice size comparisons. At the magic blackboard, they select a noun, a verb, and an adjective to make a silly sentence. (The sillier the better at this age.)

Figure 3-10:
In *JumpStart Preschool,* clicking on a familiar object in the classroom transports kids to a learning game.

As kids play in a *JumpStart* title, the software measures their success in different activities and automatically adjusts the level of difficulty. (Parents or kids can set the level, too.) And parents can check a Progress Report that records which activities your child has spent time playing.

The Progress Report feature in the *JumpStart* series can be useful when you can't spend as much time as you'd like observing your child play and learn. This feature can show you, for example, whether your child is avoiding certain activities. That's your cue. Ask about them. You may discover that they're too easy, too silly, or too boring. If your child says they're too hard, try playing the activities together.

Making your own learning games

You don't need a huge library of CD-ROMs to help your child master each and every school-readiness skill. Try using an art program to make up learning games tailored to particular skills. The personalized playtime will mean a lot to your child. We used *Kid Pix Studio* for our examples, but you can use any program that lets you paint or stamp numbers.

Number lines

In *Kid Pix Studio,* select the Paintbrush tool. Then use the Number Brush to fill the screen with numbers. Switch to the line tool, and then ask your child to find a 1 and draw a line to 2, then find a 3 and draw to it, then find a 4 and draw to it, and so on. Count aloud together, and hold up your fingers as your child connects the numbers. If you use different colors as you paint the screen with numbers, you can play variations on this game, such as "Draw a line from a blue 1 to a red 2." Don't forget to encourage counting backwards. Also try starting with numbers other than 1. Try the same kinds of games with ABCs, too.

"I Spy"

Select the Alphabet or Number Brush, and hold down the mouse to fill the screen with numbers, letters, or both. Be sure to change colors as you paint. Then ask your child to point to the correct spot on the screen when you say things like these: "I spy with my little eye a green 5," "The first letter of your name," "A yellow 6 next to a purple 9," "Two letters that make a word," "Two numbers that add up to your age," "The first letter of the alphabet," "The numbers in our address," "The numbers that make our phone number," and so on.

"Mother May I?"

Our adaptation of this perennial playground game uses the stamp tool. Tell your child to stamp six stars or eight birthday cakes or what have you. Count out loud as the stamping progresses. If you don't hear the magic words "Mother May I?" first, you get to "blow up" a screenful of stamps.

OPEN

Other Great Programs for Little Kids

When you're considering software for little kids, don't overlook these two classics. You can read more about them in later chapters of the book.

✔ *Just Grandma and Me*: This Mercer Mayer story was the very first book in the Living Book series, and we think it's still a good choice for a young child just starting with the computer. The software's simple booklike design is familiar, and its easy-to-find "hot spots" (where kids click and discover a fun animation) give little ones lots of practice in aiming and clicking the mouse. In Chapter 4, you find more details about all the Living Books and how they help to nurture your child's love of reading. (Living Books, Ages 2-6)

✔ *Kid Pix Studio:* *Kid Pix Studio* is a creativity funhouse filled with zany graphics, funny animations, sound effects, and musical fanfares. For little kids, it's a wild environment to explore. For every button they push, something wacky happens, from talking ABCs to exploding patterns and dancing aliens. You can read about *Kid Pix Studio* in Chapter 15. (Broderbund, Ages 3 & up)

Part III
Building the Basics

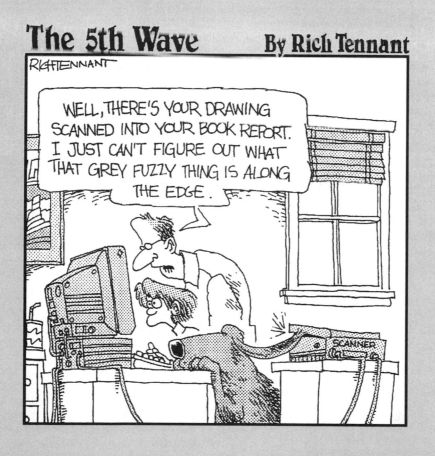

In this part . . .

The 3 'Rs — reading, 'riting, and 'rithmetic — have long dominated kids' software titles. In the early years of home computing, *basics* usually meant drill-and-practice programs. The focus: number facts, phonics rules, spelling words. Today the notion of basics has blossomed. Schools are as concerned about arming kids with critical-thinking skills, instilling a thirst for knowledge, stimulating their imaginations, and sparking their creativity as they are with the 3 'Rs.

And, happily, a wealth of inspired software is available to help. Thanks to an ambitious new generation of programs, toddlers are "reading" animated storybooks. Kids as young as 3 are exploring Boolean logic. (That's math, in case you haven't played with kids' software lately!) Four-year-olds are creating comic strips. Seven-year-olds are writing haiku.

In Part III, we tell you about software that can help your kids master the basics we knew as kids, the new basics, and the most basic skill of all — cultivating a lifelong love of learning.

Chapter 4
Using the Computer to Help Raise Readers

● ●

In This Chapter

▶ Nurturing a love of reading

▶ Enjoying stories-on-screen
  The Living Books series (ages 2–7)

▶ Learning letters
  Zurk's Learning Safari (ages 2–5)
  AlphaBonk Farm (ages 3–6)
  Dr. Seuss's ABC (ages 2–5)

▶ Practicing Phonics
  Reader Rabbit's Interactive Reading Journey (ages 4–7)
  Kid Phonics and *Kid Phonics 2* (ages 4–9)
  Reading Blaster Jr. (ages 4–7)
  Reader Rabbit 1 and 2 (ages 4–8)

▶ Reading on the Web — super sites for books and stories

▶ Other language arts programs — spelling, grammar, and more

▶ The reluctant reader — and how the computer can help

● ●

*W*hen it comes to reading, what kids learn at home is just as important as what they learn at school. And of all the things parents do, none is more important than getting kids hooked on books. Study after study shows that kids who've been read to are eager to read for themselves. And school-aged kids who read books for pleasure, not just for school, become better readers.

Here are some other things you can do to help your kids grow into readers.

___ *Read wonderful books out loud.*

Reading to kids is the best way to help them get ready to read. But make sure reading is a treat, not a 20-minute-a-day dose of academic medicine.

___ *Surround your kids with books.*

Encourage relatives to give books as gifts. Take kids to the library and let them choose the books they want to bring home.

___ *Make sure kids see you reading every day.*

Whether you're reading a mystery or catching up on the sports standings, show your kids that reading is important to you.

___ *Turn off the TV, limit the VCR.*

When kids have to find other ways to entertain themselves, reading often has more appeal.

___ *Try using the computer.*

You can find stories and information, on CD-ROMs and the Web, that can inspire kids to read more. You can find games to help kids learn letters, practice phonics skills, strengthen word recognition, build vocabulary, and more.

In this chapter, we profile two kinds of reading software. The first kind, stories on-screen, helps you spark a child's interest in books. When kids become enthralled with a story on-screen, they bring that same enthusiasm to a story in a book. We also cover skill-building reading games, which can be a painless way for kids to practice the fundamentals, from beginning ABCs to phonics and spelling.

Stories On-Screen

Imagine that as you read a book, the story comes to life right before your eyes. That's the magic kids experience in an electronic storybook. As the computer reads the story aloud, kids click the book's on-screen pictures in search of animated ssurprises.

The best electronic storybooks share many of the same qualities as a good children's book. In fact, all our favorite stories on-screen began as a much loved book. If you're worried that interactive stories might steer your kids away from real books, relax. Make the right selections, and storybook software can help make kids eager to read more, both on and off the computer.

But you have to choose with care. Not all titles foster that all-important connection to the printed word. Some skimp on the words of the story — or leave them out altogether. Others are so TV-like that children become passive viewers, not involved readers.

How can you tell what's good? We suggest you approach these programs the way you'd choose a book: Let the appeal of the story, the characters, and the artwork be your guide. Here's a checklist with questions to ask yourself as you look at storybook programs:

___ Is it a good story — the kind you'd read to your kids off the computer, night after night?

___ Will the artwork spark your child's imagination?

___ Do the program's multimedia effects (music, narration, animation, video) extend the words of the story — or eclipse them?

___ Does a copy of the "real" book come with the software?

___ Do the story's characters appear in other books? Has the author written other stories for children? In other words, does the software steer kids toward more reading?

Stories on-screen are high on replay value — if you buy them at exactly the right point. We've found that kids between 2 and 6 — contrary to the suggested age range on many a package — are the biggest fans.

The Living Books series (ages 2–7)

Living Books was the first publisher to transform children's books into CD-ROM software. And it's still the best. No one, not even Disney, can match Living Books simple charm or wildly clever wit. (You can see many of the demos of the Living Books on the *Great Software For Kids & Parents* CD-ROM.)

Living Books combine the wonderful characters and appealing artwork of children's literature with the animation of a cartoon. Each Living Book faithfully reproduces a popular children's book and brings its illustrations to life. As the computer reads the story aloud, the characters talk and move. In fact, in a Living Book, everything takes on a life of its own: trees chat, lunch boxes tell jokes, bananas dance the tango, and flowers sing a cappella.

Kids get so involved in these animated stories that they invariably want more. Be sure to hand them the paperback that comes in every box. But don't stop there. Head to your library or bookstore to find other books by the same author. Kids will read them all, over and over again. We know. It happened to us.

When Alison's daughters first met Arthur on the computer (he's the aardvark in glasses in Figure 4-1), they couldn't get enough of him. Together, mom and daughters read every Arthur book in the library. They bought Arthur books for special occasions like Valentine's Day and summer vacation. They even went to see Arthur's creator, Marc Brown, when he made an appearance at a local bookstore. Three years later, the girls are still (re)reading every Arthur story in the collection.

Here are some things you can do to turn your child's fascination with a story on-screen into a love of real books.

- ✔ Read the book together when your child is finished playing the CD-ROM. Or ask your child to "read" the story to you.

- ✔ Turn a favorite electronic book into a coloring book by doing screen captures and printing their favorite pages. (Turn to Chapter 17 to learn how to print what is on your computer screen.) Encourage your kids to trace over favorite words. Or have them circle certain letters (like the first letter of their names).

- ✔ When your kids begin to read on their own, get reacquainted with the Living Books. Although they may have "outgrown" the software, they can finally read the words.

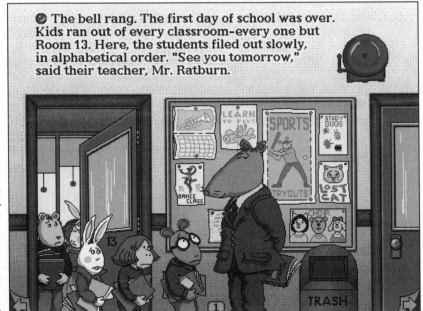

Figure 4-1: In *Arthur's Teacher Trouble,* Arthur faces third grade with the dreaded Mr. Ratburn.

Even youngsters too little to use a mouse on their own can enjoy a Living Book. Just choose the Read to Me option in the opening screen. The computer will turn the pages as it reads the story. Click the Play button so older kids can explore the hidden animations as they listen to the story. Be sure to encourage kids to click on words as well as pictures.

Happily, you'll find an ever expanding library of Living Books. Here are some of our favorites. (*Note:* The recommended ages are ours, not the publisher's. In general, we think these CD-ROMs have a shorter "shelf life" in your software library than their publishers do.)

Just Grandma and Me (ages 2–5)

Young children love Mercer Mayer's critter family. In *Just Grandma and Me*, Little Critter and his grandmother spend the day at the beach swimming, building sand castles, flying kites, and eating sandy hot dogs. The story is simple and sweet, and the words have a satisfying cadence for young children. The on-screen antics in this title are some of the best. Click on a star fish, for example, and it becomes a top-hatted, tap dancing Fred Astaire.

Little Monster at School (ages 2–6)

If your kids like Little Critter, introduce them to Little Monster, another Mercer Mayer character. In *Little Monster at School,* kids get to spend the day at school with Little Monster and his eccentric friend Yally, pictured in Figure 4-2. This story provides a funny, winsome look at school for kids who wonder what really goes on there.

Figure 4-2:
In *Little Monster at School,* kids get to share a school day with Little Monster and his friends.

The first thing we do is sing a morning song and then we practice our letters. Yally makes some of his letters backwards and then he gets mad. But I help him.

A B C D E F G H I
J K L M N O P Q R
S T U V W X Y Z

Sheila Rae, the Brave (ages 3–7)

It's always great to find a story starring spunky girls, and this tale also has nice insights into sibling relationships. With its seven sing-along songs, this CD-ROM gives kids a musical way to practice reading. Older kids enjoy the treasure hunt game, too.

Arthur's Teacher Trouble and Arthur's Birthday (ages 3–7)

If your kids haven't met Arthur and his friends, then one of these titles should top your list. And if your kids have already met Arthur, they'll enjoy these programs all the more. The *Arthur* books poke light-hearted fun at familiar people and situations in a child's life, such as school, teachers, friends, and pesky little sisters.

Arthur's Reading Race (ages 3–7)

When Arthur challenges his little sister, D.W., to a reading contest, she accepts. Joining in the challenge, kids play games with Arthur and D.W. as they move through the story. In I Spy, for example, kids match words to objects D.W. spies in the story. In Let Me Write, kids drag rebuses (pictures that represent words) onto a writing tablet to create sentences. In each activity, kids can choose their own level of play, from no reading required to reading words on their own.

The Berenstain Bears Get in a Fight and The Berenstain Bears in the Dark (ages 3–6)

The Berenstain Bears Get in a Fight and *The Berenstain Bears in the Dark* deal with kid issues like sibling conflict and kids' fears of the dark. If your kids like these stories, introduce them to other *Berenstain Bear* books. (There are more than one hundred.) If your kids are already Berenstain Bear fans, be sure to watch the on-screen interview with authors Stan and Jan Berenstain in *The Berenstain Bears Get in a Fight*. It's neat to hear the authors talk about what they do and watch them create illustrations.

Dr. Seuss's ABC and Green Eggs and Ham (ages 2–6)

When we heard that Living Books was bringing Dr. Seuss to the computer, we were skeptical. His books are so clever and riotously funny, a CD-ROM was sure to pale in comparison. Wrong! These programs bring even more Seuss-like antics to each story with all the memorable Seuss characters like Sam-I-Am (pictured in Figure 4-3) and Izzy and Ichabod joining in the fun. You'll read more about *Dr. Seuss's ABC* later in this chapter.

Figure 4-3:
Green Eggs and Ham includes games for practicing beginning phonics skills.

The New Kid on the Block (ages 3–7)

Before your kids decide poetry is not cool, introduce the zany humor of Jack Prelutsky. His rhythm and rhymes encourage kids to listen and read along, and the animations (triggered by clicking words, not pictures) add a cartoonlike quality that captivates even reluctant readers.

Stellaluna (ages 3–7)

Stellaluna, a young fruit bat, falls from her mother's hold and finds safety in a nest of baby birds. In order to survive, Stellaluna must learn to act like a bird, eating grasshoppers and sleeping in the nest instead of hanging upside down from a tree branch. Through their friendship, Stellaluna and her bird siblings come to admire each other's ways and wonder at the mystery of "being so different yet feeling so alike." In addition to the story, kids can take the Bat Quiz to learn about bats and how they live.

Many Living Books are bilingual. Kids can read and listen in either English or Spanish. (*Just Grandma and Me* offers Japanese, as well.) For more ideas about using Living Books to help kids learn a language, see Chapter 13.

Other Notable Stories On-Screen

Kids play in a Living Book by uncovering hidden animations sprinkled throughout a book's pages. Other electronic books let kids move through a story in different ways. In these programs, kids can join in the antics of two well-lored storybook characters.

Curious George Comes Home

Like a Living Book, this CD-ROM remains true to the distinctive illustrations of Curious George's creator, H.L. Rey. But instead of reading a story on the screen, kids direct new adventures for Curious George and print them as books to color and read (or pretend to read). This simple storymaking product is most appropriate for kids ages 2-4. But they'll need your help to print their book. First exit the game and save your child's story. Then open the Storybook Publisher (called CGBook) in the HMI program group and follow the instructions. You can bind your child's book in the familiar bright yellow cover included in the software package. (Houghton Mifflin Interactive, Ages 2-4)

Big Anthony's Mixed Up Magic

Strega Nona is a good witch who heals headaches and plays matchmaker for the people in Calabria. Big Anthony is her well-intentioned but bumbling assistant. Kids will find lots to do in this story-on-screen. They can listen to author Tomie dePaola read his story aloud, they can wander through the Calabrian countryside, they can assist Big Anthony (pictured in Figure 4-4) with his jobs, they can learn magic tricks, or they can choose to play several games. (MECC, Ages 3-6)

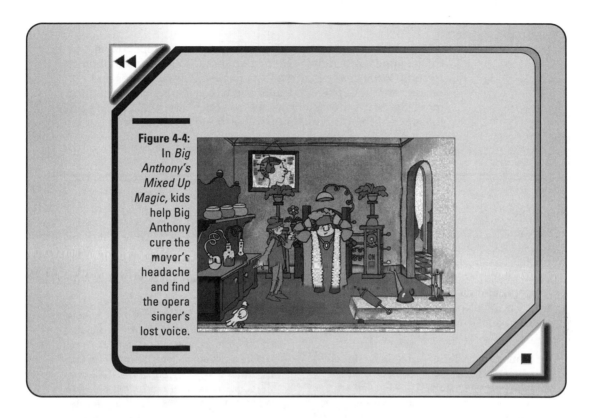

Figure 4-4: In *Big Anthony's Mixed Up Magic*, kids help Big Anthony cure the mayor's headache and find the opera singer's lost voice.

Building Reading Skills

Learning to read is hard work. Step-by-step, kids must unlock a mysterious code, using a host of wonderful but sometimes puzzling new skills. For kids who are learning the basics, computer software can disguise the repetition of skill-building exercises with fun and games.

But which skills — and which games — are the right ones for your kids? Here are some things to consider before you choose a title:

___ *Educational approach*

Most reading software is closely linked to the kindergarten and 1st and 2nd grade curriculums. Even so, software may not exactly match what your child is doing in school or what your child needs to practice. So talk to the teacher to get an idea of what's best. For some kids, an alternative approach to regular classroom fare is a welcome change. Or they may have mastered classroom lessons and are ready to move ahead. Other kids may prefer software that's more in sync with school.

___ *Fun Factor*

A kid's willingness to use skill-building software depends on one thing: games. Kids don't give a hoot about the on-screen phonics lessons. What really matters is gameplay. Choose games and characters that appeal to them, and kids will play longer and learn more. Software with aliens works for some kids, while others prefer talking rabbits. (And, parents, we've found it best to keep our opinions to ourselves.)

Reading on the Web!

It's no secret. Experts agree that reading to your kids is one of the most important things parents can do. And don't stop when your kids begin reading on their own. Read them books that are too hard for kids to tackle on their own. Take turns reading aloud. And check the Web for ideas and resources for family reading. Here are some reading sites we like:

✔ **Parents and Children Together Online:** A project of The Family Literacy Center, this site publishes stories, poems, and articles for families to read and explore together. You can read the story on the web and find links to related sites, or you can print it to read later. Check out the site's Global Campfire, too. Remember how you'd start a story and let the next person in the circle add on? Kids can read a mystery, science fiction, or adventure story and write the next part. Or have everyone in the family write the next section and see which one gets published online. (http://www.indiana.edu/~eric_rec/fl/pcto/menu.html)

✔ **Great Family Read Alouds:** Offers family recommendations for wonderful books to read aloud with preschool and elementary-age kids. The titles are organized by subject, including fantasy, folklore, and timeless stories. Besides title and author, you also find a short synopsis of each book and the ages for which it's most appropriate. (http://picard.dartmouth.edu/~cam/ReadAloud.html)

✔ **Children's Literature Web Guide:** Here's a wonderful collection of information for parents and teachers looking for good books for all ages. It has lists of best books from librarians, steachers, and children, plus best-selling children's titles from *Publishers Weekly,* Newberry and Caldecott Medal winners, and more. You also find excellent links to sites that publish children's writing. (http://www.ucalgary.ca/~dkbrown/index.html)

✔ **Reading Rainbow:** The Reading Rainbow public television show has a knack for finding books that kids want to hear and read. Its Web site features a list of more than 100 picture books with authors and publishers, a short description, and (sometimes) an activity idea. (http://www.pbs.org/readingrainbow/rrlist.html)

✔ **The Internet Public Library:** Here's the place to find entire books on the Web. Use the library's index to Online Books. Search by title or by author. Then download and print. All for free! (http://www.ipl.org/reading/books/index.html)

While educational software can help kids master new skills, kids need practice applying these skills off the computer. Spend some time with your kids' reading software so you can understand what they're learning. (Many have excellent parent sections.) Then bring up these skills as you read and talk with your kids each day.

Learning letters

We're overrun with ABC books. Colorful letter magnets cover the refrigerator door. Alphabet puzzle pieces litter the floor. And all our magazines and catalogs have holes where the kids cut out word pictures for their alphabet books. But letters really clicked for our kids thanks to the computer.

ABC software is a great complement to all the things you already do to help your kids learn to read and write their letters. The software is so much fun that kids return to play again and again — and learn their letters in the process. Here are some of our favorites.

Zurk's Learning Safari (ages 2–5)

Using *Zurk's Learning Safari* is like playing inside a beautifully illustrated children's book — with a technological twist. As kids play hide and seek with a funny little guy named Zurk, they see letters "morph" into animals. An F becomes a flamingo, a Z turns into a zebra, and the like (see the picture in Figure 4-5). Other letter activities include an ABC book of jungle animals (H is for hyena, hippo, and hyrax) and a jigsaw puzzle of lowercase letters. (Soleil/Maxis)

AlphaBonk Farm (ages 3–6)

AlphaBonk Farm offers up the ABCs in a delightfully different way. First there's the unusual vocabulary: *U* for udders, undershirt, and utility pole; *J* for jalopy, jersey cow, and jeans. Then there's the program's distinctive looks: A mingling of photos, line drawings, and zany graphics fill the screen like the picture you see in Figure 4-6. Then there are the program's inventive games. Seek and Find challenges kids to find hidden objects that begin with certain letters (hidden *P* words include peas, a pumpkin, a pony, and a potbelly pig), while Poke 'n Prod offers 13 offbeat activities, from concocting ice cream cones to inspecting animal innards with an x-ray machine. We love the Headbone style, but we have to tell you: It's a little too off-the-wall for some parents. Check the Headbone Interactive Web site (http://www.headbone.com) first to see whether you like its looks. (Headbone Interactive)

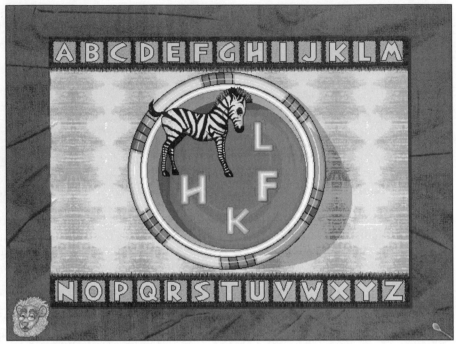

Figure 4-5:
In *Zurk's Learning Safari,* kids play hide and seek with Zurk as he dives into a magical bowl of alphabet soup.

Figure 4-6:
In *AlphaBonk Farm,* Bungie the Frog invites kids to play with pictures and words in unexpected ways.

Dr. Seuss's ABC (ages 2–5)

While clicking around this CD-ROM, kids find all the rhyming words and kooky characters from the original book, plus lots of additional adorable alliterations. The book features two *C* words, for example, but the CD-ROM has 24, complete with cartoon antics. Click the camel, and watch it dance a conga on the ceiling. Or click the crazy costume closet, and see who comes out. Will it be a cowboy, a captain, or a cook? (Living Books)

You can easily adapt these on-screen ABC games for off-the-computer fun. And when the pediatrician's running late, you're stuck in traffic, your plane's delayed an hour . . . that's the perfect time for some wordplay. Not only will you distract the kids, but you'll also be reinforcing reading skills. Here are some activities our kids enjoy.

- ✔ Look around and try to stump the kids with "I Spy something that starts with the letter , , ," or "I Spy something that rhymes with. . . ."

- ✔ Challenge your kids to think of as many things as they can that start with the first letter in their own names (or tougher, things that end with this letter).

- ✔ Start with a short word — such as *hat.* Then challenge the next player to say a word that starts with the last letter of the first word — such as *tack.* The next person has to find a word that starts with *k,* and so on.

Remember those 1st grade workbooks filled with pages of phonics exercises? Today the skills are much the same. But on the computer, silly games, bouncy songs, friendly aliens, and talking animals enliven the repeated practice. The multimedia pizzazz of reading programs is an especially big plus for beginning readers. It lets kids *hear* the sounds while they're trying to decode written letters, letter blends, and words. And it lets them *see* the "sound-it-out" process in a new way. Watching animated letters knit themselves into a single word makes concepts like blending letter sounds easier to understand.

Reader Rabbit's Interactive Reading Journey series (ages 4–7)

Reader Rabbit's been helping kids learn to read for more than 10 years, and he's still going strong. While the first Reader Rabbit programs turned phonics practice into computer games, the newest titles encourage practice in the context of real stories. In fact, each program in this series comes with a set of paperbacks that are perfect for little pockets.

The *Interactive Reading Journey* titles (from The Learning Company) offer a carefully planned sequence of on-screen books and games designed to introduce all the skills kids need for reading. This comprehensive approach has its pluses and minuses. On the plus side, kids feel good about their progress because the software presents small, easy-to-master tasks. On the minus side, the program's rigid step-by-step structure can frustrate free-wheeling kids who want to control where they go, what they do, and when. But if kids stick with the program, the *Interactive Reading Journey* really can help them grasp the basic elements of reading.

Reader Rabbit's Interactive Reading Journey Volume 1 (ages 4–7)

The Learning Company is a master at creating skill-building games that kids love to play. You find games that help kids learn to recognize whole words, games to reinforce letter sounds, games to help kids combine sounds, and games to help kids sound out words. In Figure 4-7, for example, kids pay a visit to the nursery of Nanny Toucanny who is caring for two eggs. One egg contains the letters "sh," and the other one holds the letters "ut." Nanny shows kids how to "smoosh" the two sounds together to hatch the new word "shut."

Figure 4-7:
Nanny Toucanny leads kids through one of the sound-it-out games in *Reader Rabbit's Interactive Reading Journey Volume 1.*

Interactive Reading Journey's first volume charts a path through 20 letters. But there's no wandering off the path to smell the roses. Kids must stop in each letter land, complete a series of activities, and read two storybooks. These stories are bare-bones fare, more like our childhood stories about Dick, Jane, and Spot than the Living Books.

After every few letters, kids reach a gate at the end of the unit. The software requires kids to complete 80 percent of a unit's activities before they can move on to the next unit. If this frustrates your kids, click the parent option (POP) icon in the bottom-right corner of the screen. Open the progress report. Then lower the completion number in the percentage box at the top.

To help your child get the most from *Interactive Reading Journey,* stay involved. Use POP to turn off the computer's voice and encourage your child to read the storybooks aloud to you. Before you read a story at bedtime, ask your child to read one of the program's little books to you.

Reader Rabbit's Interactive Reading Journey Volume 2 (ages 5-8)

Kids who enjoyed the first *Reading Journey* are good candidates for the second. Volume 2 takes kids to 15 reading lands filled with phonics games and stories. But you find some new twists, too. The program can record kids' voices as they read aloud and capture their response when Booker the Frog pops a question about a story. Because kids love the sound of their own voices, this feature is a great incentive for them to practice reading the title's stories on their own. (The software comes with a coupon for a free microphone in case your computer doesn't have one.)

Want to take a more active hand in teaching your child to read? Consider *The Reading Lesson,* a program designed to help parents act as teachers. This comprehensive program for ages 4 and up combines software and lesson books to help kids build phonics and word-recognition skills. With this program, the parent, and not the computer, is the teacher. (MountCastle)

Phonics fun

No, phonics fun is not an oxymoron. On the computer, kids practice the basics like consonants, vowels, words, and sentences, or prefixes and suffixes by singing songs and playing games. Here are some solid programs for helping kids to build reading skills.

Kid Phonics (ages 4–7)

Kid Phonics (from Davidson) is great for 4- and 5-year-olds who are learning to connect the look of letters and words to their sounds. Kids listen as five odd-looking but lovable "busters" croon tunes filled with alliteration and rhyme or play with sounds in two activity areas — the Sound Buster and the Word Builder. In Sound Buster, kids match what they hear to what they see to practice 10 different kinds of word sounds, including beginning and ending consonants and rhyming words. In Word Builder, kids select a picture and then build the corresponding word — letter sound by letter sound.

When kids spell a word correctly, they get to build a sentence around it like the one pictured in Figure 4-8. Show kids how to print the page for their personal word dictionary. This is a good way to help them build up a personal set of words among the more than 200 in the program.

One of the best features in *Kid Phonics* is the animated tutor that takes kids through the whole sound-it-out process. Encourage your kids to click the Show Me button to take advantage of this lesson.

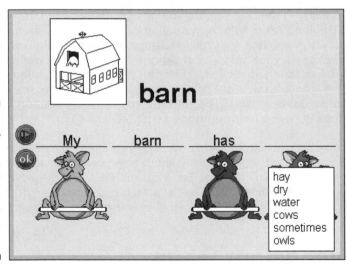

Figure 4-8:
Kid Phonics teaches kids how letters build words and how words build sentences.

Kid Phonics 2 (ages 6–9)

In *Kid Phonics 2,* kids graduate to a new level of phonics skills with seven new Buster songs and activities in a Wild West setting. In the Word Builder game, kids build words like "antelope" or "teaspoon," syllable by syllable. In the Word Rodeo, kids experiment with creating compound words like airplane and football. And in the Jailhouse, kids help desperadoes like Scrambled Sam or Sound It Outlaw get out of jail by listening to syllable sounds to unscramble words. This program also gives kids practice with prefixes and suffixes, silent vowels, and homonyms.

Reading Blaster Jr. (ages 4–7)

Reading Blaster Jr. (from Davidson) has the jazzy look of a Saturday morning cartoon, but the activities are pure phonics. Kids get lots of practice with beginning and ending word sounds, letter blends, and word families (mat . . . hat . . . sat). When kids play in the Toy Station in Figure 4-9, they spin beginning and ending sounds and then determine if the combination creates a real word. On the Planet of the Storyheads, kids move the parts of the story into the right sequence and then listen as the software reads it out loud. Also included in the program are 20 storybooks, which kids can print or read on the screen, with or without the computer's assistance.

With five levels of play for each game, *Reading Blaster Jr.* will keep many beginning readers going until they can read a real book. Most kids love the program's space setting and its raucous rock-and-roll music. But for kids who are easily distracted, *Reading Blaster Jr.,* with its spaceship full of gadgets, may not be the best choice.

Reading Blaster Jr. has a few quirks that interfere with its ease of use. There's no exit button, so kids need to press Ctrl+Q to quit. And to explore freely, kids must select Free Play when they start the program. When the program's new at home, show kids how to click the Blaster Shield button, which looks like a little shield in the top left corner of the screen, to change activities or levels of play. After they've played a few times, consider changing to "mission mode" so they'll be sure to practice all the skills.

Figure 4-9:
In *Reading Blaster Jr.,* kids see and hear how beginning and ending letter sounds combine to make a word.

Reader Rabbit phonics games (ages 4–8)

For some kids, multimedia is more of a hindrance than a help. These kids find it easier to concentrate when there are fewer on-screen distractions.

If this sounds like your child, the older *Reader Rabbit* games (from The Learning Company) may be a good choice. In contrast to *Reading Blaster Jr.,* they're quieter and slower paced. Unlike *Interactive Reading Journey,* both *Reader Rabbit 1* and *2* let kids choose freely among four phonics games.

In *Reader Rabbit 1* (ages 4-6), kids learn sight words and practice memory skills, initial letter sounds, and ending sounds. *Reader Rabbit 2* helps kids ages 6 through 8 practice 1st- and 2nd-grade skills including letter blends, short and long vowels, rhyming words, homonyms, and alphabetizing.

Kids will get more out these software games if you help them practice the phonics skills off the computer as well. Here are some activities you can try:

- ✔ While you're riding in the car or going through the getting-ready-for-bed routine, play phonics games. Can your kids think of three things that start with the *mmmm* sound, that rhyme with wall, that end with the *tttt* sound?

- ✔ Point out words your kids have "built" in *Kid Phonics* or *Reading Blaster Jr.* You may find their words in magazines, road signs, cereal boxes. How do you know the words your kids have learned? Simple! Print the program's dictionary. One copy for you. One copy for your child.

- ✔ Have kids keep a list of words they know by sight. They can circle their sight words in the software dictionary you printed and then transfer the words to their list.

Phonics practice isn't the only way to build reading skills. Writing is good for reading, too. You find lots of suggestions for storywriting programs in Chapter 5, and we encourage you to add one to your beginning reader's library. After the structured experience of skill-building software, kids will enjoy time with more creative software.

Other Language Arts Programs

After kids have learned to read and write, the challenges change. Now they're expected to focus on reading comprehension, grammar, and spelling. Here are some software programs that encourage kids to practice these less-than-popular subjects by playing games.

✔ *Reading Galaxy:* In this wacky intergalactic game show, kids compete with celebrity aliens who claim they've written some of the best children's books on Earth. To prove the aliens wrong, kids read sections from the book and answer questions, all in a puzzlelike format. For kids who need practice with reading comprehension, this program is a fun exercise. But the gameplay is reading-intensive, so you may need to play along with them to keep them involved. (Broderbund, Ages 8-12)

✔ *Cooper McQue Breaks Through!:* A grammar-skills-meet-arcade game, with the action set in a lively cartoon world. The hero, Cooper McQue, is dawdling at the chalkboard, diagramming the longest sentence ever written, when suddenly he's sucked into a mysterious Chalk World. To save Chalk World from the evil Chalk Miser, Cooper must separate sentences from fragments, rescue synonyms, and more. (DreamWorks Interactive, Ages 6-9)

✔ *SuperSolvers Spellbound:* This program looks a bit dated, but you can do something *really* useful: Enter your kids' weekly spelling words. That way, kids can use the program's spelling-bee game to study for Friday's test. (The Learning Company, Ages 7-12)

✔ *Word Munchers Deluxe:* Like its counterpart, *Math Munchers Deluxe* (Chapter 6), this popular old program has been re-released with updated 3-D looks. It plays like an old-fashioned video game, but Word Munchers is a fun way to practice phonics, grammar, and vocabulary skills for kids who like fast-clicking gameplay. Be sure to set the game to match your child's grade level. (MECC, Ages 6-11)

The reluctant reader — and how the computer can help

Some kids are avid readers right from the start. Others may need some nudging. If you've got a reluctant reader, here are some ways the computer can help:

- **Find the right books:** Help your kids find stories they like. For older kids, consult "Quick Picks for Reluctant Young Adult Readers" from the American Library Association (http://www.ala.org/booklist/best.html). For younger kids, try the recommendations from Reading Rainbow (http://www.pbs.org/readingrainbow/rrlist.html).

- **Try reading on the Web:** The World Wide Web is such an amazing resource, chances are it's got something that matches your child's personal interests.

Like sports (http://www.espnet.sportszone.com) or horses (http://www.horseweb.com) or music (http://www.mtv.com) or even television shows (http://ptd15.afionline.org/CineMedia/cmframe.html). Help kids explore the possibilities with a keyword search. Then bookmark the best sites so your kids can return and read on their own.

- **Play games!:** Software titles for younger children are light on text so that kids who can't yet read can still play. But in many programs for older kids, reading — and writing — can help kids win the game. And that motivates them to practice both skills!

Chapter 5

Using the Computer to Help Kids As Writers

● ●

● ●

*A*s you can see, we put software about reading and software about writing in separate chapters. We had to — because each category has so many programs! But real life is different. Listening and speaking, reading and writing are closely linked. Inseparable, in fact. They're all ways of using language to understand and express ideas.

Many teachers, particularly in the early grades, combine all these language-arts skills in their classroom activities. Their reason: All these skills reinforce one another. Listening makes kids better speakers. Reading makes them better writers. And vice versa.

A school day may begin, for example, with kids listening as their teacher reads a story. The kids may then reenact the story with figures on a felt board, with puppets, or with dress-up clothes. They may create their own illustrations for the story. They may copy the title, add a few words, and "read" their versions to the class. As they master letters and sounds, they progress to a few creatively spelled words and then to a sentence or two. Later they invent new endings to familiar tales. Still later, they create "pattern" books that mimic the repeating rhymes of popular children's stories. Before too long, they'll be writing solo.

Your mission, should you choose to accept it, is to make your home one that encourages kids as much as possible as they go through the learn-to-write process. Why? Because starting in 1st grade and continuing throughout adulthood, writing is the way we relay information, send messages, keep records, and express feelings.

You can do a lot to encourage emerging writers.

___ *Take an interest in the stages kids go through before they're ready to write.*

Admire their artwork. Applaud the puppet shows. Watch the playacting. All these activities are the precursors of kids' writing.

___ *Read to your kids.*

Encourage them to read solo, too. Study after study has shown that readers become writers.

___ *Provide a place for kids to write.*

The place doesn't have to be expensive or set apart from family goings-on. But a kid-sized chair, smooth work surface, and good light are conducive to writing.

___ *Encourage "real" writing — stuff that's meaningful to your kids.*

Ever notice that kids' penmanship is often at its best in Christmas lists? By the same token, kids often express their ideas better when they're writing about what they really care about.

___ *Brainstorm together.*

For kids, it's a tall order to simultaneously coordinate the mechanics of writing — penmanship, spelling, punctuation, grammar — not to mention the most important thing of all, *ideas*. You can help by encouraging your kids to describe their impressions — of people, events, places, books, movies — and use these impressions as a springboard to the written word.

___ *Respond to your kids' efforts.*

Writers (young and old) need an audience. So read what your kids write. And be kind, not judgmental, in your comments.

___ *Consider software.*

> You can find computer programs that encourage every stage of your kids' development as writers. Little kids love being able to express themselves with on-screen writing — even before they can reliably wield a pencil. Older kids appreciate the many ways software sparks their imaginations and steers them through the stages of the writing process. And kids of all ages love the way software makes their writing look. By making their writing attractive, the programs covered in this chapter *invite* kids to write. And the more kids write, the more they read, and the better they become at both.

Now here's that perennial question: How do you choose? For the very young, you'll find two good programs in Chapter 3: *Stanley's Sticker House* and *Paint, Write & Play!* After that, some kids may be ready for your word-processing program! They like total freedom. And that blank page may be invitation enough to tell a story.

For other children, one look at a blank page, and their minds go blank, too. They prefer a little structure. So the software we recommend in this chapter strikes a balance between freedom and structure — because most kids probably need some of both. The titles fall into four groups that roughly parallel what goes on at school and kids' developmental needs. (But don't feel obligated to choose titles in order.) You can find "Storytelling" software, "School Programs," "Wordplay" titles, and "Diaries."

Writing Stories

Recognizing that children begin "writing" with pictures and sounds as much as with text, storytelling programs encourage expression in a great many forms. There's the language of art with its abundance of backgrounds, stamps, and tools; the languages of sound and music with their scene-setting overtures, musical interludes, and sound effects; the language of the spoken word with its "recordable" narration in kids' own voices or text-to-speech playback. And, of course, there's the language of the written word.

Here's a look at some of our favorites, plus suggestions for how you can use them to incorporate writing into your family activities and help kids with school work, too.

The Imagination Express series (ages 5–12)

The *Imagination Express* series (from Edmark) is perfectly named. With its exceptionally beautiful artwork, equally compelling showcase for words, inventive store of ideas, clever use of technology, and polished-looking results in printed or electronic form, this series does a fabulous job of encouraging kids (ages 5-12) to express what's in their imaginations.

The starting point for many an *Imagination Express* story is an illustration, like the one in Figure 5-1. Kids begin by choosing one of many backgrounds and then "populating" it with stickers representing flora, fauna, objects, and characters. All too often, sthe stickers or stamps in kids' software are fuzzy-edged caricatures. Not so in *Imagination Express*. Its stickers are crisp, richly colored, and highly detailed — like real storybook pictures.

Often kids are frustrated because the pictures they create on the computer screen don't measure up to the image in their mind's eye. If a knight is going to skewer a dragon, for example, his lance ought to be pointed at the fearsome beast, and the dragon ought to retaliate by breathing fire. Most storytelling programs don't cooperate, however. *Imagination Express*, in contrast, has the uncanny capability to scale stickers to just the right size and to pose them facing front, back, left, or right — all while your child is moving them into the scene. Kids can also attach short, animated sequences to stickers so their audience will see a steed rear up and whinny, a whale spout, or a macaw flap its wings.

When parents see a lot of art tools in writing products, they sometimes worry: What if my kids spend all their time on illustrations? How can I get them to devote more attention to words? Teachers say readiness to move from pictures to words is a developmental thing; you shouldn't — indeed *can't* — rush it.

But why not play the "Page Per Person" game to encourage kids to write a little bit more? After your child finishes one page, *you* author the next one. That way, you can advance the plot a little or introduce another character. And on the next page, your child can take up the challenge.

The good looks of *Imagination Express* have a galvanizing effect on kids: Just minutes into a title, and they're bursting to tell a tale. Happily, their text looks equally good. It might appear on realistic-looking parchment in *Destination: Castle* or on a papyrus scroll in *Destination: Pyramids,* for example. The different backdrops for words offer subtle encouragement for kids to try different *voices* in their writing — a first-person account, a historical narrative, a story told through letters, and the like.

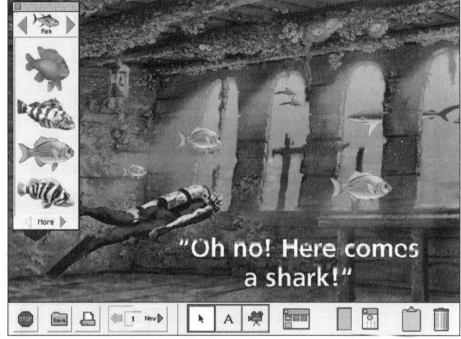

Figure 5-1:
Diving for
sunken
treasure
with
*Imagination
Express:
Ocean.*

What if your kids can't write yet? The *Imagination Express* series is still a great choice, provided you're willing to be involved. Offer to take dictation when your child is finished creating an illustration. Or help record a sentence or two. (This may take a little practice because the narration needs to be kept short; the program limits the narrative to about 30 seconds per page.) Or try the Configure for Young Child option in the Adult Options section. This choice lets kids use all the stickers they want, but only five preset backgrounds.

Imagination Express strikes a nice balance between "open-ended" and "assisted" storytelling: freedom for kids who know what they want to do as well as unobtrusive help for kids who need a bit of a jumpstart. To help inspire kids with an interesting reason to write, for example, each title has a built-in fact book. Some kids like to skim the fact book as they would a historical handbook or a field guide. Others never consult it — until they run into a particularly intriguing sticker. Then they can click into the fact book, adding to their fund of knowledge as they spin their tale.

What do kids do when their stories are complete? They share them on the computer or print them to create a book. The benefits for on-screen viewers are scene-setting music, sound effects, narration, and animation. For off-the-computer readers, *Imagination Express* produces the best-looking books we've ever seen from a computer.

The *Imagination Express* series gives kids lots of options, as you can see from the following list. Your choice of titles depends on your kids' interests and what's going on at school. A diehard in-line skater may be happier with the *Neighborhood* title than with the *Castle* title, for example. Many of the following programs make excellent complements to classroom social studies units.

- ✔ *Destination: Castle:* Fanciful and factual at the same time, the fairy-tale looks of this title make it a good choice for young children, who often start writing by retelling cherished tales. Older kids can easily use it to spin more complex fantasies or more realistic tales about society in medieval times.

- ✔ *Destination: Neighborhood:* The familiarity of the people and places in this program make it a good choice for young children. But it can also be satisfying for older kids, who often enjoy creating different endings for real-life conflicts at school or events at home.

- ✔ *Destination: Rain Forest:* Quite a crop of rain forest-related products is on the market, and this is one of the best. The sights and sounds of the jungle are especially lush and realistic. When your child tackles the delicate issues of ecological preservation versus economic growth at school, this is a good at-home complement.

- ✔ *Destination: Ocean:* You can find as much information in this program about marine life, ocean habitats, and the human impact on underwater ecosystems as you can in an oceanography CD-ROM.

- ✔ *Destination: Pyramids* and *Destination: Time Trip, USA:* These are school products, but Edmark *will* sell them directly to parents. Just call Edmark's 800 number, listed in Appendix B. If your child loves history or you're trying to encourage an interest in times past, either or both of these titles make a great choice. We've found that the challenge of writing from the vantage point of an ancient Egyptian (shown in Figure 5-2) or an American colonist can really inspire kids to delve into history.

The space allotted for text in *Imagination Express* is smaller than the space allotted for the artwork. So what do you do when kids have a *lot* to write? Encourage your child to accompany an illustration with a single sentence, or maybe two, and save the rest of the text. Then select a blank or bordered backdrop for the next page and use it entirely for text. That way, kids who are bursting with words can alternate picture pages with story pages.

Kids can try out any style of writing with *Imagination Express*. Beginners can write captions, and nothing more. Older kids can try writing narrative, in the first-person or third-person. They can write poetry, dialogue, a news story, a diary entry, a speech. In short, anything at all.

Figure 5-2:
In this story, the author has adopted the character of an Egyptian boy.

The *Hollywood* series that we describe next also gives kids plenty of scope. But it focuses on one particular form of writing, the screenplay — perhaps the single most popular genre in our culture — and makes it instantly accessible to kids.

The Hollywood series (ages 9 & up)

Here's what we like best about *Hollywood* and *Hollywood High* (from Theatrix Interactive). They've got characters and scenarios with *attitude,* the kind that 9-year-olds and up find funny, relevant, and irresistible. These titles deliver *immediate gratification.* Kids instantly see their writing and their directing come alive on the screen. And these titles put *way-cool technology* into kids' hands, enabling characters to move the way kids tell them to and speak the lines that kids write, complete with lip-synching. The programs build stage directions, sound effects, and music right into the script.

Casting call

Hollywood production starts with a choice of backgrounds. In the original *Hollywood,* 20 different backdrops inspire the action: a talk show set; a diner; a sports arena; a space ship; a mad scientist's lab; and a school auditorium, cafeteria, or classroom. *Hollywood High*'s 20 settings have a teenage twist: a mall, an arcade, a school dance, a beach. Next come the characters: wacky animals in *Hollywood* and teens in *Hollywood High*. Kids assign each character a name, a hobby (heavy-metal music, bungee jumping), a mood (bored, paranoid), a speaking voice (nerdy male, whispery female), and a role (student, bicycle messenger). Kids then move the characters into a scene.

Scripting the show

With characters on-stage, scripting begins. To accompany lines of dialogue and narration, like those you see in Figure 5-3, kids can give each character facial expressions of all sorts, body language (shrugging shoulders, crossing arms), and actions (talking on the phone, eating a pizza). For added realism, kids can include sound effects and theme music. And every gesture, action, and sound is automatically written into the script and updated whenever kids make a change. During both the creative process and the performance, the *Hollywood* programs lip-synch the dialogue and read the characters' lines with one of the best text-to-speech voice generators we've heard.

Figure 5-3:
Kids find that scripting lines in *Hollywood* is a satisfying way to handle homework, propose an increase in allowance, resolve a fight with a sibling!

Where to share your stories

For kids (and adults, too), having an audience is an important part of the writing process. Kids learning to talk need someone to listen; kids learning to write need someone to react. And the newest place for young writers to find readers is the World Wide Web.

Publication is a good incentive for kids to edit and polish their work. And reading stories written by other kids their age may inspire your kids' efforts to write. When you and your kids agree their work is ready for a wider audience, check out the following sites:

✔ **Children's Literature Web Guide:** Probably the best resource to consult when you're looking for a place to post and read kids' work. The Children's Writing section of this site suggests many excellent places to share diary entries, artwork, poetry, sound clips, puppetry scripts, folktales, news stories, picture books, and more. (http://www.ucalgary.ca/~dkbrown/index.html)

✔ **Internet Public Library:** You can find all kinds of good stuff in the Youth Division of the Internet Public Library. Click the World icon, and kids can enter a story in the Young Writer's Competition. Winning entries become part of the IPL collection; they're more ambitious and better written than many of the two- and three-line tales posted on many other sites. The Story Hour icon steers kids to good books; the Dr. Internet icon routes kids to pages of quizzes and fun and facts connected with math and science; the Ask the Author icon puts kids in touch with children's authors and illustrators. (http://ipl.sils.umich.edu/youth/)

✔ **KidNews:** What if your child wants to post something other than a story? KidNews is a place to share new articles, features, profiles, creative writing, sport stories, reviews, and more. All postings are by kids, for kids. This site has a chat area for kids and another one for adults. (http://www.vsa.cape.com/~powens/Kidnews3.html)

✔ **KidPub:** Simply e-mail a story to this site, and in a matter of hours, your child will see it on the Web. When kids visit their story a week or a month later, they can see how often it's been read. KidPub will even set up an e-mail link so your child can receive reviews from readers. (http://www.Kidpub.org/Kidpub/)

Performing the show

Kids can run through their production at any point in the creative process by clicking the Playback button. They can invite friends and family to the theater for a show. They can print a script. And they can even share their production via floppy or e-mail by including the projector program from the *Hollywood High* CD-ROM with their saved file.

Is this education or entertainment?

The *Hollywood* programs don't offer formal instruction in writing. So where's the educational value? Don't worry, it's really there. But it's subtle and indirect. (And maybe that's why kids respond so enthusiastically!) By clicking and exploring, kids discover for themselves the essentials. Just compare their first script to their fourth or fifth scripts, and the improvement will show you just how well your kids are taking those implicit lessons to heart.

If your kids need help getting started with *Hollywood,* try this: Pick a scene, add a character or two, and write some dialogue that you think will get a rise from your kids. (A family debate over a child's weekly allowance — with the kid winning! — or a comic newscast about a kid being elected president will usually do the trick.) Then let them take over. Invite a friend or two to contribute, and you've got a social event. We've even heard of *Hollywood* parties where guests — kids and adults — collaborate on funny skits and present them to the group.

The Process of Writing

Once kids are comfortable writing a few sentences or paragraphs, teachers often introduce a multistep process that helps kids extend and improve their writing. These steps apply equally well to all kinds of written work — for example, reports for school, thank-you notes, creative writing. And while they vary somewhat from classroom to classroom, the following process should come pretty close to the method your child is learning.

- **Brainstorming and prewriting:** This is the stage when teachers assign topics or kids cook up ideas of their own. What if kids get stuck? Remind them about recent real-life events. Talk about their favorite stories and how to end them differently. Have kids start drawing (on or off the computer) and let a story evolve from the picture. Explore their storytelling software for ideas.

- **Drafting:** Once they have an idea, kids capture it on paper or on-screen. Younger kids may have more pictures and fewer words, and that's okay. The balance will shift to words as kids develop more confidence in their writing. Keep your distance while kids are drafting their stories or reports (unless they ask you for help). And allow plenty of time for their ideas to flow. Older writers spend lots of time thinking, and so should kids. What looks like dawdling to you — sharpening pencils, fiddling with margins, flipping through the dictionary or thesaurus — may just be your child's way of getting ready to write.

✔ **Response:** Kids don't learn how to talk without hearing someone talk back. And they can't learn how to write without having an audience to respond to their efforts. When you read a draft, offer specific, positive comments. Try to focus on *what* your child has written (ideas, perceptions, descriptions, and so on) rather than on *how* it was written. "Creative" spelling and grammatical errors are okay at this stage.

✔ **Revision and proofreading:** This is one of the hardest stages; kids (and many adults, too) are inclined to dodge the process of revising a draft. How can you encourage the habit of revision? Remind kids that a "clean" draft is easier to share with others; and sharing, after all, is the ultimate goal. And introduce some tricks for catching errors: using a spell checker, reading a draft out loud, reading it word by word — backwards!

✔ **Publishing:** Here's the fun part for kids: deciding what form they want their work to take (cursive script and hand-drawn artwork, printed report illustrated with clip art, on-screen presentation with music and animation, and the like) and sharing it with others.

While both the *Hollywood* and the *Imagination Express* series, discussed earlier in this chapter, reflect aspects of this process, the product we profile next incorporates *all* of the preceding steps.

The Ultimate Writing & Creativity Center (ages 6–10)

A good choice for schoolwork, *The Ultimate Writing & Creativity Center* (from The Learning Company) steps 6- to 10-year-olds through each stage of the writing process. At the prewriting stage, for example, the program supplies rain forest, desert, outer space, and ocean environments for kids to explore in search of inspiration. By clicking creatures and objects within those settings, kids trigger an animation and a writing suggestion. In fact, more than 1,000 suggestions relate to art, music, literature, math, science, and kids themselves.

In the drafting stage, kids can choose templates that automatically format their words as a school report, newsletter, sign, storybook, or journal. The program supplies a paint module, pictured in Figure 5-4, with both freehand art tools and an abundance of stickers, lets kids express their ideas in pictures, before or after they've written some text. They also can use hundreds of clip-art pictures to enliven their documents, plus sounds and animation for online presentations.

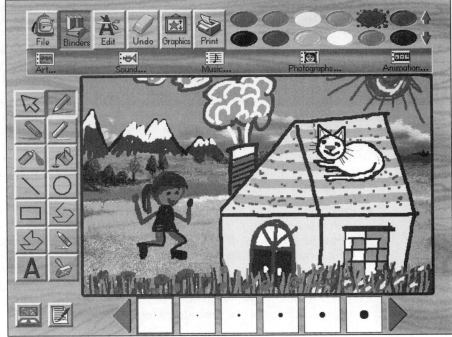

Figure 5-4:
Art tools
like these
add fun to
the drafting
stage of the
writing
process.

At the response stage, parents, teachers, and classmates can write comments on on-screen yellow sticky notes. The Read Words feature reads kids' text out loud, making it easy for them to hear when words are missing or unpronounceable. (And the computer's robotic voice is fun and never critical, the way adults sometimes can be when they're proofreading.) The program also lets kids click into a dictionary, a thesaurus, and a spell checker. And in a thoughtful twist, parents can set the spell checker to ask kids to try spelling a word again on their own *before* the spell checker provides the correct spelling.

Writer's Block? Try Playing with Words

When beginning writers get bogged down, you never can tell what's going to get them unstuck. Sometimes it's as simple as going to the kitchen and getting a snack. Sometimes it's a reminder about the step-by-step process to follow. Sometimes gazing off into space does the trick. Sometimes a bit of wordplay can help kids lighten up and get back on track.

Our prescription? Try *The Amazing Writing Machine* and *Top Secret Decoder*, profiled in the following section. These titles spark kids by giving them some highly unusual tools. In very different ways, these programs let kids rediscover the sheer fun of words.

The Amazing Writing Machine (ages 6–12)

With its amazing array of "cool tools," *The Amazing Writing Machine* (from Broderbund) turns close encounters with grammar, composition, and school assignments into irresistible fun.

Getting started

Kids start by making some initial choices. Deciding on a writing project — essay, letter, poem, journal, or story — is the first step. Second, kids choose whether to start from scratch or to create a variation on prewritten projects. Each choice brings with it a new set of options. Story writers, for example, can opt for eight different genres, including mystery, romance, fantasy, and adventure, each with a special set of stamps for illustrations. Would-be poets can experiment with haiku, limericks, cinquains, and couplets — all forms that kids work with in school. One last decision, and the fun can begin: With their chosen project on the screen, kids click either the text area to start writing or the graphics area to start illustrating.

Cool tools

Our favorite part of this product is the wealth of tools specifically for writing. There's the Reader Robot tool to read text aloud, the Rebus Picture tool to change words into pictures, the Secret Coder tool to encrypt text into one of eight codes. But the best is the Bright Ideas tool. Click it, and kids see 14 different buttons on the bottom of the screen.

The Quotes button produces an endless supply of quotations; for example, "The thing that impresses me most about America," said Edward, Duke of Windsor, "is the way parents obey their children." The Fun Facts button generates information kids can plug into their work. (That's how we found out a cockroach can live for 10 days without a head!) The Brainstorm button offers story starters: for example, suppose a dog became a detective or what if a spaceship landed in your backyard? These buttons are endless fun for kids to explore. But better still, these buttons give *you* a painless way to reinforce lessons about grammar, sentence structure, punctuation, and all those other essentials kids resist learning!

Here are some suggestions for using Bright Ideas buttons to create at-home lessons:

> ✔ Has your 2nd grader forgotten what an adjective is? Don't tell! Instead of defining it, try clicking the Descriptive Word button a dozen times. Seeing a succession of words like *crunchy, graceful, late, talented,* and *angry* will make the meaning clear.

✔ Does your 4th grader's opening sentence leave something to be desired? Don't criticize. Generate a sentence (or two or three) by clicking the Who, What, Where, When, and Why buttons. You wind up with some pretty inane sentences, but the humor underscores the essential elements of a complete lead sentence.

✔ Does your child's work have pitiful punctuation? Click the Quotes button till you have a couple of intriguing comments. Delete *all* the punctuation. Then ask your child to supply the quote marks, commas, and periods.

Family fun

The opportunities for wordplay in *The Amazing Writing Machine* are best shared. Write toddlers a story they can "read" themselves by using the Rebus Picture tool. (A rebus is a picture that stands for a word or part of a word: an eye for the word I, a heart for the word love.) Just write your story, highlight the text, click the Auto-Rebus button at the bottom of the screen, and pictures automatically appear in place of words.

Try writing poetry with your 7-year-old, with the first line by you, the second by your child, the third by another family member, and so on. And don't forget! After writing a line of poetry, whenever you or your kids press the Return key, six words that rhyme with the last word you wrote appear on the screen, as shown in Figure 5-5.

Figure 5-5:
For a poem that began "On a hot summer's day," the program suggested jay, neigh, say, hooray, clay, and Monday as rhymes.

Use *The Amazing Writing Machine* to create homemade Mad Libs. Start by writing a silly story, including lots of adjectives, things like a quote or a joke, a random fact or a proverb, colors, and numerals. Then delete some words and phrases, and give kids a word list (but *not* the story itself) to fill in. They can do this by hand or by using the program's Bright Ideas buttons. Copy their suggestions into your story. And finally, click the Robot Reader button to hear the nonsense read out loud.

Kids who are in their secretive stage (ages 8-12) love putting their words into code. They do it when they pass notes in class, and they can do it when they write on the computer, too. For some kids, the eight codes in *The Amazing Writing Machine* satisfy the itch for secrecy. Others prefer the more extensive options in *Top Secret Decoder,* profiled in the next section.

What do codes have to do with writing — and learning to write better? Rest assured, they provide a very real form of mental exercise. When you think about it, kids spend lots and lots of time decoding. After all that's the process that helps them learn to read, figure out new words, solve math problems, play music. We think working with codes can help strengthen kids' skills not only in language arts but also in math and critical thinking. In fact, one of *Top Secret Decoder*'s developers spent many years as a math teacher.

Top Secret Decoder (ages 7–14)

Segassem terces gnikcarc dna gnitaerc rof loot suolubaf A!

Z ezatkntr snnk enq bqdzshmf zmc bqzbjhmf rdbqds ldrrzfdr!

Gibberish? No. It's a secret message, encoded in two of more than a dozen inventive ciphers kids find in *Top Secret Decoder* (from Houghton Mifflin Interactive). (By the way, both messages say the same thing: "A fabulous tool for creating and cracking secret messages." To read the first one, just look at the words from right to left. To figure out the second, substitute A for Z, B for A, and so on.)

Top Secret Decoder gives kids the feel of operating high-tech spy equipment. Kids type their messages into an on-screen laptop computer. A control panel to one side lets them select a code. Then one click, and their words are instantly encoded and displayed in the bottom half of the screen.

The results range from pretty obvious to fairly devious to downright ingenious. On the easier end of the spectrum are pig Latin (igpay atinLay), reverse coding (esrever), a top-down code, which is read from top to bottom; and Trick Jump, shown in Figure 5-6. You find visual codes like

Letterfold, Reverse Mirror, or Fakeout that are "crackable" only by folding or tilting the paper on which they're printed or by holding them up to a mirror. And then there are alphabetical offset ciphers (A=C, B=D, C=E is one possibility).

To break these codes the old-fashioned way, kids need an eye for patterns, some knowledge of the incidence of letters in the English language (E is most common, followed by T and S); and some problem-solving smarts. Or kids can crack them on the computer, using the program's animated "cipher wheel." Toughest of all are messages that utilize two or more codes.

Don't worry; kids can click a button to get tips about codes and deciphering techniques. And they can write hints (which appear in very, very tiny type at the bottom of the page) when they print coded messages for friends. Be prepared for kids to do lots of printing with this software; its printing features are pretty amazing. One code, for example, shows up on paper as a jumbled blur of indecipherable letters. In fact, the result looks as though the printer has gone haywire. But if you put a comb on top and slide it around, the ink pattern turns into words.

Besides challenging you or their friends, kids can also earn secret agent credentials by decoding messages from the Code Master, a cyber-spy who dishes out more than 300 code-cracking challenges at ten levels of difficulty.

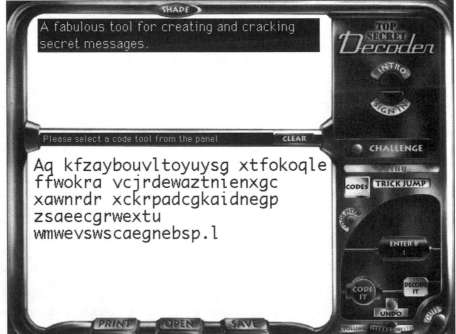

Figure 5-6:
The Trick
Jump code
inserts
random
letters
between
the real
letters in a
message.

Try using the Alphaglyphs code for some fun with a kindergartner or a 1st grader who's mastering initial letter sounds. Alphaglyphs is a substitution code in which pictures stand for letters. For example, an elephant represents E, a turtle is T, a koala is K, and so on. Code the word "Hi," and you get a horse and an iguana. Demonstrate how the code works by using your child's name; after all, those are the letters kids know best. Messages that are short and sweet (I love you) or silly (My cat eats purple mice) work best for starters.

Great sites for word lovers

Chances are, kids (and parents) who like codes also like anagrams and puns, knock-knock jokes, and crosswords. Here are some examples of wordplay and Web sites to surf for them:

- ✔ **Palindromes:** A palindrome is text that reads the same backwards as forwards, like "Madam I'm Adam" or "Able was I ere I saw Elba." If your child finds those silly sentences intriguing (and if those are the only two you know), check out this amazing site for links to hundreds and hundreds of palindromes. You and your kids will find such gems as:

    "Flee to me, remote elf."

    "Was it a cat I saw?"

    "Are we not drawn onward to new era?"

    "He did, eh?"

    "No lemon, no melon."

    The Web address is `http://freenet.buffalo.edu/~cd431/palindromes.html`

- ✔ **Anagrams:** An anagram is a word or phrase made from the letters of another word or phrase. Ideally, the new words should also shed some light on the meaning of the original words. Because anagrams are an exercise in mental agility — and good for vocabulary, too — teachers often have students practice making them. They're fun at home, too. Start kids off with simple words, and after they get the hang of anagrams, have kids compete with each other or with you by using longer words or names. We surfed the Web for inspiration and found these wonderful examples:

    The Morse code = Here come dots.

    England's Queen Victoria = Governs a nice quiet land.

    Funeral = Real fun.

    Eleven plus two = Twelve plus one.

There are many anagram sites. Try `http://www.awarenet.com/graphic/anagram/examples.html` or type **anagram** in the search field of your favorite search engine to find other sites. For an instantaneous Anagram Generator, check `http://www.wordsmith.org/awad-dgibin/anagram`

- **WordSearches:** Every week this site posts new crossword and word-search puzzles that are just right for 3rd through 6th graders. (`http://www.smartcode.com/puzzle/`).

- **Word finds, analogies, and more:** The `http://syndicate.com` site features word-find puzzle contests (how many words of four letters or more can you make from "trestles" or "charisma," for example); word analogy puzzles (child is to mother as symphony is to . . .), rebuses, and more.

Don't be surprised if your browser can't find a Web address you type. It's not your fault, and it's probably not our fault either! Blame it on the World Wide Web itself: Web addresses (and sites themselves) can be pretty fickle. Try looking for a "missing" site with a search engine. And try shortening the address by deleting everything after the `.com` (or `.org` or `.edu`).

On-Screen Diaries

Wordplay, coding, and decoding are classic kids' fun, but at the same time, they're great for making kids more agile thinkers, appreciative readers, and accurate writers. Diaries — another all-time kids' favorite — can also help stretch the mind and flex writing muscles.

Keeping a journal encourages kids to develop the habit of reflection and self-expression. It sharpens their eye for detail. It helps ideas flow. Even writing grumpy remarks about homework assignments, household chores, or pesky siblings is good writing practice.

And as with practically every other form of writing these days, diaries are now on the computer. It's true, of course, that computer-based journaling is missing one of the most appealing things about a diary: the little lock and key. But computers have passwords and so do software diaries. If your kids like doing writing assignments or storywriting on the computer, consider an on-screen diary. When they're midstream in other computer activities, they'll appreciate having a place to capture a random thought. And on-screen diaries, as you'll see in the brief profiles that follow, have many appealing features that add pleasure to recording the day's events.

Let's Talk About ME! (ages 10–14)

This CD-ROM (GirlGames Inc./Simon & Schuster), which is an interactive handbook on adolescence for girls, is packed with information and activities that address girls' questions about their bodies, their personalities, their futures, and more. The Backpack section has the most upscale on-screen diary we've seen. And in a nice touch, every time girls open the diary, they see a thought-provoking quotation, such as Oscar Wilde's remark, "Life is too important to be taken seriously." The CD also has an interactive scrapbook for collecting photos and recordings of friends' voices, an e-mail/phone book, connections to cyber pen pals plus candid information from successful women about their own adolescence.

The Amazing Writing Machine (ages 6–12)

Profiled earlier in this chapter, this program (from Broderbund) makes journaling easy for kids who can't get started or are unsure what to write. With its Spin feature, kids can personalize four partially written diary entries (My Day, When I Grow Up, My Dream, What I Like). Altering an entry is a matter of clicking on choices such as "I love to wear jeans, T-shirts, sneakers, or snowshoes." When kids select all the variation they want, they can continue writing by clicking the Transform Spin to Write button.

The reluctant writer — and how the computer can help

Writing on the Walls!: It's so easy to send a message to your kids about your pleasure in their writing. Try showcasing a child's short story, written on or off the computer; display the no-error spelling test on the refrigerator; frame a nice example of their penmanship.

Write Yourself: When you get a letter in the mail, aren't you inclined to write back? Same with kids. Slip a note under the door, and they'll slip one under yours. Post a question on the refrigerator, and sooner or later, you'll find an answer there. You can play these same communication games with kids' computer programs. Start a story in their favorite writing program, and leave it for kids to complete. Encourage friends and relatives to send e-mail or a fax to your kids, and talk to your kids about how they'll respond. If you have a desktop utility like *KidDesk*, you can record voice mail for your kids and leave notes for them to discover when they turn on the computer.

Get some Web Advice: We've found that an Internet publication from the U.S. Department of Education called "Helping Your Child Learn to Write Well" is an excellent resource for parents. (http://www.ed.gov/pubs/parents/Writing/index.html)

It's Not Writing Software, but It Has a Lot of Writing (and Reading) Practice!

Zurk's Rainforest Lab

This visually stunning program has a unique combination of math activities, science explorations, language arts, and writing. Set in a lush rain forest, *Zurk's* encourages writing by sending kids on a virtual journey with a photo album and a log book. As kids scroll from the rain forest floor to the canopy, they discover different rain forest dwellers. Kids can hear text read, hear the animals' names and realistic sound effects, or read all about them. (To encourage reading, turn off the program's sound.)

For every picture kids snap for the photo album, they can write captions, comments, or their own made-up stories. The program suggests a different story starter every time kids use the photo album. We've found that even reluctant writers like making entries in their albums. We think this is an especially good choice for rain forest aficionados; their special interest will help spark their writing. The printed album looks great, too. (Soleil/Maxis, Ages 5-9)

Oregon Trail II

Hands-down, this is the best history simulation program, and it just so happens the program also provides a compelling opportunity for reading and writing (along with the "usual" challenges of shooting the rapids and surviving blizzards, cholera, and other hazards of pioneering). As kids make their way westward, they hear pioneers reading from real diaries, "talk" with fellow emigrants, and explore different locales along the 1,000-mile trail. By noting advice in their on-screen diary, kids boost their chances of making better decisions. And the online guidebook is a must-read for tips about surviving the journey. (MECC, Ages 10-16)

Chapter 6

Using the Computer to Help Kids Master Math

Cuddling up with the kids to read, flopping down on the rug for a game of Monopoly — these are some of the fun times in parenting. But who has "warm and fuzzy" feelings associated with doing math?

For many parents, the very word math conjures up painful memories: rote memorization, flash cards, lightning-fast answers, timed tests, double-digit problems on the blackboard in front of the whole class, getting the right answer — or else!

But take heart. You can help your kids grow up math literate — even if you're not. That's where great math software comes in. On the computer, math always feels like fun.

And you have lots of choices. If your kids detest time limits, have we got suggestions for you! If they crave fast action, need a patient tutor, prefer puzzles to problem sets, want to challenge a fiendish opponent, you can find just the thing.

So how do you choose?

✔ First, always look for titles based on the newest standards of the National Council of Teachers of Mathematics (NCTM). That way, your child's at-home computer activities will be in step with what's going on at school.

Here's what the NCTM likes to see in the classroom (and we think you'll see it in good software, too):

- Activities that involve kids in the mathematics of everyday life.

- An atmosphere that encourages questions and hands-on discovery: Kids need to explore, conjecture, and reason, *not just learn rules and procedures by rote*.

- Opportunities to become mathematical problem solvers, to see more than one way to approach a problem.

- Encouragement to apply mathematical ideas to other situations, make generalizations, see patterns.

✔ Start your kids off with the kind of programs in the "Having Fun with Math Explorations" section of this chapter. These titles offer a playful, hands-on introduction to number facts, rules, and formulas, as well as to the "new basics," such as patterns, estimation, attributes, spatial visualization, and more.

✔ Provide additional opportunities for your kids to practice the concepts they discover. The "Practicing Math Facts" titles later in this chapter are a respected source of drills — and you can easily tailor them to this week's math facts.

✔ Challenge your kids to apply their improving skills to new and unfamiliar situations. The programs you find in the "Building Thinking Skills" section are great at helping kids gain confidence as problem solvers.

Head to the World Wide Web for more tips on helping your kids grow up math literate. Absolutely *the* best source for math advice and ideas is an online booklet called "Helping Your Child Learn," from the U.S. Department of Education. It provides pointers for parents, plus family math activities that you and your kids can do at home, in the grocery store, or in the car. You find activities for both young children and older kids at this site. Some of our favorite little-kid suggestions include: the "More or Less" game played with a deck of cards, a variation on 20 Questions called "Name That Coin," and a "Money Math" game that helps kids count change. For older kids, check out this site's "Math on the Go" activities. In the car, kids are a captive audience and easier to involve in a game. Not surprisingly, many of these games use license plates! We love "Total It" because of its mental math practice. (http://www.ed.gov/pubs/parents/Math/index.html)

Having Fun with Math Explorations

When we were in grade school, our teachers were on a mission: to make us fast at number facts, rules, and formulas. Today, schools have shifted their focus from memorizing math facts to understanding concepts. What's more, teachers believe that kids tend to learn best about concepts while playing mathematical games, using concrete materials, and solving real-life problems. (Almost sounds like fun, doesn't it?)

The titles in this section take this changing philosophy to heart. These programs invite kids to explore concepts, play, experiment, and figure things out for themselves. As a result, these programs make math approachable — even for kids who say they hate math.

Which kids benefit from "Math Exploration" titles? Almost all of them. But check these questions to get a better idea about whether these programs can help *your* kids:

___ *Does your child need a different approach?*

A teacher or parent can do only so much to help kids understand a concept. But with technology, the sky's the limit! "Math Exploration" titles take a fresh look at familiar facts and concepts. If inches, feet, and yards just aren't making sense for your child, try a program that lets kids measure with shovels or boots. Using bubbles to explain place value or fireworks to express fractions may be just the breakthrough your child needs.

___ *Does your child enjoy free play?*

Many kids learn best from open-ended challenges; the things they discover on their own are what they really remember. Others prefer more structure, patterns to follow, or problems to solve. "Math Exploration" titles strike a balance between free play and directed activities.

___ *Does your child freeze under pressure?*

Kids need repeated experience in all areas of math, every year, at every grade level. But practice doesn't always have to be fast. "Math Exploration" titles provide plenty of no-pressure practice.

___ *Does your child like wacky scenarios?*

Math teachers say it's very important to present ideas to kids in context, that is, within a situation or scenario that really grabs their interest. That way, kids get involved and stick with a problem until they make sense of it.

Did you answer *yes* or *sometimes?* Then read on. The titles we profile next are geared for kids in their early- to late-elementary school years. They're the logical step *after* the early-math programs in Chapter 3 and *before* the fast-action drills you find in the "Practicing Math Facts" section later in this chapter.

In math classes today, kids spend lots of time dragging manipulatives around. The theory is that *manipulatives* — things kids can move around, such as beans, pennies, blocks, bottle caps, and sometimes even their classmates — foster an atmosphere of playfulness and give kids a hands-on, concrete way to grasp abstractions.

Kids of *all ages* should use manipulatives, according to math teachers. They help kids understand concepts better and kids develop abstract-thinking skills more readily when they manipulate concrete objects to solve math problems.

The Mighty Math series (ages 5–14)

Edmark has made manipulatives the cornerstone of its *Mighty Math* series, creating innovative, on-screen manipulatives for *all* the areas of math that kids encounter between the ages of 5 and 14. (See Appendix C for information about the software on the *Great Software For Kids & Parents* CD-ROM.)

Virtual manipulatives

Six-year-olds playing *Carnival Countdown,* for example, can explore the concept of place value with instruments that toot musical bubbles. Little bubbles with a trumpet tone represent units of one. Medium-sized, baritone bubbles are units of 10. And big, bass-note bubbles represent units of 100. As the instruments play, the bubbles melodiously float into the ones, tens, or hundreds section of a band shell. And whenever there are 10 ones or 10 tens, the bubbles cluster into a larger, single unit and move over in place value. This transformation really helps kids visualize what *regrouping* (the new term for "carrying over") is all about.

Other manipulatives with lots of appeal for younger kids include giggles (believe it or not, they help kids learn the meaning of the symbols for equal, less than, and greater than), clowns, cups, shoes, crayons, bathtubs, ostriches, whales, bears, and horses. Older kids can assemble toy robots and stretch on-screen rubber bands to solve geometric challenges. Or they can launch fireworks, like those shown in Figure 6-1, for a noisy, animated lesson in the relationship between a fraction's numerator and denominator, and more.

Figure 0-1. Launching fireworks is a fun way to understand fractions.

Tried-and-true math with a new twist

The *Mighty Math* series gets high marks for enlivening time-honored math activities with multimedia pizzazz.

Take Quizzo in *Number Heroes*. This game show parody puts a new spin on a standard software activity: problem sets. First, there's no time pressure. Kids 8-10 can take all the time they need with hundreds of problems in addition, subtraction, multiplication, division, patterns, shapes, analogies, and more. Second, they can control the level of difficulty in a new way: by choosing the number of points they want to try for. (Don't worry, they won't always opt for the easy stuff. If they want to win badly enough — and eventually they will — they'll begin opting for higher points and wind up with harder questions.) Third, kids have to do more than just get the answer. They have to pay attention to their opponent's answers, too, and click a Yes or No button to indicate whether their rival is right or wrong. (For information about software on the *Great Software For Kids & Parents* CD-ROM, see Appendix C.)

Try playing Quizzo with your child as a *collaborative* rather than a competitive game. How? Simply make accumulating the highest combined score of the two players the goal of the game. And before the two of you click the Yes or No button, talk through your analysis of each other's answers.

Mighty Math skills span K–8th grades

The six programs in the *Mighty Math* series give kids a new perspective on the curriculum they encounter in kindergarten through 8th grade. Here's a rundown of the programs and the concepts they cover:

- ✔ *Carnival Countdown:* Set in an amusement park where 5- to 7-year-olds can do things they never could in real life, this program covers 2-D geometry, patterns, place value, equivalency, attributes, addition, and subtraction.

- ✔ *Zoo Zillions:* Also for 5- to 7-year olds in grades K-2, this program introduces money concepts, story problems, the number line, spatial awareness, multiplication, and division.

- ✔ *Number Heroes:* The pleasantly "warped" heroes in this title create fun and fascinating situations that involve 8- to 10-year-olds in plane geometry, chance and probability, fractions and decimals, plus basic number operations.

- ✔ *Calculating Crew:* Aimed at 8- to 10-year-olds in grades 3-5, this title progresses to multiplication and division of whole numbers and decimals, the properties of 2-D or 3-D shapes, and money transactions.

- ✔ *Cosmic Geometry:* Intended for 11- to 14-year-olds in grades 6-8, this program provides a comprehensive introduction to middle school geometry.

- ✔ *Astro Algebra:* With introductory algebra for 11- to 14-year-olds in grades 6-8, this title covers variables, expressions, equations and inequalities, patterns, functions, graphing, ratio and proportion, plus operations with fractions, decimals, and percentages.

Prove to your kids that mistakes really are okay!

Chances are, you've said something like this to your kids: "It's okay to make mistakes — that's how we learn." But do they believe you?

The Logical Journey of the Zoombinis (from Broderbund) is one of the best titles we've seen for proving to 8- to 12-year-olds that mistakes really are okay. In fact, kids have to make mistakes in order to figure out the right things to do.

Here's the context: When the Zoombinis' happy lives are disrupted by greedy, holiday-hating Bloats, the Zoombinis decide to escape and build a new community. Here's the challenge: Kids have to get the Zoombinis through 12 perplexing puzzle regions. And here's the kicker: This program doesn't offer a single word of advice. Kids figure out what to do entirely on their own.

What kids see going on at Allergic Cliffs, for example, is pictured in Figure 6-2. Standing at the edge of a cliff, a band of Zoombinis looks hopefully over the chasm. Two bridges span the gap. Obviously, the Zoombinis want to journey across. So kids click a Zoombini, and set it down near a bridge. The Zoombini might skitter safely across the bridge, or the cliff (with an ominous face etched into the rock) might sneeze the Zoombini back to where it started. After a couple of successes and sneezes, kids readily deduce which bridge has an "allergy" to which kind of Zoombini, and they quickly get the rest of the band across.

That process requires a guess or two. Yet even when kids guess wrong, they don't feel like they've made a mistake. Instead, they feel as though they've experimented. The result: Kids are willing to risk mistakes in order to figure out what combination of Zoombini attributes will get the Zoombinis through each puzzle. Playing this game not only drives home that all-important lesson about mistakes but also helps kids master logical thinking, comparing, grouping, forming and testing hypotheses, sorting, graphing, and using set relationships — skills kids need when they get to algebra and statistical analysis.

Sometime around age 9 (later if you're lucky, earlier if you're not), it's bound to happen. Kids develop an *attitude*. Good software for the 8- to 14-year-old crowd plays to their new, biting sense of fun. The software uses

Figure 6-2:
Only certain Zoombinis can cross each bridge, and figuring out which ones gives kids a workout in logic.

hip, irreverent characters, snappy comments, and droll situations to draw kids deeper into academic challenges. You see it in writing programs like *Hollywood High* (Chapter 5), thinking challenges like *Dr. Brain* profiled later in this chapter and geography adventures like *Carmen Sandiego* (Chapter 9).

The newest math titles also have a sense of humor that's just right for kids with *attitude. Number Heroes,* from Edmark's *Mighty Math* series, is one of these titles. And *Math Heads,* from Theatrix Interactive, goes even further.

Math Heads (ages 9–13)

This pre-algebra program is so hip, irreverent, and in-your-face that parents may be taken aback. (This may be the program that persuades you to buy headphones for the computer.) But it's got some great things going for it: first, a really cool context for doing math; second, a focus on mastering problem-solving techniques — rather than simply performing correct calculations. Unlike many other math programs, this one gives equal time to teaching as well as to testing. The list could go on — but let's get specific.

Taking its cue from the TV shows kids watch (and watch and watch), *Math Heads* is a high-spirited parody that pokes fun at every television convention. As with any TV show, contestants pass through makeup and wardrobe before going on the air. In a funky twist on playing dress-up, kids combine faces and wigs, hats and outfits to create their own panel of contestants. Best of all, they can use *their own photos.* They'll find step-by-step instructions in the *Make-A-Head* application (mini-program) that comes on the CD-ROM.

Sounds like fun, but not much like math, you say? Yes, but there's a method to this madness.

When kids have a stake in a game — when their faces are on-screen — they pay more attention. They play more often, on their own initiative. They persevere with tricky problems. They remember the math. And that's the whole point, right?

The actual math happens when kids start using an on-screen remote control to channel surf and select a program. Here's a look at four "channels" and the activities they feature.

Go Mental

Mental math skills get a terrific workout in this hip game show, pictured in Figure 6-3. The idea is to win a tic-tac-toe game, but not merely by solving wacky word problems. Instead, kids have to decide whether celebrity contestants are giving the right answers or just bluffing. That two-step

Figure 6-3:
Word
problems
aren't so
bad when
they're as
wacky as
the posers
in Go
Mental.

process — doing the math *plus* evaluating someone else's reasoning — is a powerful learning technique. And it's not easy. Sometimes the contestants have the right idea but do their math wrong. Sometimes they calculate correctly but misunderstand the problem. Or they may just try to trip up kids.

Infomercials

Who can resist critiquing TV commercials? This channel features nearly a dozen wicked parodies. But instead of promoting cars, soda, or fast food, these "commercials" pitch techniques for solving math problems. Silly as it is, this is *the* place to go for more insight into the math that comes up in Go Mental.

Dance 'Til You Drop

Kids do a lot of estimating in math class these days (and in good software programs, too). Estimation gives them a leg up on counting, measurement, and problem-solving of all sorts. That's because kids who can make a good estimate — who can sense which answers are reasonable and which are outrageous — clearly understand the problem. In *Dance 'Til You Drop*, players answer math questions by selecting the right range on a huge number line. And the game is so fast-paced that kids have no time to work out the entire calculation. So they've got to estimate.

Home Shopping

Here's where kids can spend the "money" they earn playing *Math Heads* games. Some products are "purchase and print" activities for doing math off the computer: tricks, jokes, math games, and do-it-yourself projects. Other merchandise encourages kids to spend more time with *Math Heads,* by letting them "buy" accessories like wigs, heads, or bodies for customizing the game show contestants.

OPEN

Other Math Exploration Programs to Consider

✔ *Math Workshop:* You hear people — math teachers especially — talk about the beauty of mathematics. But do you believe them? (Don't answer that!) You'll be a believer when you see *Math Workshop.* Its puzzle-solving and patterning activities are a visual delight, as you can see in Figure 6-4. But don't be fooled: This stuff really is math. Putting puzzles together — on or off the computer — helps kids develop spatial visualization skills and paves the way for geometry. (Broderbund, Ages 5-12)

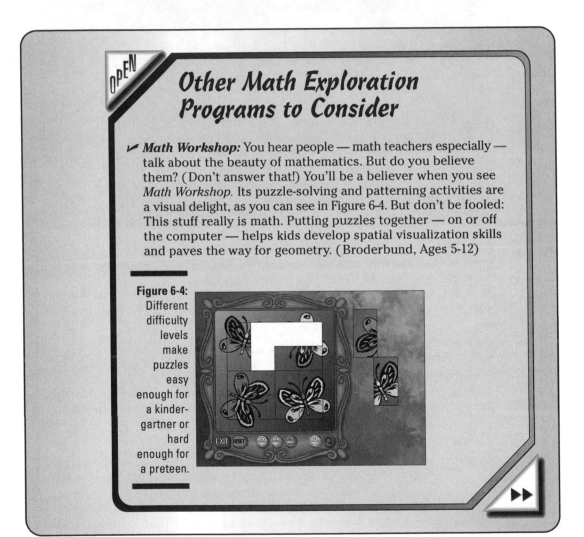

Figure 6-4: Different difficulty levels make puzzles easy enough for a kinder-gartner or hard enough for a preteen.

✔ *Interactive Math Journey:* This title takes a distinctive, three-step approach with every math concept it presents. First there's a short, interactive "book" that presents the concept in a story. Next comes a hands-on activity that lets kids explore the concept. And finishing off each lesson is a fast-action drill to test kids' proficiency and encourage repeated practice. The program's carefully sequenced activities cover patterns and shapes, addition and subtraction, measurement, fractions, and multiplication. This title is big on manipulatives, both in the software itself and inside the box it comes in, which includes a nifty calculator, a bag of pattern blocks, a set of interlocking cubes, and an excellent activity book. (The Learning Company, Ages 6-9)

✔ *Snootz Math Trek:* Great story, great math. If the Snootz can find all the items on their Big List, they can return to their home planet and play — for the rest of their lives. Kids aid the Snootz by exploring five math activities where the items are hidden. These games provide a wacky yet balanced diet of contemporary classroom math challenges: decoding symbols, interpreting maps, solving puzzles, planning strategies, identifying and remembering patterns, and sequencing. (Theatrix Interactive, Ages 5-9)

Practicing Facts, Remembering Rules

Ever worry that your kids just don't seem to know their number facts the way you once did? Do "Math Exploration" titles strike you as too much play and not enough practice? Do your kids enjoy beat-the-clock challenges? Then this section may be right up your alley.

These practice-makes-perfect titles are a much-respected source of drills. They feature thousands (actually, tens of thousands) of problems — in addition, subtraction, multiplication, and division, plus exercises in estimation, prime numbers, algebra, factors, multiples, and other basics — all dressed up in Nintendo-like games of high-speed, shoot-'em-up pursuits and escapes. Because you can tailor them precisely, these titles are especially helpful if your child needs some highly targeted math practice. And because they play like games, they're a good choice for fast-action aficionados.

Which drills are right for your kids?

___ *Do your homework!*

Find out how (and when) your child's teacher introduces math concepts and skills. Together decide which particular skills your child needs to practice.

___ *Pick some titles that target your child's grade level.*

Of all the available kids' programs, math software has been around the longest and most closely mirrors the curriculum used in schools. So it's relatively easy to find titles that reinforce the topics your child is studying. The packaging for most drill products provides details on the curriculum they cover.

___ *Put yourself in your kids' shoes.*

Ask if you (as a kid) would be hooked. Download some demos; shop at try-before-you-buy stores; request sampler disks from the software publishers.

___ *Ask your offspring.*

Since these titles are popular in schools, kids may already have a preference.

Munchers and Troggles (ages 6–12)

Thought you were going to be reading up on math drills? But now you're seeing weird words like *Munchers* and *Troggles*? Don't worry, you're in the right place. Munchers means math for thousands of school kids.

Munchers are the quirky green heroes of a long-running math series. Troggles are the bad guys, always popping up unexpectedly to thwart kids in their quest for right answers. The basic gameplay is similar in all *Muncher* titles: Kids have to make the Muncher eat correct answers off a game board while steering clear of trouble-making Troggles. Remember Pac-Man? That's what playing with Munchers and Troggles is like — move, munch, and move some more.

Math Munchers Deluxe (ages 8–12)

Math Munchers Deluxe (from MECC) gives a 3-D facelift to the original *Number Munchers* game. *Math Munchers Deluxe* features lots of color and animation, more Troggles, a section of geometry problems, plus a parent video guide right on the CD-ROM. The action takes place on a playing field of squares, each containing an answer: a number, an equation, a symbol, or shapes like those shown in Figure 6-5. Kids have to figure out which answers correctly match a target rule (like "multiples of 9" or "equals 5/8") at the top of the grid. Then they maneuver their Muncher to gobble up right answers — and outmaneuver the Troggles that pop up anywhere, anytime.

Troggle Trouble Math (ages 6–12)

Troggle Trouble Math (from MECC) has more of a storyline. The evil Dr. Frankentroggle is holding the Muncher captive, and players have to help Sparky the math dog search for clues to the captive's whereabouts. But Sparky's in danger, too; gangs of Troggles are after his dog treats. Kids have to protect Sparky and get rid of the Troggles by creating equations like the one in Figure 6-6. Depending on difficulty level, equations can use addition, subtraction, multiplication, division, or a combination of these. The computation takes place on an on-screen Troggulator, which kids must "recharge" periodically by solving (rather than creating) a series of equations.

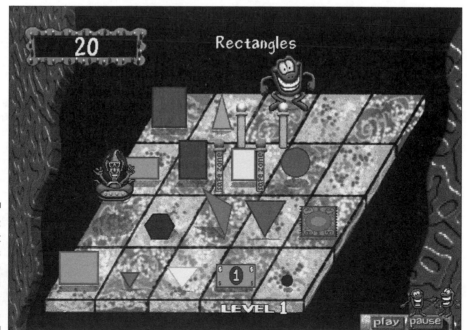

Figure 6-5: The object of this game is to munch all the rectangles.

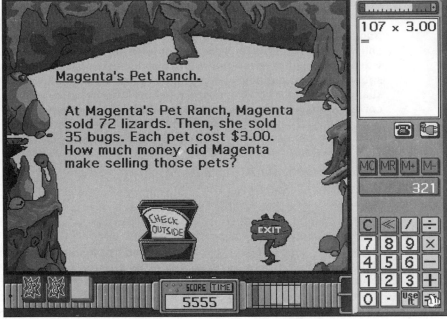

Figure 6-6:
This
program
encourages
kids to think
word
problems
through by
requiring
kids to
show all the
steps they
use to get
an answer.

What if your kids still don't "get" the math they're supposed to learn? *Never ever* assume that math just isn't your child's subject. Many kids simply need lots of different kinds of explanations before mathematical understanding really sinks in. So your job is to look for titles that come at similar concepts with different approaches.

If your kids don't like Muncher-style gameplay but still need math-facts practice, you have other options. For practice with no time pressure, try the Bowling for Numbers activity in *Math Workshop,* the Quizzo game in *Number Heroes,* or Go Mental in *Math Heads,* all described earlier in this chapter. Or for math in shoot-'em-up-style games, try the *Blaster* titles in the next profile.

The Math Blaster series (ages 4–12)

Math Blaster (from Davidson) is the oldest series of math drills around (since 1982), and still going strong.

Its success is based on a simple formula: Math drills plus video-style gameplay add up to repeated practice. Kids who love defeat-the-evil-alien adventures will always do the math in these titles — just so they can be rewarded with some fast-action gameplay.

Math Blaster Jr. (ages 4–7)

In *Math Blaster Jr.,* kids gain familiarity with the basics by counting constellations; using alien inchworms to explore concepts of greater than/less than; practicing equations, subtraction, and addition with number lines (see Figure 6-7); constructing rocket ships from colored geometric shapes; and more. Nice touch: an age-appropriate free-play option that enables kids to switch games and change difficulty levels whenever they want.

Mega Math Blaster (ages 6–12)

Mega Math Blaster is a bigger, better version of the most popular games in the original Blaster titles, including the *Space Zapper* and *Equationator,* pictured in Figure 6-8. (These may be Greek to you, but chances are your kids will know — and love — these games from school.) *Mega Math Blaster* is bigger, thanks to the addition (so to speak) of hundreds of new problems at six levels of difficulty. And the program is better because of a great new 3-D graphics look. Math topics include addition, subtraction, multiplication, division, fractions, decimals, percents, estimation, and number patterns. Nice touches: a separate CD-ROM parent's guide filled with math tips and resources, plus the capability to customize sets of math problems for your kids.

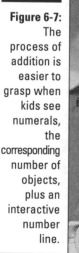

Figure 6-7: The process of addition is easier to grasp when kids see numerals, the corresponding number of objects, plus an interactive number line.

Figure 6-8:
Kids choose numbers and operations from the vertical tubes to make equations.

Older but still appealing for fast-action kids are *Math Blaster: Episode 1: In Search of Spot* (ages 6-12), with four games and thousands of math problems; *Math Blaster: Episode 2: Secret of the Lost City,* aimed at slightly older kids (ages 8-12); and *Math Blaster Mystery: The Great Brain Robbery,* with pre-algebra and word problems for kids 10 and up.

Just out for older students is *Geometry Blaster,* which brings a jazzy 3-D look to a new breed of bad guys and the geometric puzzles kids must solve. The title covers a year's geometry curriculum.

Without doubt, the computer is a great way to help kids practice computation. But don't limit their computer experience to skill-and-drill software. Research shows that kids benefit most from open-ended software that encourages them to explore, experiment, and solve problems. So serve up a well-balanced diet by choosing titles from all three math categories: "Math Exploration" titles, "Math Practice," and "Thinking Skills."

Building Thinking Skills with Math Challenges

You won't see math facts or problem sets in the programs in this section. But wait! Don't skip it, because its challenges will make your kids much better at math. These programs focus on reasoning, devising several different ways to get an answer, and applying skills to new and unfamiliar challenges. In a word, they're about problem-solving.

Kids who are good problem solvers, according to the National Council of Teachers of Mathematics, share certain characteristics. And the titles in this section nurture them all:

✔ An eye for detail and the ability to pick out the important features in a problem

✔ Flexibility, a willingness to try many approaches, and the ability to transfer their learning from one problem to another

✔ Perseverance

✔ A sense of whether their solution is a reasonable one

Don't expect your kids to toil in silence over these programs. Time was, kids worked alone, quietly, with math workbooks or ditto sheets. Today, collaborative problem solving is the norm. Encourage your kids to use math software with friends or siblings — even with you. Discussing and defending their solutions really helps kids extend their thinking and cement their understanding.

The Thinkin' Things series (ages 3–13)

Even if you tried day in and day out, you couldn't possibly teach your kids all the factual information they'll need for the future. There's just too much of it. But you can help them learn *how* to approach the future. Both in school and at home, you can encourage them to uncover facts, take on new situations, think critically, deal effectively with information, and become confident problem solvers.

That's the philosophy behind the *Thinkin' Things* titles (from Edmark). They don't focus on 3 'R skills such as addition facts, initial letter sounds, or spelling rules. Instead, they introduce a broader set of far-reaching skills — the kind kids can use wherever they are and whatever they're doing. Kids can't solve *Thinkin' Things* puzzles with memorized math facts; children have to tackle the activities with educated guesswork, developing hypotheses and discovering what works. Another plus: The five activities in each title are wonderfully diverse. Some involve musical skills. Others are wildly artistic. Many present logical challenges. They're all fun and inventive. And they feature unusual characters, with appeal for kids, from 3-year-olds all the way to 13-year-olds.

You can see activities from each of the three *Thinkin' Things* titles on the *Great Software For Kids and Parents* CD-ROM. Refer to Appendix C for information about the CD-ROM.

Our favorites, the Fripples

Of all the critters in kids' software, some of the most endearing are in the *Thinkin' Things* series. They're called the Fripples.

What's so special about the doodlelike creatures you see in Figure 6-9? For starters, they're irresistibly cute. They come in different colors. They sport a variety of patterns, hairstyles, and eyeglasses (or attributes, in mathematical parlance). And they need your child's help.

From their perches in the Fripple Shop in *Thinkin' Things Collection 1,* the Fripples squeak and wink and grin and fidget like winsome puppies hoping to be adopted. In fact, finding homes for the Fripples is what the game is all about. When customers order a Fripple — "I like purple or spots but not straight hair, please" — kids eyeball 12 candidates and click their choice. If they're right, a Fripple wobbles happily out the door to its new owner. With their subtle antics, the Fripples keep kids playing over and over again. And that's where you'll see a tremendous educational payoff. With repeated play, 3- to 8-year-olds develop an eye for detail. They become skilled at comparing and contrasting attributes.

In *Thinkin' Things Collection 2,* the Fripples challenge 6- to 12-year-olds to Frippletration, one of the toughest, most inventive games of concentration we've seen. And in *Thinkin' Things Collection 3,* the Fripples need help finding which of nine rooms on three floors they belong in. Working with as few as one written hint and two or three "thought balloons," 7- to 13-year-olds have to solve the logic problems posed by the clues. Try it yourself, and you'll be amazed at the challenge.

If your preschoolers or kindergartners love the Fripples the way ours do, try playing the Fripple game *without the fripples and without the computer.* Let your child drag out an armful of favorite toys. Then you play customer and place an order: "I want a cute toy with brown fur and button eyes and white paws." This is a great way for little kids to make a (manageable) mess in the kitchen while you make dinner. And it gives them good practice identifying attributes and following directions.

Figure 6-9:
Only one of these 12 Fripples is right for the customer, and kids have to make the choice.

Other Thinkin' Things favorites

Thinkin' Things Collection 2 is great for musical games that let kids create rhythmic patterns, test their ear for rhythm, make up melodies, or learn to play up to 15 familiar tunes. Best of all are *Snake Blox* and *2-3D Blox,* in which kids boost their visual perception and spatial awareness by exploring 2-D and 3-D space, experimenting with optical effects, and manipulating visual images.

Thinkin' Things Collection 3 gives kids in the double-digit ages tough logic puzzles and artistic challenges. Best of all, you find an inspired encounter with computer programming (the process of writing instructions that tell a computer what to do). By challenging kids to create a half-time show with marching bands, cheerleaders, and football players, the Half Time activity introduces the concepts of computer programming. Kids design the formations and set them in motion by linking programming codes represented visually as puzzle pieces.

Computer programming for kids makes a comeback

Whatever happened to computer programming for kids? Once upon a time, students used to march off to the computer lab for an hour's close encounter with programming languages like BASIC or APL. Yet today many labs have given way to classroom computers, and lessons in programming are few and far between.

But thanks to a great new crop of kids' software titles, programming skills are back. Only now, they have unprecedented graphic pizzazz, funky characters, playful scenarios, and plenty of appeal — for both girls and boys. These new products don't teach programming per se.

Instead, they present playful scenarios that encourage kids to use the thinking skills important in programming — logical sequencing, analyzing patterns, and planning and creating actions and designs.

More important, kids don't need to learn a special programming language. Instead, they make things happen by manipulating visual icons. This combination of fun scenarios and new, nonverbal "languages" gives kids a great reason to exercise and master programming skills. Then kids can put these skills to work in creations of their own.

✔ *My Make Believe Castle:* With a handful of clicks, even preschoolers can "program" the antics of a prince and princess, a witch and wizard, a dragon and horse, and other castle characters in a whimsical play world. (Logo Computer Systems Inc., Ages 4-7)

✔ *Zurk's Alaskan Trek:* The Moviemaker activity lets children explore how Alaskan animals really interact in the wild or "program" the way they want the animals to behave. The result: an animated story complete with script. (Soleil/Maxis, Ages 6-10)

✔ *Snootz Math Trek:* The outfit-the-Snootz activity starts out as a dress-up game, but in fact turns out to be a challenging exercise in analyzing and constructing a complex set of attributes. It teaches sequencing and lets kids "debug" the sequence, both underlying skills of any programming language. (Theatrix Interactive, Ages 5-9)

✔ *Cocoa:* An innovative environment that lets kids build on-screen "worlds" filled with characters and objects that do exactly what kids tell them to do. Easy to understand, fun and powerful, this software is *the best* introduction we've seen to programming and simulations. For a full profile, see Chapter 13. (Apple, Ages 10 & up)

The Lost Mind of Dr. Brain (ages 9 & up)

Here's what we learned from Dr. Brain: Never underestimate the power of a silly scenario and a challenging, addictive set of puzzles to give kids (of all ages) a real mental workout.

The story of *The Lost Mind of Dr. Brain* (from Sierra) is hokey but appealing. Dr. Thaddeus P. Brain (that's *P* as in puzzle) has inadvertently transferred his intellect into Rathbone, his laboratory rat. To reverse the brain drain — and win the game — players have to complete brain teasers in ten different puzzle areas. All told, kids confront hundreds of word and logic puzzles, memory and strategy games, problem-solving adventures, and visualization and musical challenges. (See Appendix C for information about the software on the *Great Software For Kids & Parents* CD-ROM.)

Here are some of our favorites:

- ✓ *Music Region:* This one is our personal favorite, probably because it's such a rare pleasure to hear classical music in a computer game. This musical memory game challenges kids to unscramble mixed-up musical measures.

- ✓ *File Sorting:* Plenty of games test kids' memory, but this one challenges them to think about strategies for remembering things. For added fun, the "things" in question range from the ordinary (light bulb, sandwich) to the absurd (procrastinator, dimwitty).

- ✓ *Motor Programming:* The challenge here is to navigate a maze by using commands like Move, Turn Left, Turn Right, and Wait. Kids who stick with this puzzle will end up knowing some of the basics of programming.

- ✓ *3D Construction:* As kids try to build an exact copy of a 3-D object, like the structure shown in Figure 6-10, they get lots of practice visualizing what things look like from above, below, front, back, and side.

Figure 6-10: Kids can get hints from Dr. Brain's niece if they have trouble getting their blocks to look like the model.

✔ *Word Surge:* In this logic puzzle, kids rotate rows and columns of letters so that several words appear simultaneously.

✔ *Pentode:* Computer matching games are all too often uninspired versions of Concentration. This one is much, much more demanding. It will also introduce your kids to sign-language symbols, Greek letters, periodic table symbols, and Roman numerals.

Play games, get smart

When you were growing up, playing games was probably just for fun. Today games may be part of your kids' homework. That's because gameplay strategies — formulating a plan, mapping out offensive and defensive plays, predicting the outcomes of different moves, second-guessing your opponent — are important thinking skills. With *Strategy Challenges Collection 1: Around the World* (Edmark, ages 7-13), your kids not only get three cool games but also savvy coaching in strategic gameplay.

These are *not* your typical board- or card-games-on-a-computer. They're unconventional, often ancient, pastimes — Mancala, pictured in the figure in this sidebar; Nine Men's Morris; and Go-Moku — each presented with a distinctive multicultural flavor and an artistic flair rarely seen in computer games.

And each has a wealth of thoroughly modern multimedia help features: a question-mark

button for learning the rules and stepping through an actual game, a globe button with historical facts about each game, coaches with game-playing tips, and an undo/redo button for reconsidering your moves.

If you don't know these games, so much the better. You have a perfect opportunity to show your kids how *you* tackle something new.

By playing with you, kids also get a chance to think out loud. At school, teachers often don't have the time to observe how a child figures out a problem. At home, you do. Talk it out. Encourage your children to tell you what's going through their minds. Thinking out loud helps kids strengthen their reasoning abilities and makes them aware of the process of strategizing. With practice and encouragement, kids will find that strategizing is a *transferable* skill. That is, the strategies they develop for one situation may well work in another.

Dealing with the "Oh no! Not math!" syndrome

An ounce of prevention: Cure the problem before it starts. Make a fun, no-pressure math program one of your child's first software titles.

Read children's books that give you a chance to "talk math." (We especially like these authors: Mitsumasa Anno, Eric Carle, Tana Hoban, and Pat Hutchins.) That way, kids will have happy math memories by the time they reach elementary school. And they'll be less likely to pick up bad math vibes from older kids.

Try togetherness: Talk to your child about how you handle math, whether you're checking change from a purchase, keeping score at a game, or mortgaging property in Monopoly. Play with your kids' math software; give them a chance to see you having fun with math and give you a chance to talk math in a no-pressure context. Instead of hovering while they do their homework, hang out while they play a math CD-ROM.

Lighten up: Humor helps. In one of our ventures on the Web, we found an interesting collection of math cartoons at http://www.csun.edu/~hcmth014/comics.html. The cartoons aren't fancy. They look as though they've been clipped from newspapers over the years and then scanned into the computer. But some of them are hysterical, and older kids especially may enjoy them.

OPEN

It's Not Math Software, but It's Got Lots of Math Practice!

Be alert for math activities within other software programs. Many history, science, and geography titles make computational challenges part of their activities and adventures. After all, math is a useful part of many disciplines. Here are a few of our favorites:

✔ *Sammy's Science House:* The Make-A-Movie activity encourages children to practice sequencing. In the Sorting Station activity, kids find similarities and differences in pictures of plants and animals. (Edmark, Ages 3-6)

✔ *Playskool Puzzles:* This is creativity software with both prereading and early math activities. The dot-to-dot activity gives kids practice in number recognition and counting. And at Levels 2 and 3, the numbers associated with the dots start in the teens or 20s. When kids count forward from 1 or backward from 10, they often go on automatic pilot. But start the sequence at 23, for example, and kids really have to think, not just recite. (Hasbro, Ages 2-5)

✔ *Zurk's Rainforest Lab:* The Puzzle Patterns activity provides a colorful opportunity for kids to visualize geometric and spatial relationships. (Soleil/Maxis, Ages 5-9)

✔ *What's the Secret?:* The "How many pieces can a pizza produce?" activity is a concrete example of fractions in everyday life; it lets kids build their understanding by manipulating numerators and denominators. It also convincingly demonstrates the connection between fractions, decimals, and percentages. (3M, Ages 7-12)

✔ *Travelrama USA:* Because calculating mileage is an important part of this geography game, kids have an opportunity to strengthen their mental computational abilities. (KidSoft, Ages 7-12)

✔ *Morgan's Adventures in Greece:* The Magic Squares activity is based on a classic game that helps kids develop analytic and computational skills. Kids can click for hints; but they're never told the answer; they're just told how to approach the challenge. (HarperKids, Ages 7-12)

Part IV
Homework!
Oh, Homework!

The 5th Wave By Rich Tennant

©RICHTENNANT

"IT'S A FOOTBALL/MATH PROGRAM. WE'RE TACKLING MULTIPLICATION, GOING LONG FOR DIVISION, AND PUNTING FRACTIONS."

In this part . . .

Not long after our kids began doing homework, we started hearing them chant the oh-so-perceptive lines from Jack Prelutsky's poem "Homework! Oh, Homework!," in which resentful students fantasize about washing their homework away in the sink!

You can find the poem in Jack Prelutsky's book, *The New Kid on the Block* (also on CD-ROM). It hits the homework blues right on the head — and makes kids smile about them. And the same thing happened when we started using the computer to help. We found our kids stopped grumbling quite so loudly. They took an avid interest in the colorful, animated tools that could help get the job done. And they were jazzed about the way their work looked when it emerged from the printer.

Part IV is all about turning your family computer system into a productivity tool for tackling homework assignments. Chapter 7 takes a look at word-processing options and suggests creative ways to approach that time-honored assignment: the book report. In Chapter 8, you see the ins and outs of electronic research. And throughout both chapters, we share practical tips from kids, parents, and teachers.

Chapter 7
Writing It Down!

● ●

In This Chapter

▶ Getting organized

▶ Finding the best writing tools
   The Student Writing Center (ages 9 & up)

▶ Learning to type
   Type to Learn (ages 8–14)

▶ Getting creative with reports

● ●

*W*hen we were kids, we didn't do our homework on a computer. (OK, so now you can guess how old we are!) But when our kids hit homework age, they had computers at school. And we had computers in our homes. So we got to thinking: Should the family computer be part of the homework routine? How — and when — should kids use it for their assignments? And how could we help?

We did some homework ourselves — among other parents and teachers, at the library, on the World Wide Web — and came up with the following checklist.

This list starts with all-purpose pointers, applicable whether your kids use the computer for homework or not. And then it offers computer-specific suggestions.

For all families

___ *Get organized.*

Establish a homework routine. Have on hand pencils, paper, and other necessities (a globe, perhaps, or the right software package). Encourage your kids to study in the same place every day.

___ *Set a schedule.*

Strive for a regular homework time. The advice about same place–same time is tough to follow with kids racing off to soccer, ballet, karate, or piano lessons. Further complications arise when siblings need the same resources (such as the computer or the dictionary) at the same time! Encouraging your kids to create an after-school calendar can help them get a grip on their busy lives.

___ *Check with the teacher.*

Find out what role your kids' teachers want you to play when it comes to homework. Here are some questions to ask at back-to-school night: Should you check kids' backpacks for assignments? Do you need to sign off on their homework? How should you handle mistakes that you spot?

For computer-using families

___ *Respect the teacher's goals.*

Ask your kids' teachers how and when they think the home computer can help. It would be inappropriate for your 1st or 2nd grader to use a word-processing program, for example, if the class is practicing penmanship! And although electronic encyclopedias can make short work of research, the 5th-grade teacher may want the kids to practice "look-it-up" skills by thumbing through a dictionary or using a textbook index.

___ *Make the computer one of many homework helpers.*

Explore lots of different approaches to your kids' assignments. Say they're supposed to practice the times tables. You may try store-bought flash cards, make some from scratch by using index cards or a computer art program, or download some shareware flash cards. Crack open the piggy bank, and let your kids use coins for their calculations. Deal out two cards from a deck, and ask for the product. Call out an "answer," and ask your kids what numbers they can multiply to get that result. Steer kids to the multiplication activities in their math software. The more ways — and the more times — kids tackle the assignment, the better they learn it.

___ *Give kids the know-how — not the answers.*

When they hit 3rd grade or so, introduce your kids to word-processing software and electronic references — the programs kids use most for homework. (Exactly when you choose to do this will depend on the length and complexity of your kids' assignments.) Guide them by asking questions as they explore the software. But don't do the work for them!

Now take a look at ways your home computer can help your kids with written schoolwork. In this chapter, we cover different kinds of writing and typing software, profile several programs worth adding to your software library, and suggest new ways to tackle traditional assignments by using writing software.

Writing Programs for Schoolwork

OK, say that your kids want to start writing their homework assignments on the computer. What should you buy?

Nothing! Not yet, anyway. You may already have a program that meets your beginning writers' needs. Consider these three options first:

🖝 Check the kids' titles you've purchased for your software library.

A great many kids' programs (even paint programs like *Kid Pix Studio*) include some writing features. For younger students — with short assignments — one of these may work just fine:

> *The Amazing Writing Machine*
> *The Imagination Express series*
> *Creative Writer 2*
> *Zurk's Rainforest Lab*
> *Storybook Weaver*
> *Davidson's Kid Works Deluxe*

🖝 Check your hard disk for programs that were preloaded by the manufacturer.

If you find something with the word *Works* in the title — *ClarisWorks, Microsoft Works, Novell Perfect Works* — you're in business. That's because these popular all-in-one *Works* programs include word processing, spreadsheet, database, and communications software. Some *Works* software also provide extras like a paint program, graphics features, and desktop-publishing capabilities. In short, they've got the basic tools students need for writing reports.

🖝 Consider the word-processing program you use. With a little instruction, kids can easily learn to use adult software. Here are some distinct advantages to all of you using the same software:

- You don't have to spend more money!

- You don't have to tackle something new. If your kids get stuck, you can help them out without going through another learning curve.

- Your kids will enjoy that touch of pride that comes from using grown-up software.

Word-processing basics for kids

Whatever program you opt for, make sure to cover a few word-processing basics with your kids. Before you do anything else, set up a special folder where kids can keep their documents. Then show them how to select options from your program's menu bar to do the following:

1. **Launch the program.**

2. **Create a new document or open a saved document.**

3. **Name and save the document.**

4. **Apply some formatting — margins, font, type size, and style.**

5. **Save the document.**

6. **Use the Edit menu to cut, copy, and paste words, sentences, and paragraphs.**

7. **Save the document.**

8. **Use tools like the spell checker and the thesaurus.**

9. **Save the document.**

By now you've gotten the point: Urge your kids to click Save a lot!

You have two good reasons to consider buying a special writing program for your kids. One reason is to stay in synch with your kids' school. If your kids use a word-processing program at school, they may prefer the same one at home. And with the same program in both locations, kids can easily work on assignments at home or at school.

Find out from your school's computer coordinator which program your kids are using now and which ones they're likely to use as they move up through the grades.

Another good reason to buy a kids-only writing program is to provide them with special homework-helper features. And that's what the following software profile is all about.

The Student Writing Center (ages 9 & up)

We like *The Student Writing Center* (from The Learning Company) because it's loaded with features that are specially designed to help kids 9 and up with their different kinds of school assignments.

At the heart of this program is a word processor with all the essentials — editing and formatting commands, fonts and type styles, and tools like a spell checker and a thesaurus. Its basic desktop-publishing features let kids design pages with columns, create personalized letterhead, and illustrate their work with clip art. But here's the best part: This program gives kids ideas, suggestions, and lots of advice for writing reports, letters, newsletters, journals, and more.

You're wise to introduce kids to homework-helper programs like *The Student Writing Center* before they've got an assignment due. That way, no one gets stressed out. Pick a fun project for starters, such as a party invitation or a family newsletter. And encourage kids to click every option in every pull-down menu — just to see what happens! In the Letter section, they can click their way through 18 different letterhead designs, plus they find step-by-step instructions on creating personalized stationery. In the Newsletter section, they can experiment with mastheads and reformat a page with up to eight columns.

Reports made easy

The Report section of *The Student Writing Center* can be a godsend when your kids are tackling an essay, book report, short story, or research paper. It's sort of like having the world's most patient teacher on-screen — anytime kids want!

Imagine this scenario: It's 9 p.m., and your 11-year-old can't remember a thing about essays, except that one is due tomorrow morning. You'd like to come to the rescue, but you haven't written an essay since college! Relax. You can figure out what to do with *The Student Writing Center*.

Click the Tips button, and you find a list of "how to" suggestions organized by assignment type. Under Essay is an explanation of the three parts of an essay, plus instructions for writing different kinds of essays (such as essays that persuade or those that explain). Under Book Report tips, like those shown in Figure 7-1, are definitions of plot, setting, characters, and theme — with examples of how to write about each.

Other practical tips include:

- **Writing samples:** Book report, business letter, news story, short story
- **Research help:** How to take notes, organize an outline, format a footnote
- **Creative-writing tips:** How to start and end a story, where to get ideas
- **The writing process:** How to select a topic, create an outline, revise, edit
- **Style rules:** For punctuation, capitalization, plurals, abbreviations, word usage

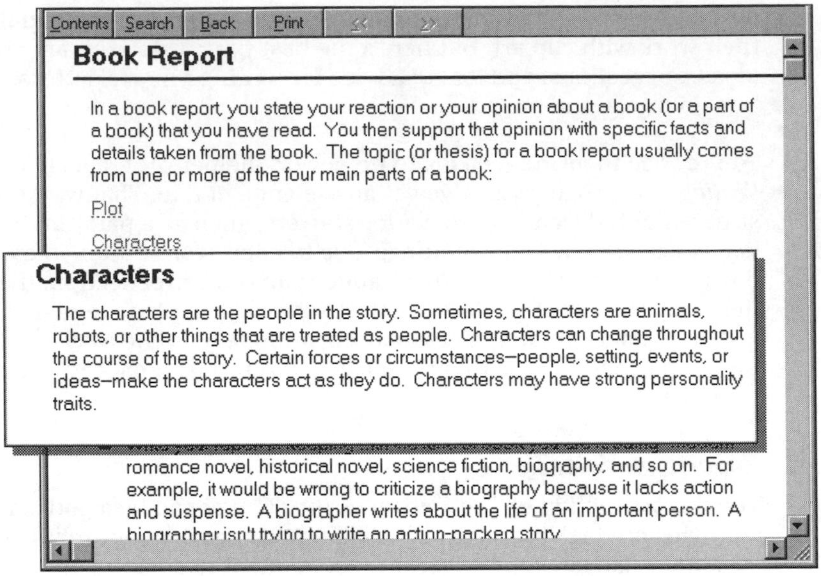
Contents
Search
Back
Print
<<
>>
Book Report
In a book report, you state your reaction or your opinion about a book (or a part of a book) that you have read. You then support that opinion with specific facts and details taken from the book. The topic (or thesis) for a book report usually comes from one or more of the four main parts of a book:
Plot
Characters
Characters
The characters are the people in the story. Sometimes, characters are animals, robots, or other things that are treated as people. Characters can change throughout the course of the story. Certain forces or circumstances—people, setting, events, or ideas—make the characters act as they do. Characters may have strong personality traits.
romance novel, historical novel, science fiction, biography, and so on. For example, it would be wrong to criticize a biography because it lacks action and suspense. A biographer writes about the life of an important person. A

Figure 7-1: *The Student Writing Center* is filled with instructive tips that can help at homework time when there's no teacher around.

Presto! It's a bibliography

The Student Writing Center is loaded with automatic features that take the tedium out of reports. Take its fill-in-the-blank approach to creating a bibliography. First the software prompts kids to identify the kind of references they use. Is it a book? Encyclopedia? Magazine article? Then the program asks kids for the author, title, publication date, and so on. Kids fill in the blanks in the entry box, like the one pictured in Figure 7-2, and click Create Entry. The software automatically formats the data, arranges the entries alphabetically, and even applies the proper punctuation.

PARENT TIP

The Learning Company also publishes *The Student Writing and Research Center,* which includes all the writing and homework features of *The Student Writing Center* plus an electronic version of *Compton's Concise Encyclopedia.* Designed for kids ages 10 and up, *The Student Writing and Research Center* is a good choice if your family does not have an all-purpose electronic encyclopedia. Another option for younger students ages 6-10 is *The Ultimate Writing and Creativity Center.* This program, which is profiled in Chapter 5, focuses more on the stages of the writing process and less on the elements of book reports, essays, and the like. It also has a spell-check feature that many parents like: You can have the software prompt your child to try again before it automatically makes a correction.

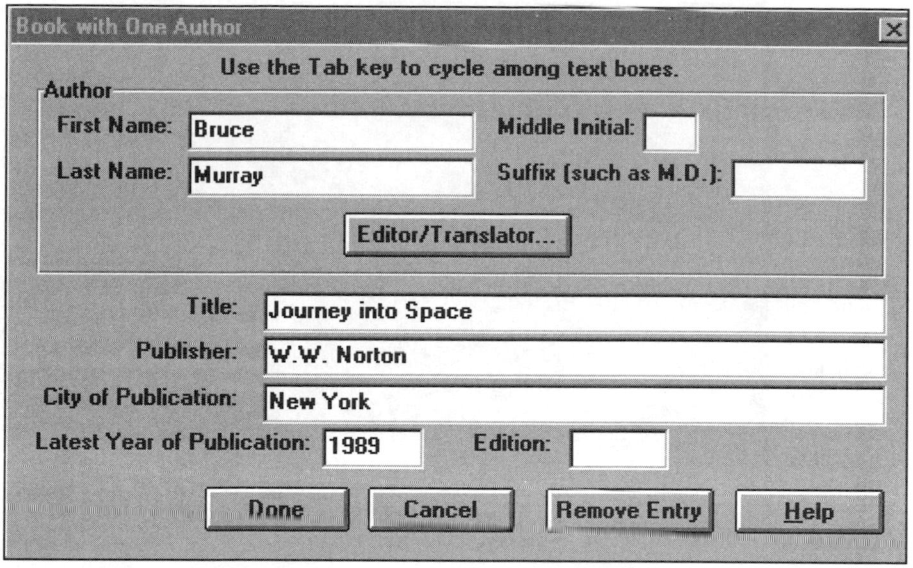

Figure 7-2:
The Student Writing Center helps kids with the details of formatting a bibliography.

Happily, all three programs make it clear that kids can't rely on the spell checker to catch every error. Proofreading is still essential. And if kids don't do it, they'll be hearing from their teacher! After all, a spell checker can't tell which homonym is right: there, their, or they're. It can't always puzzle out a child's phonetic spelling. And it doesn't inform kids about missing apostrophes, run-on sentences, or misplaced modifiers.

Type to Learn (ages 8–14)

After your kids are writing their homework regularly on the computer, it's time to move beyond the "hunt and peck" approach to typing. Most typing programs cover pretty much the same ground: a sequence of lessons and practice sessions to teach finger placement and build speed and accuracy (kind of like the typing classes we took in high school, only more fun).

If your kids like the program they use in school, get that one. Or consider our favorite: *Type to Learn* (from Sunburst Communications). It isn't flashy, but it works! Schools across the country have been using it for years to teach kids to type.

This typing program is designed for kids, and that shows. Its lessons and practice sessions are the right length for a 10-year-old's attention span. It introduces new keystrokes with verbal instructions and an animated pair of hands showing kids where to place each finger, as in the "T" and "Y" lesson you see in Figure 7-3. And best of all, its games not only reinforce new typing skills but also help kids with math, social studies, and other school subjects.

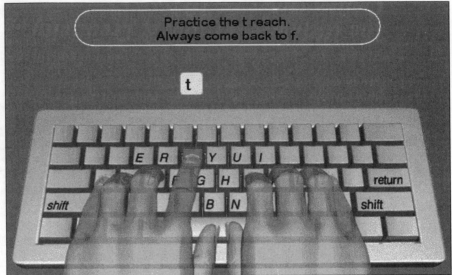

Figure 7-3:
Sound and graphics help kids learn keyboard skills in *Type to Learn*.

In the How Many? game, for example, kids are challenged to think as they practice typing numbers in response to questions like "How many musicians in a duet?" or "How many teeth in an adult's mouth?" Each correct response fills part of a picture. In Map Games, kids travel the world — and practice using the Shift key — as they fill in missing capital letters of countries, cities, mountains, and rivers. They also get practice locating different states as they type their abbreviations.

After kids have mastered the program's lessons, the exercises in Warpspeed help them develop speed and accuracy. Another winning feature: Clicking Notepad opens a basic word processor where kids can practice typing anything, from the lyrics of their favorite CD to this week's list of spelling words.

Sooner or later, most kids who use the computer genuinely want to improve their typing skills. But practicing A-F-J-U is a bore, even on the computer. You need to help kids stick with a typing program long enough to develop sufficient skill. Setting up a practice schedule may help. Try taking turns using the program — it's fun for your kids to see how imperfect you are! Every so often, excuse them from a chore so they can practice.

Having Fun with Book Reports

In many classrooms today, teachers encourage kids to approach old standards — like book reports — in new ways. First graders may draw their reactions to a book. A 3rd grader may review a poem by writing one of his own. A 5th grader who's read *The Diary of Anne Frank* may come to class in costume and field her classmates' questions as though she were Anne. Writing software fits right in with this approach, giving kids sophisticated options for enlivening their reports: inventive formatting, graphics, scanned photos, charts, and illustrations from a CD-ROM or the World Wide Web. Here are some book-report variations your kids can easily produce — provided the teacher approves — by using the software from this chapter or elsewhere in the book.

The book report as a picture book

Encourage children in the early grades to show what they know about a book's setting and characters by creating illustrated reports like the one pictured in Figure 7-4. Use a program that combines lots of artistic options with some writing tools. Good options: *Paint, Write & Play!* (Chapter 3), *The Ultimate Writing and Creativity Center* (Chapter 5), and the *Imagination Express* series (Chapter 5).

Figure 7-4: Younger students can write and illustrate reports in programs like *Paint, Write & Play!*

. . . as a news article

Using software such as *The Student Writing Center* or *ClarisWorks,* kids can create a news article or an entire front page about the book they read. Take *Tom Sawyer,* for example. Kids might run an interview with Becky, presenting her views on the night in the cave. They can devote a banner head to Injun Joe's demise. And if they're really ambitious, they can even make the newspaper look like one from 1876 by scanning in old-time photos from a product like *Vintage Prints* from *The Print Shop Photo Folios* series (Chapter 15). (*Print Shop Photo Folios* are packages of artwork that work with *The Print Shop.* For more information, look at `http://www.broderbund.com`.)

. . . as a debate or quiz show

The backdrops from a program like *Hollywood* (Chapter 5) are a great starting point for writing a script instead of a book report. Using the auditorium background, kids can stage a debate between commentators on the merits of the book. Or, they can create a quiz show where the host asks contestants questions about the book.

. . . as a "real" review

Challenge your kids to write a review that really "sells" a book to other children. And then publish it on the World Wide Web! Start by finding some Web book reviews written by other kids, reading them together, and brainstorming about what makes them interesting. Then let your kids start writing. You can post your kids' reviews at sites like The Internet Public Library Youth Division (`http://www.ipl.org/youth/`); Midlink Magazine, an electronic magazine geared for kids 10–15 (`http://longwood.cs.ucf.edu/~MidLink/`); and The Book Nook, sponsored by Canada's SchoolNet project (`http://I-site.on.ca/bookbbk.html/`).

The bottom line: Kids really have to know a book inside out to write about it creatively, in the form of a script, news article, or review. And that's exactly what teachers (and parents) want!

Chapter 8
Looking It Up!

- -

In This Chapter

▶ Building a software reference library

▶ Choosing all-in-one reference CD-ROMs
  Ultimate Children's Encyclopedia (ages 7–9)
  Microsoft Bookshelf (ages 9 & up)

▶ Using a CD-ROM encyclopedia
  Microsoft Encarta (ages 9 & up)

▶ How to find (almost) anything on the Web

▶ Taking a study break online

- -

*W*hat's the difference between a fruit and a vegetable? How about the greenhouse effect? Which was the first state? What's the definition of recalcitrant?

Never mind about the answers. (This isn't a spot quiz, after all!) The real question is: Are you prepared for your kids to start bringing home questions like these? If not, it's time to assemble a home reference library where kids can look up answers and find homework facts. And today much of that library is accessible on your family's computer.

Computer references have a lot going for them. They're less expensive than many reference books. They're up-to-date. And they appeal to kids. But with hundreds available, from CD-ROM encyclopedias to atlases to online libraries, where should you start? And which ones do your kids *really* need?

That's what this chapter is all about. We recommend kid-friendly software resources. And we share practical tips about electronic research, what you need to get kids started, how you can help them, and what works best.

Building a Software Reference Library

When it comes to reference software, parents almost always ask questions like these:

Q: When will our kids need reference software?

A: Most kids don't need to look things up much before they're in the third grade. Still, you may want to invest in an electronic encyclopedia before then. That way, you'll be ready when your kids bring home a question you can't answer. Your kids will probably request a dictionary, an atlas, and an encyclopedia once they start using them regularly in school.

Q: How big a reference library do we need at home?

A: A few CD-ROMs will suffice. You can always supplement your resources by surfing the Web.

Q: Can kids handle computer references on their own?

A: Electronic references are complex products, packed with information and features. You need to get kids started by showing them the kind of information each resource offers and demonstrating electronic look-it-up techniques. (We explain those techniques later in this chapter.) But after kids get the hang of using multimedia resources, they can take off on their own.

Q: What should we buy first?

A: That's easy! Choose from one of the two all-purpose reference CD-ROMs we recommend. These collections cover all the basics. For more in-depth information, add an electronic encyclopedia and an atlas.

Great Reference Software for Families

If you're looking for one general reference source to help your kids with school assignments, consider one of the following choices. They're not only chock full of information, they're also fun to use.

Ultimate Children's Encyclopedia (ages 7–9)

A good choice for younger kids, this program (from The Learning Company) combines an easy-to-read encyclopedia with an atlas, a thesaurus, and an illustrated children's dictionary, plus lots of biographies and word facts. Kids pursue information by clicking a subject category, such as science, machines, the human body, or the solar system; or they can type a specific word or phrase. When they reach the topic they're looking for, the *Ultimate Children's Encyclopedia* takes care not to overload them with a dense, text-filled screen. Instead, kids find a manageable paragraph of text and lots of buttons like the ones visible in the lower-left corner of Figure 8-1 to take them to short videos, narrated animations, maps, pictures, and related articles. If you're an America Online subscriber, this software also links your kids directly to *Compton's Living Encyclopedia* on AOL.

Microsoft Bookshelf (ages 9 & up)

This collection may see your kids through college! Nine different sources are packed on this CD-ROM: *The American Heritage Dictionary of the English Language, Roget's Thesaurus, The Columbia Dictionary of Quotations, The Concise Columbia Encyclopedia, The Hammond Atlas of the World, The People's Chronology, The World Almanac and Book of Facts, The Concise Encarta World Atlas,* and the Microsoft Internet Directory. If you have an online connection, the Internet Directory is a great way to link kids to thousands of subject-related (and prescreened) Web sites. You can update the Internet Directory monthly at the Microsoft Web site.

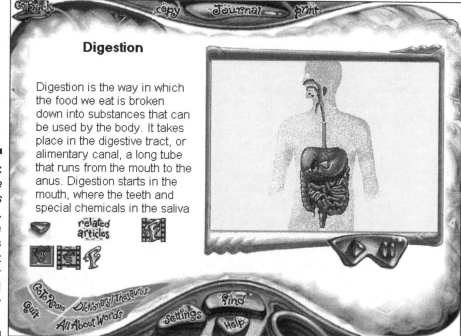

Figure 8-1:
In *Ultimate Children's Encyclopedia,* simple buttons make it easy for kids to find their way around.

Microsoft Encarta (ages 9 & up)

Among the several reliable encyclopedias on CD-ROM, we like *Microsoft Encarta* the best. It's easy enough for kids 9 and up to use but extensive enough for adults. Its layered design helps kids navigate through tens of thousands of articles and graphics without getting lost. And its articles direct kids to additional resources where they can learn more about a topic — in other *Microsoft Encarta* articles, on the World Wide Web, and in the library.

Browsing information

When we were kids, we loved to pick a volume of the encyclopedia, open it to any spot, and then idly turn the pages and look. We'd zero in on the pictures and maps, occasionally skimming a caption or absorbing a random fact, fascinated by the incredible breadth of an encyclopedia's information. When curious kids browse the "pages" of a CD-ROM encyclopedia, they find plenty of pictures to view. But these days, there's lots more to see — and hear. In *Microsoft Encarta,* kids can hear the words of Mahatma Gandhi, Malcolm X, and John F. Kennedy; or they can listen to the sounds of calypso music, Brazilian samba music, or a Buddhist chant. They can experience real-life videos of an earthquake and a hurricane. They can view maps that animate Magellan's voyage around the world or the movements of the Allied forces in World War II.

Microsoft Encarta invites kids to explore its multimedia information in several intriguing ways. We like the Guided Tours where Encarta introduces kids to a topic by leading them from one article to another. Take the Extremes tour, for example. By clicking on the Next button in the Guided Tour box shown in Figure 8-2, kids jump from the world's deepest lake (Lake Baikal in Siberia) to the coldest continent (Antarctica), the longest river (the Nile), and to the largest island (Greenland). Other Guided Tours include deserts, the Wild West, Olympic medalists, dinosaurs, the ancient world, and dangerous animals.

In the *Microsoft Encarta* Timeline of World History, kids explore world events and cultures from fifteen million B.C. to the present by scrolling through a timeline (pictured in Figure 8-3) and clicking illustrations they find along the way. Some clicks summon a short essay about the significance of a historical person, place, or event — Pepin the Short, Catherine the Great, Jamestown, Stonehenge, ENIAC, the Battle of Hastings, elections in South Africa. Others show a location on the globe — the Olmec civilization in Mexico, the Hellenistic age in Greece. Others offer up a bit of historical trivia: Invented in 2000 B.C., ice cream was a favorite dish of the Chinese emperors. All provide hypertext links to a *Microsoft Encarta* article about the subject. (See the sidebar "Web talk" later in this chapter for more about hypertext.)

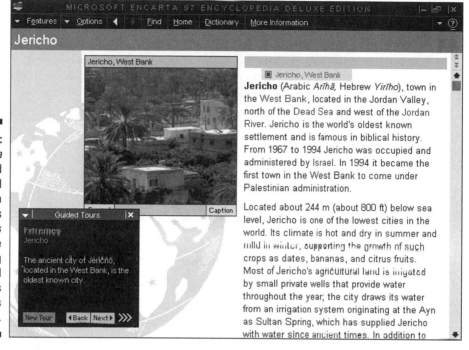

Figure 8-2:
Encarta Guided Tours and Multimedia Collages invite kids to explore by looking and listening as well as reading.

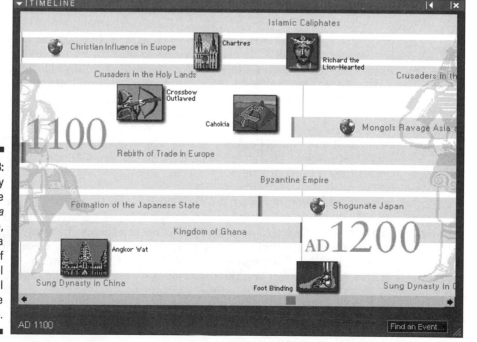

Figure 8-3:
When they explore the *Encarta* Timeline, kids get a sense of historical events all over the world.

When kids can't come up with a topic for their school report, *Microsoft Encarta is* a great place to browse for ideas. If the assignment is a country report, have your kids explore the sights and sounds in the *Microsoft Encarta* Atlas. From the *Microsoft Encarta* main screen, select Media Features and then Atlas. Next choose a continent from the world map. Zoom in to see the different countries, and click on one that's of interest. Kids can get a feel for any country in the world by clicking through *Encarta* photographs and sound clips.

Finding information

What if kids want to go straight to the facts about a topic they're studying? Click on the Find button to display Pinpointer, the *Encarta* search tool. Pinpointer lists alphabetically every article in the encyclopedia. But for more efficient searching, kids should learn to use the *Encarta* search options, called filters. Kids can mix and match these five filters in any combination.

- ✔ **Word Search:** Search for articles that contain certain keywords or phrases.
- ✔ **Category:** Find articles by subject area, such as history, geography, sports, or life science.
- ✔ **Media:** Search for articles that contain specified media elements, such as videos, sounds, or charts and tables.
- ✔ **Time:** Target a search to a specific year or span of years.
- ✔ **Place:** Search for a specific geographical location.

Each search returns with a list of *Encarta* articles like the one in Figure 8-4. By combining filters, kids can really zero in on a topic. To find pictures of nineteenth century English poets, for example, select Category: Art Language, Literature: Writers and Poets; Media: pictures; Time: 1800-1899. To find out more about the recent history of Nicaragua, select Category: History: History of the Americas; Time: 1970-1990; Place: Nicaragua.

Because it's so small, *Encarta's* text can be tough for kids to read. So make it bigger. Show your kids how to change the text size by choosing text size under the Options menu.

What if kids can't locate what they're looking for in the first article they find? Sometimes, information about a topic may be scattered in different articles. With *Encarta,* looking up these other articles is as easy as clicking the mouse. Kids just click the More Information button to see a list of Related Articles. Clicking on any title in the list takes them directly to that article. Kids also can find related articles by clicking on the highlighted words in an article's text. In the *Encarta* article on human nutrition, for example, kids can click to related articles about proteins, carbohydrates, vitamins, and glucose. Kids also can find definitions for unfamiliar words in the *Encarta* dictionary.

The 1997 version of *Microsoft Encarta* adds links to more than 5,000 related Web sites to many of the encyclopedia's articles. If your kids are curious about research on the Web, the *Encarta* connection is a great way to get started. From any article, just click the More Information button to see a list of related Web resources like the one pictured in Figure 8-5. Instead of you and your kids combing the Web to find the best sites about a certain topic, Microsoft editors have done it for you.

For many articles, *Microsoft Encarta* also provides a bibliography of books where kids can find more information about a topic they're researching. Just click on the Further Reading button. Then print the list of recommended books and head for the library.

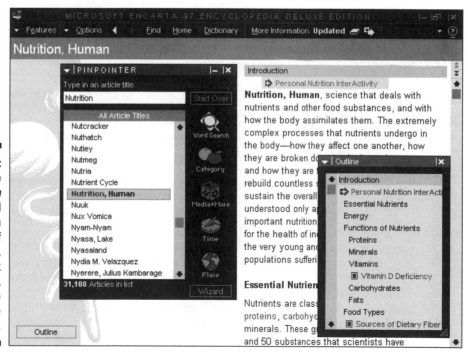

Figure 8-4:
When the *Encarta* search tool returns with a list of articles, kids click the title, and the article opens.

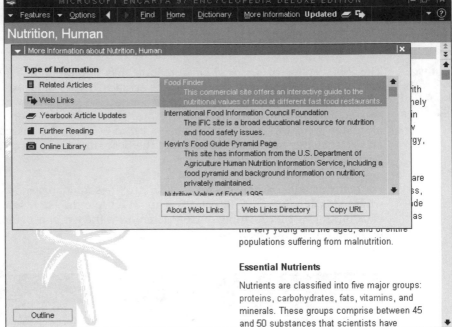

Figure 8-5:
Encarta
directs kids
to other
resources
where they
can pursue
further
information
both on and
off the
computer.

Taking notes

If your kids are using *Microsoft Encarta* to do research for a school report, they'll need to find a way to take notes on what they read. Here are two approaches to try.

✔ **From a printed page:** Some kids find it easier to work the old-fashioned way — taking notes from a printed page. To print an article (or selected sections), click on the Print command under the Options menu.

✔ **On the computer:** *Microsoft Encarta* offers two ways to take on-screen notes. Under the Tools menu, kids find a Word Processor and Notemark, a kind of virtual "yellow sticky" note. After kids get the hang of it, Notemark notes are easier to manage. When kids find a fact worth noting, they click on Notemark, and a yellow note square appears on the screen (as pictured in Figure 8-6). Kids can type in the note just as they would in a word processor. *Encarta* keeps a list of Notemark notes, a helpful way for kids to keep track of which articles they've read. Before kids exit the software, remind them to cut and paste their Notemark notes into a word processor and print them.

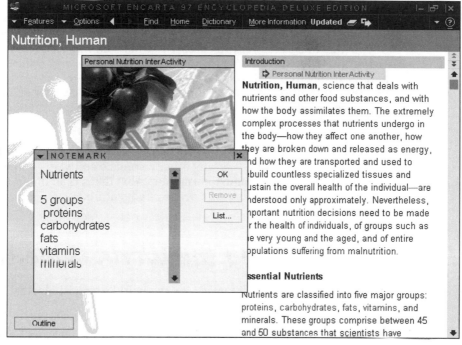

Figure 8-6:
Kids can take electronic notes right on the screen by using the *Encarta* Notemark features.

No doubt your kids hear this from their teachers: "Write reports in your own words." But they should hear it from you, too. Because it's so easy to copy text and pictures, kids can get lazy about summarizing what they've read and citing their sources. You can help by reminding them to write from scratch and by showing them how to document their sources. Here's the kind of bibliography entry librarians recommend for an electronic encyclopedia: Human Nutrition. Microsoft Encarta. CD-ROM, Windows. Seattle: Microsoft, 1997. (You can find guidelines for cybercitations at http://kalama.doe.hawaii.edu/hern95/rt007/.)

Staying up to date

If you're connected to the Web, Microsoft makes it easy to keep *Encarta* up on current events. Each month, the *Encarta Yearbook Builder* lets you download updates to articles in the encyclopedia. Every month you can also download new and updated Web addresses. Each of these monthly update services is free if you buy the 1997 *Encarta Encyclopedia Deluxe* edition. If you own an older version of *Encarta,* call Microsoft to learn about upgrades to *Encarta 97.*

If you want to extend your family's home reference resources beyond *Microsoft Encarta,* check out the *Encarta* Online Library. From within *Encarta,* kids can link to more than 800 additional periodicals and reference sources. At the time this book went to press, the Online Library had a monthly subscription fee of $6.95. To learn more about the *Encarta* Online Library and its 10-day free trial, visit its Web site (`http://www.encarta.cognito.com/about/index.html`). And be sure to check out another online reference database called The Electric Library. You'll find more information and a Web address at the end of this chapter.

Encarta is one starting point for looking up information on the Web. But your kids don't need *Encarta* — or any other reference software — to venture into the dynamic world of online information. All it takes is an online connection, some parental assistance, and a sense of adventure.

Doing Research on the World Wide Web

Welcome to the World Wide Web! It's the world's biggest electronic library. It's always open. And it's lots of fun.

The World Wide Web is a compelling online resource for kids. Here's why:

- ✔ It's got way-cool multimedia — photos, sound effects, music, video clips, animation, and artwork.

- ✔ It's got something called *hypertext links* that let kids jump from one Web site to another with a simple click of the mouse.

- ✔ And it's dynamic — open all the time, everywhere, for anyone. Every day, people are adding to the Web's collection of pages, from IBM to the Library of Congress to Mrs. Warrington's 6th grade class at Hillview School in Menlo Park, California!

The result: Some wonderful resources, and some mediocre ones, too. Navigating this eclectic mix is part of the fun. In fact, research on the Web is a bit like playing scavenger hunt via computer. There's no guarantee kids will find exactly what they're looking for. But the process is sure to be interesting.

Web talk

Just like computers, the Internet has its own set of buzz words. If you're new to the online world, you may not be familiar with all the words or terms we use in this section. So here we provide you with some short definitions to help translate Web talk into real words.

- **World Wide Web:** A graphical interface to the Internet, the Web lets you access pictures, animation, and sound in addition to text.

- **Hypertext:** A special technology that creates links between different locations on the Web. Clicking on a hypertext link (sometimes called hot spot) on one page takes you to another page in the same Web site or to an entirely different Web site.

- **Web site:** A Web site is a location on the Web composed of one or more pages. Think of the World Wide Web as a huge library and Web sites as the books that fill the library's shelves. Just as you browse through the pages of books in a library, on the Web, you browse through the pages of different Web sites.

- **Home page:** This is the first page of a Web site.

- **URL:** Every Web page has its own address or URL (which stands for Uniform Resource Locator). A Web address is the string of letters and numbers starting with `http://` that you see wherever we refer to a Web site.

- **Browser:** To move around the Web, you need special software called a browser. People are probably most familiar with either the *Netscape Navigator* or *Microsoft Internet Explorer* browsers.

- **Surfing:** To surf the Web means to jump from one linked Web page to another.

- **Search engine:** Also called a search service. On the Web, you use a search service's software to help find Web pages related to a particular subject. Search services like AltaVista, Lycos, InfoSeek, and Excite are available free through your Web browser.

- **Directory:** A directory is a database of Web sites organized by hierarchical subject categories like the card catalog in the library. It's another way to find Web pages related to a particular subject. Popular directories include Yahoo! and Magellan.

- **Bookmark:** You use a bookmark to mark a page on the Web to which you'd like to return just as you'd mark a page in a book. Your browser lets you bookmark any Web page and store its address in a bookmark list. When you want to go back to the site, you just click on its name.

- **Server:** A server is a computer that holds content (in the form of Web sites) that can be accessed by other computers on the Internet.

- **HTML:** Short for HyperText Markup Language, this language is used to format Web pages so that they support hypertext links and can be read by Web browsers.

- **Modem:** A modem translates your computer's digital data so that it can be transmitted over the phone lines. Modems come in different speeds that are measured in bps (bits per second).

- **ISP:** An ISP, or Internet Service Provider, leases you a connection to the Internet just like the phone company leases you access to the phone network. There are many ISPs, both local and national, including companies like AT&T, Netcom, and Pipeline.

Getting connected

First things first. To reach the Web, you have to get connected. Here's what you'll need:

- ✔ A modem
- ✔ A commercial Internet Service Provider (ISP) to provide the connection between your computer and the Web
- ✔ And a browser, such as *Microsoft Internet Explorer* or *Netscape Navigator*

Chances are you already have a modem since this device is often included with a computer system when you buy it. If not, we suggest that you call around to get the best price on a 28.8 Kbps modem. (At the moment, 28.8 Kbps is the fastest modem technology you can buy. So it will cost you more than others. But it's worth the investment if you want to view the great graphics on the Web.)

After your modem's in place, you have two easy alternatives for your Web service and browser:

- ✔ **Join an online service:** You can reach the Web through any of the major online services — America Online, CompuServe, Prodigy. In addition to their own content, these services provide everything you need to reach the World Wide Web.
- ✔ **Purchase an Internet starter kit:** These starter kits, available wherever you buy software, provide everything you need to get connected to the Web. Some of the most popular starter-kit packages are *Netscape Navigator, Microsoft Internet Explorer,* and *Internet in a Box.*

You can also start by contacting an Internet Service Provider. Many, like Netcom, provide subscribers with the software they need to connect to the Web. To locate an Internet Service Provider in your area, talk to friends who are online or look up service providers under Internet services in the Yellow Pages.

Web safety

When your kids use CD-ROM software, their experience is private. The only people involved are sitting with them in front of the computer. Kids need to understand that the Web is different. It's a public place, so your kids should be as careful online as they are at the bus stop or the mall.

Here is a list of some common-sense precautions for parents and kids:

___ *Take time to understand what kids can do on the Web and on your family's online service if you use one.*

Then set clear guidelines about when and how your kids can use online resources.

___ *Spend time with your kids while they are online.*

Have them show you what they are doing.

___ *Caution your kids.*

Make sure they know they should never ever give out anything personal like their real name, address, phone number, photograph, or e-mail address while they're online.

___ *Ask your kids to check with you if they encounter a site that requires their name or e-mail address to enter.*

Some Web sites require special identification and sign-in procedures. Make it a family policy for kids to check with you first if they want to use one of these sites.

You can find more parent guidelines, plus a list of kids' rules for online safety at the Web site for Child Safety on the Information Highway (`http://www.4j.lane.edu/InternetResources/Safety/Safety.html`) and the Web site of the University of Oklahoma's Department of Safety (`http://www.uoknor.edu/oupd/inetmenu.htm`).

Let's go surfing now . . . everybody's learning how

When can kids start doing school research on the Web? You can find fun stuff for kids of any age. But for independent research, kids must be competent readers. Locating useful information takes persistence, the ability to skim through lots (and lots) of information, screen out the extraneous stuff, and find the pertinent facts.

Plan to spend time with your kids helping them to learn the ins and outs of Web research. If you're new to the Web, you and your kids can figure it out together. Like anything else, it's a process of learning by doing. The more you venture on the Web and explore, the more proficient you'll become.

Here's a four-step process to follow when you're ready to show your kids the ropes. It works for any research topic kids select. We illustrate the process with a topic suggested by our 9-year-old friend Erik who wanted to go high-tech with his science report.

Step 1: Ask questions

Web research works best for kids when they're looking for answers. Pursuing specific details helps kids stay focused while they scroll through pages and pages of information. So help your kids turn their assignment into a list of questions. After first considering ants, praying mantises, and pill bugs, Erik settled on butterflies as the subject of his report. Here are the questions he wanted to answer:

- How long does a butterfly live?
- What do butterflies eat?
- How many different kinds of butterflies exist?
- What kinds of butterflies live in California?
- Why do butterflies have colored wings?

Step 2: Create a list of key words

To find resources on the Web, kids start with a search service (also called a search engine) such as AltaVista, Lycos, InfoSeek, or Web Crawler. The search service asks kids to type keywords. Then its search software scans millions of Web pages (AltaVista, for example, scans 30 million) looking for keyword matches.

Keywords are so central to research on the Web that we suggest your kids spend some time thinking about them *before* they go online. Encourage kids to create a list of keywords (and phrases), the more specific the words, the better. Here are the words Erik started with: butterflies, length of life, diet, world, California, wings, colors.

Step 3: Start the search

With most browsers, kids are just one click away from a choice of search services.

If your browser is *Netscape,* kids can get to a search service by clicking the Net Search button in the menu bar. If your browser is *Microsoft Internet Explorer,* they click the button with the little magnifying glass in the menu bar. When kids reach the search service, they type a keyword (or words) in the blank space and click on the button next to the blank (depending on the service kids are using, it might say Submit or Seek Now or Go Get It) to start their search.

In seconds, the search service returns with a list of the pages that contain the same keywords. Pages that contain the highest number of matches are listed first. To visit any site on this list, kids just click on the highlighted page name.

Step 4: Experiment

Warn kids that they won't find everything they're looking for on their first search. A keyword search can easily produce thousands of matches. And many will be unrelated to your child's project. When Erik used AltaVista to search for "butterflies," the search service informed him it found 10,000 matching pages. Among the pages at the top of the list, he found How Butterflies Came To Be, which was a Native American story, and another called Feeding Like Butterflies, which sounded promising at first but turned out to be all about a Canadian rock band!

Here are some different ways to experiment with and improve keyword searches.

Add more keywords to help focus the search

When Erik added the words "diet" and "food" to "butterflies," a site called Designing Gardens for Butterflies appeared at the top of the new list of matches. Created by the Brooklyn Botanic Garden, this site told him what butterflies and caterpillars like to eat.

Try different word forms

When Erik tried "butterfly" instead of "butterflies," he discovered a whole new set of sites. Near the top of the list was The Butterfly Website.

Within a site, look for links to other URLs

Even if a site is not quite right, it may serve as a rich source of links to other ones that are useful. Despite its name, The Butterfly Website didn't answer Erik's questions. But it did provide a list of Other Internet Resources which in turn led him to the Entomology Index of Internet Resources, created by an entomologist at Iowa State University.

Check anything labeled K-12 for useful sites for school projects

As we skimmed the Entomology Index, we spied K-12 Educator Recommended Resources. Score! It listed two pages of insect resources for kids. Erik first linked to Butterflies of the U.S, a page in the Northern Prairie Science Center's Web site. And there, he found a list of all butterfly species in California, plus a huge selection of color photographs. Other sites on this K-12 list helped answer most of his remaining questions.

Urge kids to try more than one search tool

Different search engines work in different ways. If your kids don't luck out with one, suggest they try their keywords with another. You can learn more about the different search services at `http://www.cnet.com/Content/Reviews/Compare/Search/`.

Most Web search services offer tips for doing keyword searches. Spend some time with your kids reading this search advice and experimenting with the recommendations. Keywords are the basis for electronic research (CD-ROM encyclopedias, for example, also use this method), and learning how to use keywords effectively is a skill your kids will use for many years to come.

Try Web directories, too

Web directories like Yahoo! and Magellan offer another way to search for information on the Web. Rather than use software to search for keyword matches, directories use human beings to assign a subject category to a site, the same way a library catalogs a book. In Yahoo!, for example, butterfly sites are listed under Science: Biology: Entomology: Butterflies.

Kids can also search Yahoo! by keyword. Like a search service, Yahoo! search results return titles and short descriptions of pages containing keyword matches. But Yahoo! also assigns a subject category that helps kids zero in on the most relevant pages to pursue. For example, when Erik searched for butterflies in Yahoo!, he realized he could skip the pages related to gardening and music (there's that rock band again) and go right to the pages in the science category.

Yahooligans! and KidZone, junior versions of Yahoo! and Magellan, respectively, are Web site directories for kids. They're organized by subject headings like Animals and Plants, Science and Oddities, School Bell, The Reading Room, and Art Soup. While they're not educational collections per se, they refer kids to many interesting, kid approved, often educationally-related Web sites.

Step 5 : From research to report

When kids find useful information at a site, encourage them to print the pages and put them in a folder or notebook. Remind them to note the source of the information, too, so they can include it in footnotes or a bibliography. Then they can underline, take notes, create an outline, and start writing.

This is a good time to introduce your kids to the outline feature in your word-processing software. It's a bit tricky at first, but it sure makes it easy to add topics and change things around. And when it's time to build a bibliography, kids will find suggestions for citing online and CD-ROM resources in bibliographies and footnotes at the Internet Public Library. (`http://aristotle.sils.umich.edu/classroom/userdocs/internet/citing.html`)

Web research may seem more convenient than a trip to the library, but it "ain't necessarily so." Getting to the right sites can be slow going. So make sure your kids leave plenty of time for online research. Last-minute surfing the night before a report is due will drive everyone crazy.

Finding educational sites for kids

Here's another way to look for great Web sites for kids. Consult Web resources developed to help students and teachers. These lists of educational sites are filled with links to help kids with homework and school projects. Most of these lists are organized by subject. Here are some of our favorites:

- **Kids Web:** This extensive listing of sites in the arts, sciences, and social studies is part of an effort to create a digital library of Web resources for school-age kids. The effort is part of an educational project funded by New York State. (http://www.npac.syr.edu/textbook/kidsweb)

- **Franklin Institute Science Museum's Educational Hotlists:** A collection of educational sites selected by the staff at the Franklin Institute Science Museum. Topics include geology, health, energy, American history, insects, weather, reference, and more. (http://sln.fi.edu/tfi/hotlists/hotlists.html or http://sln.fi.edu/tfi/welcome.html)

- **Link Library:** These lists of Web sites for teachers, parents, and students are part of the excellent collection of resources at Houghton Mifflin's Education Place. Look under Resources for Teachers for a useful list of social studies resources. (http://www.hmco.com/hmco/school/links/index.html)

- **Cool School Tools:** A subject index of selected resources created by librarians for kids in grades K-12. (http://199.76.61.8:80/cooltools/)

- **Classroom Connect:** Use keywords to search GRADE, this site's library of educational Internet links. (http://www.classroom.net/cgi/rofm/eduFind.html)

- **Arts and Social Sciences Gateway:** These lists of resources for K-12 educators were created by librarians and computer specialists at Cornell University. (http://www.tc.cornell.edu/Edu/ArtSocGateway/) A second gateway lists mathematics and science sites recommended for high school students. (http://www.tc.cornell.edu/Edu/MathSciGateway/index.html)

- **4Kids Treehouse:** Reading, science, and social studies resources particularly well suited for elementary school kids. (http://array.4kids.com)

- **6th Grade Brain Bank:** Patrick White created this homework page for his school science fair project. He's looking for new links, so if you find a new resource you like, let him know. (http://www.zygomedia.com/61wc/index.html)

Did your browser fail to find a Web address you typed? It could be a fickle Web address. Try looking for a "missing" site with a search engine. And try shortening the address by deleting everything after the .com (or .org or .edu).

PARENT TIP

Don't forget the library. School libraries and local branch libraries offer lots of reference materials created especially for kids and aimed at a range of reading levels. Younger children and kids with reading difficulties may have an easier time with these resources.

Great Web research resources — for a fee

If your kids are overwhelmed by the Web, you may want to consider investing in The Electric Library. For a monthly fee of $9.95 (when this book went to press), this site gives your family unlimited access to a wealth of reference materials. Among them are *Compton's Encyclopedia, Monarch Notes,* newspapers, magazines, academic journals, TV and radio transcripts, and photography collections.

For parents concerned about letting kids loose on the Web, The Electric Library offers a more controlled alternative. Although kids enter The Library via the Web, once they're in its database, they can link only to other Library sources, not to other sites on the Web. Check out The Electric Library's free two-week trial offer. If you're a member of Prodigy, look for the same service under the name Homework Helper. (http://www.elibrary.com)

ELECTRIC LIBRARY

Welcome to the new Electric Library-Read all about our new Design!

begin your **Research**

Welcome
About Electric Library
Research vs. Net Search
Free Trial Offer!
Download Software

Information
Content
Common Questions
News
5% for Kids

Subscriptions
Monthly
Schools & Libraries

Help
Search Tips
Help Index
Customer Service

Go

Enter a question or some keywords. Select source types. Click Go!
Try it now and receive a free two week trial. Click here for details.

☒ **Magazines**
Nearly 800 full-text

☒ **Maps**
Hundreds available

☒ **Books**
Over 2,000 works

☒ **Newspapers & Newswires**
More than 150 full-text

☒ **TV & Radio Transcripts**
Television transcripts

☒ **Pictures**
Over 28,000 Photos

(More Options...)

Online diversions

When kids need a break from studying, they can find plenty of entertaining diversions on the Web. Look for sites listed under "Entertainment" in Web directories like Yahoo! (http://www.yahoo.com/Entertainment/) or Magellan (http://www.mckinley.com/browse_bd.cgi?Entertainment/). When your kids find a site they really like, create a *bookmark* so they can find their way back tomorrow. We offer these three fun sites for starters:

✔ **Famous birthdays:** What famous people were born this very day? Stop by Britannica's Lives, shown in Figure 8-7, for brief biographies of sports stars, historical figures, famous literati, and celebrities of all kinds, arranged by date of birth. (http://www.eb.com/cgi-bin/bio.pl/)

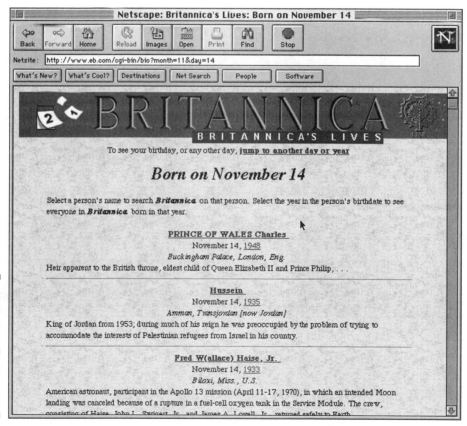

Figure 8-7:
Impress
your friends
with the
names of
famous
people born
on this day.

✔ **Insult of the day:** "Oh thou spleeny toad-spotted knave!" Shock siblings and friends with erudite insults. You get a new one every time you visit the Shakespearean Insult Server. (`http://www.nova.edu/Inter-Links/cgi-bin/bard.pl/`)

✔ **Comics of the day:** Catch up on your favorite funnies! Kids can read Nancy, Peanuts, Marmaduke, and more at The Comic Strip site pictured in Figure 8-8. (`http://www.unitedmedia.com/comics/`)

Figure 8-8: Take a comics break at The Comic Strip site.

Part V
Explorations for Inquiring Kids

The 5th Wave   By Rich Tennant

"From now on, let's confine our exploration of ancient Egypt to the computer program."

In this part . . .

This is one of the biggest sections of *Great Software For Kids & Parents* — for the simple reason that there's so much great software for kids in this category!

Exploration software — thanks to photographic images, informative animation, video clips, realistic sounds, and kid-friendly text and narrative — takes kids to places they can't ordinarily go. And it makes them feel as if they're really there.

But we're talking about more than multimedia wizardry here. The titles we like "hook" kids with a quest, a mystery, or an adventure — something that gets them all fired up about delving into history, geography, and science. And our favorite programs go even further, offering children a hands-on opportunity to experiment with their on-screen surroundings.

In Part V, you find software that takes kids on explorations around the world (a.k.a. geography). There are titles that transport them back in time. Some give kids control over virtual environments, where they can simulate events. Others give them a chance to experiment with scientific concepts on-screen. Still others make it easy for kids to learn a foreign language.

Chapter 9

Using the Computer for Explorations around the World

● ●

In This Chapter

▶ Discovering geography today — it's more than state capitals!

▶ Having great fun – gameplay + geography
　　　The *Carmen Sandiego* series (ages 5–12)

▶ Making facts stick — after the game's over!

▶ Doing cartography with kids
　　　My First Amazing World Explorer (ages 4–9)

▶ Getting geography smarts on the Web

● ●

*Q*uick! Name the 50 states in alphabetical order. What's the main export of Madagascar? What's the capital of Zimbabwe? What countries border Azerbaijan to the west? What's the world's longest river (and why should we care)?

That's the kind of geography we memorized as kids (except that Zimbabwe was Rhodesia back then and Azerbaijan was part of the Soviet Union). Facts like these are still important. (And far too many kids don't know them.) But equally important today is an emphasis on "thinking geographically": growing up observing and appreciating the many people and places around the globe, asking questions about the complex interactions between people and their environment, understanding why certain events unfold in particular places. After all, it takes a geographically informed person to get home from a bus stop, find a place on a map, plan a vacation, make sense of the nightly news, vote intelligently on political issues that affect the environment, manage a business, and so much more.

How can you help? Actually, you can find many ways to include geographic thinking in your children's experiences.

If you follow all the tips in this book, you won't have any space left on your walls at all! Because now in addition to kids' artwork and written work, we're suggesting that you make room for a map or two. According to the U.S. government's Office of Educational Research and Improvement, kids who grow up around maps are more likely to get the "map habit" than kids with limited exposure. Which map(s) should go up? That depends on your kids' ages and family activities. A map of your vacation destination is an obvious choice; so is a map showing where grandma lives. Placemat maps are lots of fun, too. They're available with U.S. and world maps, international flags, and the like.

Of course, using the computer is another way you can help your junior geographers. We find that computer-based geography experiences tend to fall into three categories: geography games, CD-ROM references, and Web encounters with distant places and people. And in this chapter, we give you a taste of all three and suggest how to integrate them with off-the-computer activities. You can find more ideas for older kids in *TakeCharge Computing For Teens & Parents,* published by IDG Books Worldwide.

We've said this before — but, hey, why not say it again: Kids learn to care about things their parents value. If you read, they'll read. If you use the computer, they'll use the computer. And the same applies to geography. If you talk about world events, if you snip the foreign stamps off postcards from vacationing friends, if you keep a globe handy, your kids are more likely to grow up with a sense of what in the world is where!

Having Great Fun with Geography Gameplay

Playing games is one of the time honored ways of reinforcing your children's knowledge, and geography has always been a natural source of fun for families. Geography facts seem tailor-made for quick questions at the dinner table or TV quiz shows. Many of the all-time favorite kids' games utilize geography smarts, too: games like scavenger hunts, activities like treasure maps and mazes, and the license-plate contests kids play on a car trip.

The Carmen Sandiego series (ages 5–12)

In the past decade, a computer game has made its way into that list of classics. Maybe you've heard of it. It's called *Carmen Sandiego*. But if you haven't, chances are your kids have — from the PBS game show, the TV cartoon series, the card games, the calendars, the board games, the jigsaw puzzles, the sweatshirts, the backpacks, the books, et cetera. Despite this merchandising industry, Carmen is first and foremost a software superstar. That's where she got her start — in 1985! And that's still where she's at her best.

We think the *Carmen Sandiego* series is smart software, and here's why. It's got abundant opportunities for learning; it's got a quest; it's got strategic gameplay; it's got visual pizzazz and pun-filled humor.

For kids, playing *Carmen* is part scavenger hunt, part snoop job, and part on-screen orienteering, complete with up-close encounters with sights and sounds from around the globe. And it has the thrill of the chase that kids love. Here's what happens: Kids play *gumshoes* by following a trail of geographical clues to recover artifacts stolen by Carmen's villainous gang. The ultimate goal: nab the thieves. Success brings a promotion (sometimes) and a more complex set of clues for the next case.

Sparked by this challenge, kids throw themselves into the pursuit of information with amazing enthusiasm. Kids who have never cracked an atlas scrutinize maps in search of the Volga. Beginning readers painstakingly sound out three-syllable words to figure out their next destination. Fourth graders who have never used a database before plunge right in, hoping to discover just where the heck Chiang Mai is. And competitive kids (even siblings!) find themselves collaborating to catch the common enemy — Carmen.

For parents and teachers, *Carmen* pushes all the right buttons, too. The series provides a fun way for kids to pick up geography facts. It throws new words at kids: follicles, nefarious, coiffure. It fosters research skills, with both electronic and traditional references. It cultivates a spirit of cooperation. It connects kids with books (since some sort of reference work comes with every *Carmen* program). And it breeds respect for knowledge — because the lesson implicit in the *Carmen* titles is that it's fun to get smart, and smart kids win.

Which Carmen?

Which of Broderbund's three *Carmen* CD-ROMs you start with depends on your child's age and enthusiasms, what's going on in school, and your family's interests.

For 5- to 8-year-olds, the *Junior Detective Edition* provides a trail of visual and spoken — versus text-oriented — clues for tracking down the villainous Carmen and her cohorts. Hidden in stunning photographs, the clues to a thief's whereabouts include pictures of national flags, local crops, native wildlife, and the like. You can see typical clues in Figure 9-1. Junior detectives have to remember what each clue looks like — and listen carefully to comments from fellow agents and the Chief — to correctly choose their next destination. Comical cartoon interludes along the way show glimpses of the suspect, followed by inept photographers who snap incomplete photos that kids must piece together into a wanted poster. But bear this in mind: it's less about getting kids to remember world geography than it is about exercising visual and auditory memory and developing reasoning skills.

Big-kid Carmens (ages 8–12)

Because it's about familiar territory, *Where in the USA Is Carmen Sandiego?* (from Broderbund) may be a better first *Carmen* program for some 8- to 12-year-olds. But *Where in the World* is a also good choice if you have relatives overseas or you bring the kids yen or pesos or rubles from business trips. And the latest release of *Where in the World* gives the program a multimedia facelift that MTV-generation kids appreciate.

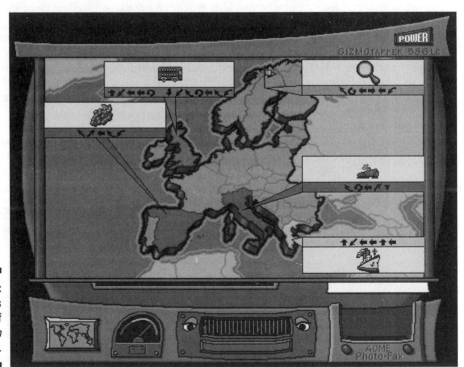

Figure 9-1:
Visual clues
tip kids off
in *Carmen
Junior.*

The photorealistic good looks of the newest edition come from the panoramic photography used as a backdrop at every location that kids visit. The cartoon characters strolling through these scenes are better looking, too. (The computer-animated bystander in Figure 9-2, for example, is pictured against a "real" image of the Eiffel Tower in Paris.) And the program's air of breathless, game-show excitement comes from using footage of TV's "real" Acme Detective Agency chief, Lynne Thigpen, who launches kids on their cases and gives them pointers along the way.

More chances to learn

But don't worry. There have been improvements in substance, too, not just sizzle. An excellent on-screen reference called the World Wiz Database is just a click away. If you're wondering whether that makes finding answers too easy for kids — good question! It's true that some questions are answered more readily with the World Wiz, such as: Is the Kyber Pass in Afghanistan or Pakistan? But the World Almanac book is better for others. Kids have to figure out how the two resources are organized, how to look up information in both, and which is better for different questions. And that's a valuable learning experience.

Figure 9-2: Kids can talk to this bystander or stroll around looking for other characters to question.

Here's another change: Clues about a suspect and where he or she is headed are divvied among more "bystanders." As a result, kids spend longer in each location asking questions, and the payoff is more geographical information. Luckily, there's now an on-screen notebook in which kids can keep tabs on all the clues.

Just for fun, shelve the almanac that comes with your *Carmen* CD-ROM and don't click into World Wiz. Play the game alongside your kids, and you be the reference, instead. Share your geography know-how by thinking aloud as you puzzle out clues. (It's also a good way to show kids how to make an educated guess when you don't know the answer.) When you're right, your kids will be impressed. But be prepared for heckling when you're in the dark and the crook gets away.

OPEN

Other Fascinating Geography Games

Here are three other geography games you may want to consider. The first is for younger children, although it has some activities that are great for family fun. The second involves strategic gameplay, not just geography smarts, making it especially appealing to game-loving kids. And the third has a cool storyline and the excitement of a time limit, which may appeal to older kids.

✔ **Gigglebone Gang World Tour:** The "gang" in this title — a frog, a hog, a raccoon, a monkey, and a tiger — create an exceptionally good-looking travelogue about Australia, China, Egypt, Ghana, India, Japan, Mexico, Norway, Peru, and Russia. In each country, kids have lots of options for learning fun: interactive folktales; matching games about landmarks, customs, and languages; and more.

◀◀

Don't let the little-kid age-range (4-8) deter you from playing with this title yourself or with the kids. It's filled with humor, with lots for little kids to giggle at — plus zingers for adults that fly over kids' heads. The Fact or Fib activity is especially good for parents and kids together. In each country, Velma the pig relates fascinating (but sometimes deliberately erroneous) information, and players have to call her bluff. For example: "Did you know that in Ghana there's a tree you can actually live inside of? Fact or Fib?" (Headbone/Broderbund Interactive, Ages 4-8)

✔ ***Travelrama USA:*** Travelrama is quick to hook kids with its good looks, lively music, and an appealing challenge: hit the road to collect five postcards — before your opponents get their postcards and before your mileage meter runs out. Besides sheer fun, this cross-country adventure for one to four players gives kids a fairly rigorous workout not only in U.S. geography but also in problem-solving, map-reading, math, and strategic thinking. If kids don't know which states are represented by the postcards on their list, they have to figure it out. Kids also have to pick an advantageous starting point, map out the shortest route to other states and outthink their opponents, too. (KidSoft, Ages 7-12)

✔ ***The Adventures of Simon Challenger:*** In this new challenge from the creators of the original *Carmen* game, kids try to prevent the theft of famous people, places, and things, past and present, by identifying them *fast* from a series of clues. Although the action takes place in a futuristic laboratory, kids actually do a lot of good old-fashioned reading in this program. And we like that a lot. After a couple of games, kids get to know the history and significance of such "cultural icons" as the Last Supper, the Easter Island statues, Mother Teresa, the Great Wall of China, Thomas Edison, the Eiffel Tower, the Sphinx, and scores more. (Maxis, Ages 8 & Up)

■

Especially for little kids

Many of the programs we profile in Chapter 3 introduce concepts that are pertinent to geography.

✔ The Edmo and Houdini activity in *Bailey's Book House*, for example, gives kids a workout with *positional* words (over, under, in, out, above, below) that are important for understanding location.

✔ The Weather Machine and Make-A-Movie activities in *Sammy's Science House* let children explore natural phenomena and their impact on people.

✔ Virtually every activity in *Trudy's Time and Place House* is geography-oriented.

✔ By helping Putt-Putt make his way to the different neighborhoods in *Putt-Putt Joins the Parade*, kids get a leg up on map reading.

✔ And the Travel Agency in *Paint, Write & Play!* introduces youngsters to ten different ecosystems or communities.

Making Facts Stick — after the Game's Over

The improvements in *Where in the World Is Carmen Sandiego?* go a long way toward correcting a long-time complaint from parents of *Carmen*-loving kids. And that is: Kids can master the game without retaining much information about different cultures and regions of the world. Once they catch a thief, do they remember that Zaire is known for its copper mines? By the time they're en route to their fifth destination, do they remember the second or third? Will they remember tomorrow that Austria is south of Germany and north of Italy?

This is a good example of why you need to stay involved in your child's computing experience — even when you've selected great software. In track-the-clues adventures like the *Carmen* titles, you need to conjure up ways to help facts stick after the end of each episode. At school, teachers often spring a quiz to make sure students have paid attention to their on-screen travels. You can't do that at home. But there's a lot you can do.

Helping "Carmen Facts" stick

Here are some activities to try with younger kids who play the *Junior Detective Edition:*

✔ Make a project of creating "what you learned" postcards or passports. Little books made from folded paper do nicely. Or you can make something a little more slick with an art program or your word-processing program. For 5- and 6-year-olds, it's best to write down the countries your "detectives" visit and the clues they collect. Older children can keep notes themselves. Kids of any age can illustrate their transcontinental adventures with freehand art or pictures cut from travel magazines. The result: something personal to show for their crime-busting prowess.

✔ The *Junior Detective Edition* handbook also suggests some good off-the-computer activities for extending the title's fun.

Consider these ideas for kids who play *Where in the World* or *Where in the U.S.A.:*

✔ Get a globe and keep it near the computer whenever your kids use geography software or at their desks when they're doing geography homework. Encourage kids to spin to different locales as they're playing *Carmen Sandiego* or when they're doing map homework. It's often hard for kids (and many adults, too) to grasp the relationship between a map that's flat on their desktop or computer screen and a 3-D model. A globe puts them more directly in touch with where places really are.

✔ Even though *Carmen Sandiego* displays the route kids take from one destination to the next, kids don't see a *cumulative view* of all the routes they've traveled. Kids can note every location in their on-screen notebook. But it's also helpful — and fun — to draw their routes by hand, destination by destination, on an outline map. A good source of printable maps is the Outline Maps pages of Houghton Mifflin's Social Studies Center Web site (`http://www.eduplace.com/ss/ssmaps/index.html`). Print a supply of maps for different regions, and it's easy for kids to record their country-to-country progress as they chase down clues.

Take a virtual vacation

Taking a "virtual" vacation — or better still, planning a real one — is one of the best ways to get geographical facts to stick with kids.

One way your kids can do this is by taking a tour with one of the Good Guides in the new *Carmen*. These seven characters provide travelogues — rich in cultural, historic, and economic detail — for every location players visit during the game. *Carmen*'s World Wiz Database (and practically every other geography CD-ROM) also works well as a source of facts, figures, and photos about potential vacation spots.

For real vacation-planning, we like a combination of CD-ROM and World Wide Web resources. Here's a real-life example recounting how our kids helped plan a summer "volcano vacation:"

From the Web

Nothing could be simpler; just follow these steps:

1. **Connect to the World Wide Web.**

   You do this simply by double-clicking the icon for your Web browser, found on your desktop. What if there's no such icon on your desktop? Then take a break, and check your set-up for Web surfing. For advice on getting connected to the Web, you may want to consult *Internet For Dummies,* 3rd Edition, *The World Wide Web For Kids & Parents,* or *TakeCharge Computing For Teens & Parents,* all from IDG Books Worldwide.

2. **Select a search engine.**

   With most browsers, you're just one click away from a choice of *search engines,* powerful tools that let you search for sites to visit by typing keywords into a fill-in-the-blank form.

   If your browser is Netscape, you can get to a search engine by clicking the Net Search button in the menu bar. If your browser is Microsoft Internet Explorer, click the Search button in the menu bar.

3. **Type** volcano **in the search field.**

   The *search field* is that fill-in-the-blank space that appears on your screen once you've linked to a search engine. You can type a single word (like **volcano**) or several (like **volcano and kids**). Most search engines offer help for doing keyword searches. These little online tutorials are well worth your time; when you do "smarter" searches, you get a better list of sites.

4. **Click the Search button.**

   This is the button that tells the search engine to start looking for sites that contain your keyword. Actually, the button goes by different names, depending on the search engine you use. But whatever it's called, you can't miss it; it's usually right next to the search field.

Just seconds after we initiated the search, we had a list of volcano-related sites to peruse. One of them in particular, VolcanoWorld at `http://volcano.und.nodak.edu/vw.html` (created by the University of North Dakota) was an absolute gold mine. We decided to stick to volcanoes in the Cascade chain (Hawaii, alas, was not in the cards), and clicked our way into pages of travel information, historical facts, stunning photos, and fun stuff (see Figure 9-3) for both kids and adults.

As believers in informative vacations, we also liked this site for its kid-friendly earth science. Tempted by pictures and video clips, clear explanations, and fascinating animations, the kids soon knew more about plate tectonics and different kinds of lava than the grown-ups knew. A special kids' section featured volcano-oriented word games, connect-the-dot puzzles, crosswords, matching games, and *virtual* field trips to volcanoes in Japan, Hawaii, Washington, and Mars! (After our trip, the kids sent volcano artwork to VolcanoWorld's Kids Art page.)

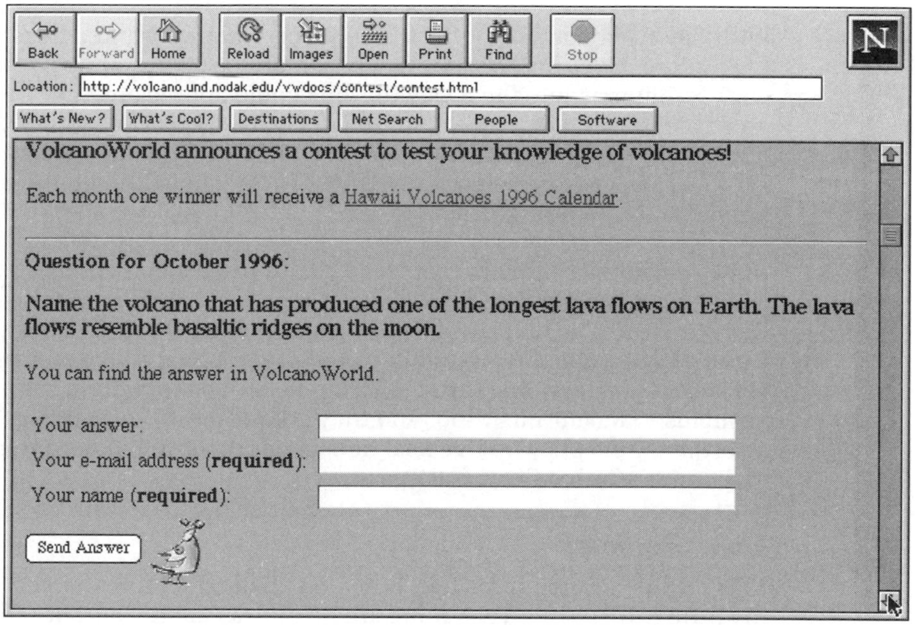
Back
Forward
Home
Reload
Images
Open
Print
Find
Stop
N
Location: http://volcano.und.nodak.edu/vwdocs/contest/contest.html
What's New?
What's Cool?
Destinations
Net Search
People
Software
VolcanoWorld announces a contest to test your knowledge of volcanoes!
Each month one winner will receive a Hawaii Volcanoes 1996 Calendar.
Question for October 1996:
Name the volcano that has produced one of the longest lava flows on Earth. The lava flows resemble basaltic ridges on the moon.
You can find the answer in VolcanoWorld.
Your answer:
Your e-mail address (required):
Your name (required):
Send Answer

Figure 9-3: Clicking deeper into this site produces more and more information, including this quiz at `volcano.und.nodak.edu/vwdocs/contest/contest.html`.

The kids also liked the challenge of VolcanoWorld's monthly contest, a question designed to encourage kids to forage for facts. Some typical questions: Name a caldera that had its last major eruption about 600,000 years ago and is also a national park. What Japanese volcano produces small ash eruptions almost every day that the people living nearby have managed to get used to? Name the glassy volcanic rock that is usually black in color and rhyolite in composition.

After using VolcanoWorld to decide which places to visit, we linked to The National Park Service Web site, http://www.nps.gov/parks.html, for regional maps, travel directions, park telephone numbers, campground information, and the like. A good resource for specific itineraries is GORP, the Great Outdoor Recreation Pages at http://www.gorp.com/gorp/. If deserts are your kind of outdoor adventure, check The Ultimate Desert Resource at http://www.desertusa.com. And if you're city bound, make sure you start your trip at CityNet (http://www.city.net/), which has Web links to more than 2,300 cities.

On CD-ROM

With day-to-day details of the trip in place, what we wanted next was the big picture. More depth, more science, more history, more personal experience — but presented in a way the kids could appreciate. And we found it in *Volcanoes: Life on the Edge,* pictured in Figure 9-4. This beautiful CD-ROM, from Corbis Corp., is nothing short of a multimedia documentary that explores the history, science, and lure of volcanoes through the eyes of people with a passion for volcanoes.

Unlike database products that leave you to make connections among an amalgam of facts, this CD-ROM takes a highly personal storytelling approach to its subject. The kids liked Roger Ressmeyer's perspective best; the CD-ROM re-creates his 14-month trip photographing active volcanoes. The kids also liked traveling through 1,900 years of history, from the eruption of Vesuvius to Mount Pinatubo. And they got to "meet" volcanologists as well as ordinary people who live near active volcanoes in Indonesia, Japan, and elsewhere. (Corbis Corp., All Ages)

From the library

This may be an electronic age, but you still need print resources. Guides to the little towns along your route are helpful, as are restaurant recommendations, AAA maps and tour books, campground directories, and the like.

Figure 9-4:
This copyrighted image from *Volcanoes: Life on the Edge* is typical of the CD-ROM's lush, fascinating imagery.

Doing Cartography with Kids

Remember daydreaming your way through an atlas, the heaviest volume of the World Book, or a stack of old National Geographics? In our mind's eye, we could feel the spray from Victoria Falls, gawk at the vibrant webbing of the blue-footed booby, bake in the sun beating down on Ayers Rock. We want our kids to enjoy the same kind of imaginary excursions. And we also want to prepare them for the very real global connections that will be part of their lives in the twenty-first century.

That's where CD-ROM geography references come in. Today you can find an abundance of colorful, intriguing, fact-packed resources for geography-minded families. Perched in front of the PC, kids can compare the eruptions of Mount Pinatubo and Mount St. Helens. They can get up-close-and-personal with the Great Barrier Reef. They can observe glacial movement through time-lapse photographs.

Amazing as these encounters are, we find ourselves pondering some worrisome questions: Are kids learning something? Or are they just new-age armchair tourists? Is what they see being translated into knowledge?

That depends on you. On their own, kids willingly play *Carmen*-styles games. But CD-ROM references and WebVentures (cool-looking though they may be) are less tempting to use solo. You need to structure your kids' experiences. These resources can indeed help kids learn, but often *not* without adult guidance. Consider using these resources to explore geography as a family project (much as we did with *virtual* vacation planning). For more together-time suggestions, just read our next profile.

My First Amazing World Explorer (ages 4–9)

Remember looking at coffee-table books? We get that same sense of visual delight with CD-ROMs from DK Multimedia. We think you and your kids will enjoy their distinctive good looks, too: dramatic photographs, crisp clear graphics, readable pages, sensibly organized information. You will also find a judicious mix of multimedia (never too much, and all of it relevant): the voices of real kids as narrators, realistic sounds, inventive animation.

Because *My First Amazing World Explorer* is aimed at 4- to 9-year-olds, we suggest that you treat it as *together* software (that is, you and your kids use it together). Challenge them to retrace the route you took on your honeymoon. Or find the town where you ran out of money backpacking around Europe and had to call home. (For information about software on the *Great Software For Kids & Parents* CD-ROM, see Appendix C.)

Exploring the product

But we're getting ahead of ourselves. Let's take a quick look at what's in this CD-ROM. Your child's exploration begins in a kid's bedroom. Clicking on the flag poster takes kids directly to any one of 163 countries from an alphabetical listing, festooned with the national flags kids find so appealing. (Quick! Can you name a country whose flag is *not* rectangular?) Clicking on the world map takes kids on a more leisurely excursion to different regions of the world.

What kids see first is a flat map showing political and physical boundaries. You know, a traditional map. But if they toggle a switch, the flat, top-down view transforms into an animated, kid-friendly topological map, pictured in Figure 9-5. A flying fish occasionally surfaces in the Indian Ocean. A beaver gnaws and topples a Canadian pine. The four presidential faces on Mt. Rushmore sing a few bars from a barbershop quartet tune. Cherry trees burst into bloom in Japan.

MY FIRST AMAZING WORLD EXPLORER

Figure 9-5:
Click the
bird to find
a hidden
animation
in this map
of South
America.

Back | Sticker book | World map | Places | My bedroom | Index | Suitcase

More clicking reveals increasingly more information; in all, 15,000 entries are in the program. But the software doesn't let kids just sit back, click, and watch. Even though there is a TV in the bedroom, for instance, kids can't start their adventures parked in front of the tube. In fact, if kids try to watch a movie about the Arctic or the Pacific Ocean, a voice from the TV says they have to search out a special submarine (yellow, of course) in that particular region *first*. We really like the message here: You can watch the video only after you've seen the "real" thing.

My First Amazing World Explorer also uses an on-screen passport, sticker book, and picture postcards to encourage kids to keep tabs on their explorations. When they happen upon entries with special icons, kids can add a sticker to their collection or write a postcard. And if they travel by plane, boat, or train, they get a passport stamp for every country they visit.

Bonus in the box

You get a lot for your money with *My First Amazing World Explorer:* a CD-ROM, two books, a jigsaw puzzle, a colorful treasure map, and lots of stickers. What's *good* about all these goodies? Each one, in a different way, gives kids a tactile and visual sense of where one place is located in relation to others. Each goodie is a bridge between the models kids see on-screen and the real things.

Other Map and Atlas Programs

Here are some useful references to have on hand — especially when your child has a geography report due the next day. But remember: While teenagers might be motivated enough to investigate on their own, younger kids may need your help to figure out how to find the information they want.

3D Atlas

A refreshing approach to presenting an earth-shattering quantity of information. *3D Atlas* organizes its vast database of satellite images, statistical information, photographs, video and audio clips, maps, and more into three perspectives: environmental, physical, and political. From the title's physical viewpoint, for example, kids see the Earth's topology at any location they choose — from the vantage of space, up close, or anywhere in between. For kids, the most inviting aspects of *3D Atlas* are its up-close-and-personal adventures: exceptionally realistic 3-D flights through four mountain ranges; a narrated series of time-lapse photographs showing the impact of various phenomena; expeditions (created from photos, satellite data, and graphical simulation) through nine different ecological regions, and much more. (Creative Wonders, Ages 8 & up)

Cartopedia

This atlas is best for adults and middle- to high-school kids with challenging homework assignments. Apart from its depth and distinctive DK looks, *Cartopedia* has some special features. Our favorite is the Compare feature that automatically produces charts and graphs contrasting information on ethnic make-up, climate, health, or scores of other topics for any two countries kids select. (DK Multimedia, Ages 11 & up)

Geography Education via the Web

It's only fitting that something called the World Wide Web is an excellent resource for geographic activities and information for kids. Our favorite sites have a distinctive flavor and special kid-appeal; they're not just repositories for information.

Helping your child learn geography. Everything parents could possibly want to know about raising geographically informed kids. This informative booklet from the U.S. Office of Educational Research and Improvement is fun to read, easy to understand, and loaded with great suggestions for off-the-computer activities. (http://www.ed.gov/pubs/parents/Geography/)

GeoNet game. The eastern coast of the United States is warmed by the . . . ? The busy port city at the mouth of the Mississippi River is . . . ? The northernmost and southernmost states in the Rocky Mountain chain are . . . ? Kids can try their luck with these and other geography questions (pictured in Figure 9-6) in the GeoNet Game that's part of Houghton Mifflin's Social Studies Center. Kids choose an easy or hard game (the preceding questions are easy ones) and questions from any of five different categories. Fun as a quick quiz if you're Web surfing. (http://www.eduplace.com/hmco/school/geo/index.html)

State facts. Suppose that your kids have to write a report about Oklahoma's state insect — or Maryland's state colors — or Wisconsin's state reptile. It's easy to start collecting data for state reports, those standard homework assignments for students in 3rd grade and up. Just type in the following Web address — http://www.state.XX.us/ — replacing the XX with the two-letter abbreviation for the state your child is learning about. Each address takes kids to a home page jam-packed with information about that state.

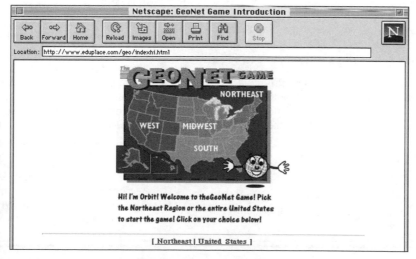

Figure 9-6: Kids choose a region to start the GeoNet game.

World Surfari. Every month, World Surfari takes kids to a different country. The clear, concise information it supplies about geography, government, economy, history, and society is well suited to kids in grades 4-6. Kids will also find neat cultural encounters — a sampling of Swahili, recipes from Kenya, and e-mail from kids their age in other countries. (http://www.supersurf.com)

How far is it? Kids really ought to practice adding up those little numbers on roadmaps or using the map's scale and a ruler to estimate distances — but in a pinch, this site provides a fun way to calculate the distance between two places. At this site, kids just type the city they're starting from and the city they're heading to. Then they click Look It Up, and the mileage appears instantaneously. (http://www.indo.com/distance/)

National Geographic. A terrific site, not just for virtual geography activities but also for close encounters with history, anthropology, archeology, and a selection of the articles, photographs, and maps that have made The National Geographic Society famous. The site features a changing array of adventures (some with time limits), a geography-oriented Question of the Day, a selection of electronic postcards, opportunities to chat with National Geographic experts, and more. (http://www.nationalgeographic.com)

Playing 20 Questions on-screen

Here's an on-screen variation of *20 Questions* you and your kids can play by using the topological map.

✔ The point of the game is to answer by asking 20 questions or fewer and to use *My First Amazing World Explorer* in the process.

✔ Players must choose something that can be found on the CD-ROM. Encourage kids to explore the software beforehand to find it.

✔ Agree on categories appropriate for your kids. Animals and oceans might be complex enough for little kids. Add continents and landmarks for older children. Check the Index for category ideas.

✔ Make up some rules that encourage kids to tap the product's resources.

  • Players must navigate to the appropriate region before hazarding a guess. If they ask, "Does this animal live in the Arctic?," they've got to have the Arctic on the computer screen. What if they're in the wrong part of the world? No penalty for little kids. Older kids might be penalized by getting to ask one less question.

  • Five- and six-year-olds get unlimited access to the CD-ROM's look-it-up resources, such as the index of capital cities or famous places, to make an educated guess. Five- and six-year-olds also get something more than Yes/No answers. If they ask, "Does it live in North America?" you might say, "No, but it lives to the south."

  • Limit the number of times per game older kids can use the index. But when they use the index successfully, perhaps reward them with an extra question in the next game.

OPEN

It's Not Geography Software, but It's Got Lots of Geography in It!

Microsoft Encarta

Probably the best computer-based encyclopedia for adults and kids, with plenty of geography-related material, such as maps and articles about different regions, countries, and cultures; environmental and political issues; and world trade and travel. *Encarta's* Language Interactivity is an especially good way for kids to make the acquaintance of other cultures. Choose any one of the CD-ROM's more than two dozen languages, and kids can point and click their way to audio clips of native speakers saying hello and good-bye, thank you, the numbers 1-10, plus common phrases and a proverb from that culture. Read more about *Encarta* in Chapter 8. (Microsoft, Ages 9 & up)

Snootz Math Trek

Hide and Seek is a map-reading game in this math product that encourages kids to use compass directions as well as grid coordinates in order to discover a hiding Snootz. (Theatrix Interactive, Ages 5-9)

WorldWalker series

This innovative series turns the spotlight on ecosystems of exotic locations such as Australia and China. But beyond flora and fauna, kids also experience "close encounters" with the people, cultural landmarks, history, and politics in each destination they explore. Read more about it in Chapter 11. (Soleil/Maxis, Ages 9 & up)

Chapter 10

Using the Computer for Explorations Back in Time

● ●

In This Chapter

▶ Using software to learn the 4 'Rs of history (that's right, four!)

▶ Reenacting history with *simulation* programs
> The *Trail* series (ages 10–16)

▶ Making facts stick — after the game's over!

▶ Exploring facts and figures with CD-ROM references
> *Ancient Lands* (ages 8 & up)
> *Microsoft Encarta* (ages 9 & up)
> *Eyewitness Encyclopedia of History* (ages 11 & up)

▶ Using the World Wide Web to learn history

● ●

Some kids are naturally interested in conventional history; they have a knack for names, dates, places, causes, effects, whys, and wherefores. Others have an instinct for the story in history, information that sheds light on the perspective of the people who lived it, how events and day-to-day lives intertwined.

History software, we're happy to say, comes in both "flavors." You can find a great many *reference CD-ROMs,* electronic resources that shine at making facts-and-figures-style history convenient and accessible. You'll also find historical *simulations* (programs that let kids reenact real events) that are personal and memorable and that make history come alive. And you can find a few truly exceptional programs that weave factual data into an on-screen drama.

How do you choose among the scores of history titles available for home computers?

___ *First consider your kids.*

What are their personal interests? Warplanes of World War II? Egyptian pyramids? The gold rush?

___ *Next consider their schoolwork.*

Is this the year they tackle state reports? Are they studying colonial America? The Civil War? The Mayan culture?

___ *But here's the most important of our criteria.*

As you add history titles to your software library, make sure that the programs, as a group, give kids lots of experience with what we call the 4 'Rs, Reading, Research, 'Riting, and Reenacting. Here's what we mean:

- **Reading:** "Real" words from original sources and literature have a way of attracting and personalizing kids' interest. Reading (or hearing) the words just as they were written, or spoken, in the past tells kids that history is about real people, real places.

- **Research:** Kids need to "do" history as well as read about it. When they uncover information on their own about events and people, the information is more likely to stick with them.

- **'Riting:** For kids, writing history as they read and research hammers home the facts and flavor of times past. Good software invites kids to "pretend on paper" — writing diaries, newspaper accounts, imagined debates, infomercials, campaign speeches.

- **Reenacting:** Stepping into someone else's shoes is a powerful way of experiencing the hopes, hardships and challenges of historical figures. Don't put this down as mere playacting! Envisioning how other people felt, thought, and acted (and understanding why) is a skill that's as important for understanding the world today as it is for grasping the significance of historical events.

One final suggestion: Don't go overboard. It's unrealistic to expect kids to absorb the whole of history in a semester or two — or even in their entire school career, for that matter! Trying to stuff too much into them will only make them rebel — against you and against history. Instead, educators suggest that in-depth encounters with a few events or eras (rather than broad coverage) give kids a better chance to understand, remember, and apply history. Happily, the best software often takes that more manageable, in-depth approach. You can find more ideas for older kids in *TakeCharge Computing For Teens & Parents,* published by IDG Books Worldwide.

What if you found history boring as a child? Now's the time to kindle an interest. That way, you won't pass on a "don't know much about history" attitude to your kids. How? We got the following great suggestions from the U.S. Office of Educational Research and Improvement. They boil down to two things: Stake a *personal* claim in history. And try doing history *with* your kids.

- ✔ Try writing your own life story.
- ✔ Along with your kids, read the real thing, such as the diary of Anne Frank or any highly personal account by other historical figures.
- ✔ Together, interview a relative or an elderly neighbor.
- ✔ Research the history of your house (or street or neighborhood) together.
- ✔ Rent a history video, watch TV history programs together.

When your kids see you rediscovering history, they're more likely to get interested, too.

Reenacting History with Simulation Programs

Simulation programs create a place, a time, and an experience that models the real thing. Then they invite kids "inside," giving them a chance to play various roles: a pioneer, a big-city mayor, a park manager, an inventor, a video-game designer. These programs are good at putting kids right in the thick of things, letting them assume an identity, allowing their decisions to make a difference in the outcome of a historical scenario.

In the world of the simulation, kids call the shots. Every choice they make has consequences. Every decision affects what happens. Kids relish this kind of involvement because, as a 10-year-old friend told us: "I really count, and I can make something different happen every time I play." Best of all, because they let kids take such an active role, simulations are a great way to learn by doing.

Simulations are available in many different branches of software: wildlife, political science, marine biology, ecology, sports, economics, game design, and more. (See Chapter 12 for some of our favorites.) And *the best* kind of history programs you can get are simulations.

In these programs, kids step into someone else's shoes and figure out — using their wits and the wealth of information provided by the software — how to think, act, struggle, and survive (if they're lucky) just as the program's character might have. These programs challenge kids to exercise their historical imagination. Creative thinking like this lets kids forge a highly personal connection between "now" and "then." And that personal stake is what helps history come alive.

Imagining yourself inside another person's skin is nothing new, of course. That's the power of historical fiction, or the craft of a great historian, or the art of a good teacher. But software brings a unique twist to the imaginative process, creating an environment kids can't quite get in any other way, as you can see from our profile of the *Trail* series of products from MECC.

The *Trail* titles were the pioneers of the historical simulation genre. And believe it or not, the original *Oregon Trail* is older than personal computers! When the software was first devised in 1971, the program relied on a teletype machine and a mainframe computer. There was no sound. No graphics. Just text. And an invitation: Step into the shoes of a nineteenth century pioneer and go West in search of new opportunities and a better life.

Today's multimedia-rich CD-ROM version of *Oregon Trail II* (as well as the other programs in the series, like *MayaQuest* and *Amazon Trail II*) gives kids an amazingly realistic "you are there" sensation, thanks to photographs, video clips, sound effects, authentic-sounding music and voices, and more. But the basic scenario is unchanged.

The Trail series (ages 10–16)

Trail players are pretty much on their own. No one tells them what to do, how to join a wagon train, what to outfit a party with for the journey, which route to travel, what to expect. Not in 1971, not 25 years later. So the perennial attraction of *Oregon Trail* (and other *Trail* titles, all from MECC) is its *double dare:* "See if you can figure this out, and see if you can win." The challenge is irresistible. Kids are motivated to develop the skills they need to play the adventure. And to discover the knowledge they need to survive in the era and environment into which they've been transported.

Re-creating history

No matter how many times kids play a *Trail* title, they can never be quite sure if they'll "make it." What makes the adventure so uncertain? What makes it feel so real? It's the complexity of the simulation; in other words, the interplay of a great many different ingredients. For example, at every decision-making juncture (and there are hundreds), the software factors in such things as weather, terrain, supplies, river conditions, wagon-train progress, pioneer skills, health, plus the choices of the player. A change in one condition can have a domino effect on many other conditions. If there's a lot of rain one month (based on actual diary accounts, histories, and other authentic documents), the rain in turn affects river depth, trail conditions, and wagon-train progress. When someone dies in a river crossing and supplies are swept downstream, the prospects of the entire wagon train are affected. And so on.

Here's the magic of *Oregon Trail:* pretending to be a historical character makes past times, places, and people seem *personal* and *real*. Kids really throw themselves into character, whether they opt to play a blacksmith, a schoolteacher, a doctor, or a carpenter. And with every challenge and decision along the *Trail,* they come face-to-face with some pretty gripping issues. Are my chances better if I ford Red Vermilion River, caulk the wagon and float it across, or pay for a ferry? How can I lessen the risk of getting cholera? Should I fix a broken axle or trade to get a new one? How many miles can my draft animals take today? Should I trade five pounds of bacon for a 30-foot length of chain? If there's no fresh fruit or vegetables, how can I combat scurvy? Should I press on in subzero temperatures or make camp?

For younger children, the consequences of "unwise" decisions on the trail can be very frightening! Their character can succumb to cholera, die in a wagon accident, drown in a river crossing, freeze to death, or starve. And that fate will seem very real to many kids. Here's one way to blunt the trauma: Suggest that your kids use a fake name when they join a wagon train. That way they'll take their "death" less personally. They'll feel up to playing again. And they'll be able to use their experience to make smarter choices.

Experiencing the "you are there" feeling

The latest version of *Oregon Trail II* brings added realism and historical complexity to the adventure. Kids can choose among 25 occupations, from baker to wainwright. They can choose one of three trails: Oregon, California, or Mormon. They can choose different kinds of wagons and draft animals, how large a party to travel with, what month and year (from 1840 to 1860) to depart. (For information about the software on the *Great Software For Kids & Parents* CD-ROM, see Appendix C.)

The endless combination of choices — plus luck and savvy decision-making on the trail — makes every game different and challenging. What's more, photographic images, 3-D graphics and animation, voice-overs and video all make kids feel as though they're actually shooting the rapids; walking into camps, forts, or towns; exploring the streets; and entering the buildings and conversing with historical figures (such as those shown in Figure 10-1).

Independence

GUIDE DIARY

Figure 10-1:
More
people and
new realism
add to the
fun in
*Oregon
Trail II.*

Many multimedia products do too much for kids and make things too easy for them. Not *Oregon Trail II.* Players aren't likely to survive unless they pay close attention to the wealth of information in the online guidebook. Otherwise, how will they know the right quantity of bread stuffs to buy or how heavy a load a team of oxen can pull? They also need to do a lot of "talking" with fellow travelers, people who live along the route, bridge keepers, ferry operators, traders, soldiers, trail guides, and others. That's where the Reading and Research parts of the 4 'Rs we mentioned before come into play.

And now comes the 'Riting part: Their chances are better still if they write in the program's online diary. Why? Well, unless they have a photographic memory, will kids remember the many tips they discover in the Guidebook? Unless they write them down, how will kids know whether a decision they made two weeks ago can help them out of a dilemma today?

The payoff of the *Oregon Trail* approach to history is that as kids travel the trail, they literally absorb historical facts, people, and places by osmosis. Kids tend to remember them because they make their discoveries under "life-and-death" circumstances. And what works best of all for kids is the "you are there" sensation — because they heard it, saw it, and read it on the computer screen and felt it on the "inside."

The Yukon Trail (ages 10–16)

In this *Trail* title, the year is 1897 and the Klondike gold rush is on. Kids take on the role of stampeders, bound from Seattle for Dawson City. The odds are pretty grim. But the adventure is so riveting that kids are willing to risk all — getting hit by an iceberg, being fleeced by cardsharps, or starving when cutthroats make off with most of their food — in hopes of striking it rich. One of the stops en route is Lake Bennett, pictured in Figure 10-2.

Amazon Trail II (ages 10–16)

Kids navigate through this *Trail* adventure as though they are seated in a canoe, experiencing the sights and sounds of the Amazon over the prow of the boat. This new version features 17 different missions and opportunities to rub shoulders with explorers, scientists, and native peoples. True to the *Trail* formula, there are a host of perils: capsizing and being bitten by a piranha, being cheated by dishonest traders, running out of supplies, getting lost in one of the Amazon's many tributaries, catching a tropical disease. But the only thing that's really infectious is the sense of adventure!

Figure 10-2: Kids decide what kind of boat to build at Lake Bennett.

MayaQuest (ages 10–16)

In a switch from other *Trail* titles, *MayaQuest* casts kids in the role of archeologists-for-hire — via a real-life bicycle trek through Central America — in a search for clues to the demise of the ancient Maya. The CD-ROM owes its realism to a 1995 cycling expedition led by adventurers Dan and Steve Buettner, who photographed, videotaped, and logged the events for each day of their four-month journey. In a first-of-a-kind educational venture, they were also in daily contact with thousands of school children via the Internet. What's more, they gave students a voice in guiding the expedition by inviting their input on where to go and asking them to research archeological problems for the cyclists.

This CD-ROM re-creates an exceptionally realistic setting for kids. There's an over-the-handlebars perspective of the rugged terrain along the bike trails. And when kids reach each of the program's seven archeological sites, more than 1,500 photographs and maps make it easy for them to believe they're face-to-face with hieroglyphics on an ancient stela, or the ruins of a temple, shown in Figure 10-3. Journal entries from the five cyclists add realism, too.

Figure 10-3: Up-close photography of Mayan landscape and ruins.

27 days to rainy season
Balance: $940.00

Kids can play *MayaQuest* two ways: the Explore game or the Adventure game. In the Explore game, kids field questions via "e-mail" and then venture into different Mayan sites in search of answers. (Don't worry: It's not real e-mail; there's no online connection.) Much as they would track down objects in a scavenger hunt, players try to answer questions like these: "How did the Maya use turtle shells?" "I am looking for evidence of internal political turmoil in Copan. Can you help me find some?" "What was the purpose of drinks made from cacao?" For added excitement, there's a time limit: Kids must try to answer as many questions as they can in the "30 days" before the rainy season begins.

The Adventure game is set in the future, at a time when the Earth's survival depends on orbiting satellites and lasers to ward off meteors. When the newest code for activating this defense system is lost, players are dispatched to find information needed to reconstruct it. What's the Mayan connection? Well, the scientist who created the code is a history buff whose specialty — you guessed it — is the Mayan civilization. Apart from this storyline, the quest for answers is much the same as it is in the Explore game. Only this time, kids have only "11 days" till meteor impact.

The *MayaQuest* CD-ROM features more than 200 questions. But in case that's not enough, kids can download new information, photos, artifacts, and tasks from the MayaQuest Web site (http://www.mecc.com/mayaquest.html). It puts kids in touch with other *MayaQuest* players and provides an excellent list of Web sites that kids can visit for more information on Mayan culture. Kids who like *MayaQuest's* over-the-handlebars perspective can even join a "live" expedition departing in March 1997; just click the Join button, located at the bottom of the *MayaQuest* Interactive Expedition page, to find out how to participate.

Other History Simulations and Games

Let your kids' school needs and tastes in games guide your choice of other history CD-ROMs. The first product we list here is a role-playing adventure in a historical setting. The second is primarily a facts-and-figures CD-ROM with a fun game to get kids jazzed. And the third is a quiz product with the good looks of a cartoon.

◀◀

Wrath of the Gods

When kids take on the role of the abandoned grandson of King Minos, they find themselves immersed in a strange world of immortals and mortals, oracles, and minotaurs. The goal: find the lad's true parents and claim the throne. At every step, kids encounter challenges and puzzles borrowed from the classic adventures of Greek heroes. Success depends on ingenuity, a knowledge of Greek myths, and persistence. For younger players who may be in the dark about Hades or other matters mythological, trips to the Oracle of Delphi and forays into an information section are essential for garnering useful facts and clues. Playing with friends or family is also helpful — and more fun. (SOME Interactive/Maxis, Ages 9 & up)

SkyTrip America

Kids fly from coast to coast and past to present, alighting wherever their historical curiosity leads. To give a little purpose to their travels, urge your kids to play the title's Pony Express game. It challenges kids to interpret messages and deliver letters to people and places around the country. Typical message for beginners: "Find the invention patented in 1873 that was responsible for taming the open ranges of the Great Plains. When you do, deliver this message to its inventor, Joseph Glidden." You can see another message in Figure 10-4. For help, kids can turn to an easy-to-use database of narrated articles, background text, photos, and video clips. (Discovery Channel Multimedia, Ages 9 & up)

Morgan's Adventure series

The games in the Morgan titles are actually multiple-choice quizzes! Your kids won't love them the way they love simulations — but consider these games as a painless way to study for history tests! *Morgan's Adventures in Ancient Greece* also features two discovery-style games. Word Builder teaches Greek roots of English words. And Magic Squares (a math activity kids encounter in school around age 7 or 8) challenges kids to make all three rows, columns, and diagonals add up to 15. Ace the questions in

▶▶

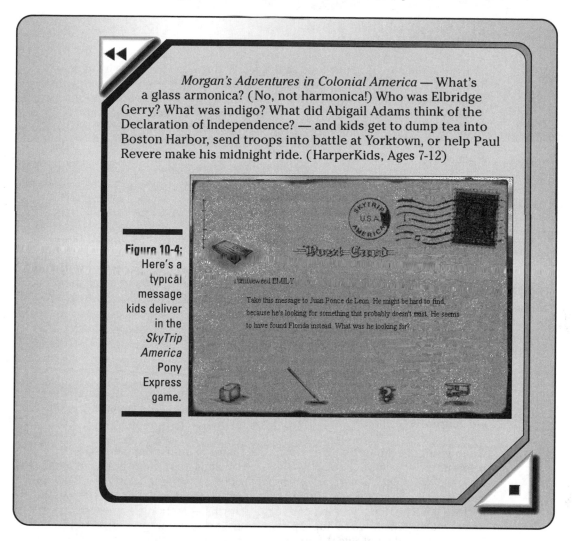

Morgan's Adventures in Colonial America — What's a glass armonica? (No, not harmonica!) Who was Elbridge Gerry? What was indigo? What did Abigail Adams think of the Declaration of Independence? — and kids get to dump tea into Boston Harbor, send troops into battle at Yorktown, or help Paul Revere make his midnight ride. (HarperKids, Ages 7-12)

Figure 10-4:
Here's a typical message kids deliver in the *SkyTrip America* Pony Express game.

Making Your Own Games to Make Facts Stick

Good as simulation titles are, you still don't have a sure-fire guarantee your kids will remember what they've encountered. Once the computer shuts down for the night, some kids' minds go as blank as the screen. Guess that's human nature. But you can do some things to help history lessons migrate from your kids' short-term memories to their long-term memories.

You play, too!

So what if the software package says ages 10 through 16. You're a kid at heart, right? So play the game yourself. Some kids will let you partner with them, especially when they're first becoming familiar with a simulation title. If your child is past that point, try playing solo. Or team up with your spouse. You'll have fun. But here's the real payoff: When you play too, you'll be able to talk the same language as your kids, compare notes, and swap advice.

Then and now

Check travel resources on the Web (think of it as the world's biggest travel agency), and invite your kids to compare the looks of a place today with the historical reality they discovered on CD-ROM. Kids are as ready to surf the Web as they are the TV, so take advantage of their interest and steer them to sites that relate to the Oregon Trail, the Klondike, the Amazon, or any place that's on one of their CD-ROMs.

Software scavenger hunts

We want to let you know up front that this activity is more parent-intensive than most of the activities we suggest. But if you're willing to put in the time, we guarantee you and your kids some smart fun!

Once you get acquainted with your kids' history simulations and CD-ROM references, you can use them as a source of clues for computer-based games of *Scavenger Hunt*. As with an off-the-computer scavenger hunt, the idea is to locate a list of items. But in this case, everything on the list can be found on a CD-ROM. The items you list can include terms, questions, names, dates, and the like. Kids have to supply definitions, answers, what people were famous for, and what event happened on a given date. With a clever list (and an appealing reward), you can subtly encourage kids to spend time with certain topics. The time spent will make them more knowledgeable players, and it will help cement their knowledge of historical facts.

Stamping history

Take a really close look at the tools in your kids' art or writing programs, and you find will lots of history-related stamps and backgrounds. Best for younger children, stamping a historical scene is a great way for artistically-inclined kids to forge another connection with the past. Here are ideas we came up with from three different programs. But these aren't the only three ideas that kids can use for this activity. Almost all kids' art and writing programs have stamps that kids can use for historical artwork.

Stamping in a few inaccuracies is fun, too, especially for younger kids. You can start the ball rolling by creating a historical scene that includes some stamps that obviously don't belong — a telephone in a caveman picture, a rocket ship in a frontier town. Then ask your kids to stump you by concealing (as deviously as they can) one or more historically inaccurate stamps in a scene of their own. Is there anything to be learned from this silliness? Yes! When kids take pains to make things wrong, they also have to know what things are right.

Kid Pix Studio (ages 3–12)

This versatile drawing and painting software (from Broderbund) includes lots of ancient Egyptian, Greek, and Roman art elements that kids can incorporate in stand-alone scenes or in comic strips. Kids find a pyramid, a sphinx, King Tut's golden death mask, Cleopatra, three different camels, a palm tree, a scorpion, a winged lion, Egyptian-style barges, a chariot, Greek vases, a mummy, crocodiles, scarab beetles, a papyrus scroll, lions, a variety of cats, a camel's head, the signs of the zodiac, and more.

Fine Artist (ages 8–12)

If your kids have this program, they've got an easy way to create comic strips about ancient Egypt. *Fine Artist* (from Microsoft) features a dozen black-and-white hieroglyphic stamps; a variety of comic-style speech balloons that can be used to convey thoughts, dialogue, or information in a comic strip, as well as background scenes that include a pyramid and a desert landscape. The title's storyboarding feature makes it especially easy for kids to turn individual cartoon scenes into a comic book. With their teachers' permission, kids can even handle their homework comic-book style!

Imagination Express (ages 5–12)

The *Imagination Express* storymaking series (from Edmark) features three "destination" CD-ROMs that take kids to times past. *Destination Castle* provides hundreds of finely detailed art elements relating to the Middle ages; some are fanciful (dragons, wizards, unicorns), others are realistic (peasants, catapults, heraldic symbols). *Destination Pyramid* (a school product that parents can buy direct from Edmark) focuses on ancient Egypt, with more than 20 exceptionally realistic backgrounds and hundreds of stickers. And *Destination Time Trip USA* (also a school product) lets kids create stories and drawings set in six different eras: 1640, 1776, 1865, 1929, 1945, and today. Because kids can mix stamps from all eras, as shown in Figure 10-5, they can easily spin time-travel stories and design truly crafty "what's wrong with this picture?" scenes.

Figure 10-5:
Kids can choose their "mistakes" from the historical stamps in *Imagination Express* or other titles.

Exploring Facts and Figures with CD-ROM References

Okay, let's be honest. Unless there's a homework assignment due, are your kids the type to spend hours with a history encyclopedia?

To be sure, it's a pleasure to flip the pages of a richly illustrated history book. And it's fun and informative to click from link to link in a history CD-ROM. But how often does that really happen? The truth is history reference CD-ROMs simply don't get the daily (or even weekly) use that simulations and other history games do. We do think it's wise, however, to have one or two history references available on CD-ROM. After all, you need to be ready when questions come up or homework comes due. Our selections are especially helpful with homework (they're a good fit with the elementary or middle school history curriculum). And they have enough kid appeal to encourage some browsing, even when there's no homework assignment to be done.

Ancient Lands (ages 8 & up)

This intelligently designed, easy-to-use CD-ROM (from Microsoft) is perfect in scope and approach for kids in 6th and 7th grades, the years when kids study the civilizations of ancient Egypt, Greece, and Rome. *Ancient Lands'* abundant use of colorful illustrations, sound, animation, comparative charts, maps, timelines, video clips, and narration makes the information in this program highly accessible to kids. Its organizing principle is good for kids, too. Kids find five icons that they can click to delve into each culture: People and Politics, Monuments and Mysteries, Work and Play, Guides, and a searchable, alphabetical Index (from abu simbel to ziggurat).

The characters in Guides are the most appealing because they lead kids on a personal journey through the data, encouraging them to see history through the eyes of realistic people. To probe ancient Egypt, for example, kids can opt to accompany characters such as an Egyptian boy, an embalmer's daughter, or a woman pharaoh. Homer, a Delphic priestess, and the queen of the gods are among the guides to ancient Greece. And kids can hear the perspective of a slave girl, a Roman chef, and a soldier, among others, as they visit ancient Rome.

Microsoft Encarta (ages 9 & up)

In Chapter 8, we recommend *Microsoft Encarta* (from Microsoft) as our favorite all-round reference CD-ROM. And we're mentioning it again because it enlarges on virtually every topic mentioned in *Ancient Lands.* You can find hundreds of photographs of archeological sites, ancient buildings and artifacts, sculpture, crafts, and artwork. Kids who are creating mosaics as a classroom project will find lots of detailed information (with photographic examples) on techniques for making mosaics (look in the Arts, Language & Literature section under Ancient History). They can also listen to examples of the modern Greek and Egyptian languages; hear a dramatic reading from the *Iliad,* enjoy excerpts from Roman poetry, play Mediterranean music.

Especially good for homework are graphical features such as the family trees of ancient gods, a comparative table of Greek and Roman deities, and a table showing the development of the alphabet from ancient to modern times. If your kids are assigned to create a Greek, Roman, or Egyptian myth of their own, they find a helpful explanation of the differences among fables, legends, and myths, with examples of all three kinds of storytelling. And kids learning about the origins of written language can find articles on all 26 letters, the origins of each one, and the evolution of its symbol.

Eyewitness Encyclopedia of History (ages 11 & up)

Part of one of the best-looking reference series around, *The Eyewitness Encyclopedia of History* (from DK Multimedia) instantly whisks kids to different time periods whenever they pull a lever on a time machine. Alternately, kids can browse through history by geographical regions. Or they can use the Quiz Master to chart a course through time. This machine tosses out random questions, and one of the questions may pique your kids' curiosity, for example, "In which country was gunpowder invented?" "What title did the Greeks give Hippocrates?"

When kids click the Look Up button beneath a question, the software charts an efficient path through its vast database, demonstrating step-by-step how to reach the answer. This feature is useful for learning the techniques for finding information in a database.

Using the Web to Learn History

No matter how many CD-ROMs are in your home software library — no matter how well prepared you are for your kids' history homework — you'll always need a larger library some time or other. And that's how we look at the World Wide Web. With a connection to the Web, you've got 24-hour access to a seemingly limitless supply of resources.

You can find page after page of information — some sites accurate and well presented, others decidedly second-rate — about marine history, the Vikings, railroads, ancient Greece, the gold rush, castles, World War II, the Industrial Revolution, the history of computing, and just about every other historical topic imaginable.

Our question is: How can ordinary parents — parents who aren't history teachers or computer wizards — make sense of such an embarrassment of riches? Answering that question is what this section is all about.

For starters, don't be intimidated! Despite the huge number of history sites on the Web, the ones that are really useful for families fall into just two categories. There are *sites for you,* expressly designed to help parents help their kids. And there are *sites for kids,* designed to present historical topics in kid-friendly fashion. (This is an oversimplification, we admit! But it's an approach that makes it easier to take the plunge.)

When you decide it's time to make the Web part of your family's history resources, head for "advice sites" first. They'll give you ideas for enjoying history with your children, suggestions for history activities to do together, and a run-down of what kids should be learning when. You'll find our favorite advice site at the top of the list that follows; you can find others by surfing curriculum, museum, and library sites.

Once you've taken the time to inform yourself, you can turn to sites for your kids. Let their interests and school assignments guide your search, and try the sites on this list for starters.

Here are some sites for both parents and kids:

✔ **Helping Your Child Learn History:** A terrific booklet from the U.S. Office of Educational Research and Improvement. It's packed with tips for making history a habit with your kids and with activities to do with kids ages 4 through 11. (http://www.ed.gov/pubs/parents/History/)

✔ **This Day in History:** A daily feature of The History Channel Web site. Just enter the month and day kids want to know about, and more than a dozen historical fun facts pop up on the screen. You also find a sizable list of people born throughout history on that date. How can you turn this activity into more than a trivial pursuit? You might encourage your child to select today-in-history facts for a personalized calendar. Like the ones you can buy in stores, the calendar might focus on people and events in your state, on a favorite hobby (baseball, Hollywood) or on a hot topic (famous women, literary figures). Kids can cut and paste their favorite facts into the family calendar program, the calendar that's part of Windows 95, or one from a kids' software title. (http://www.historychannel.com/historychannel/thisday.html)

✔ **Who Said That?:** Every week, the cable TV History Channel posts a fiendish quotation quiz, like the one shown in Figure 10-6. Players have to decide which of four people actually said things like: "It's the orders you disobey that make you famous." "A fanatic is one who can't change his mind and won't change the subject." "The single most exciting thing you encounter in government is competence, because it's so rare." The hardest part is waiting a week for the answers! So why wait? Encourage your kids to pick their favorite quote and do a little sleuthing online or off-line on the four possible answers. Isn't that cheating? Well — probably. But we think kids will learn a more valuable lesson about research by trying to ferret out the answers than by making an educated guess! (http://www.historychannel.com/historychannel/games/thequiz.html)

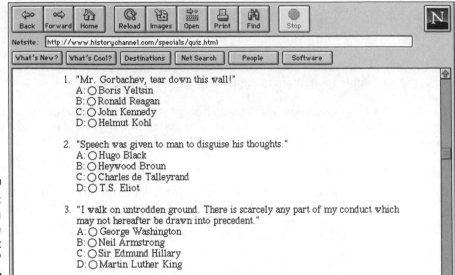

1. "Mr. Gorbachev, tear down this wall!"
   A: ○ Boris Yeltsin
   B: ○ Ronald Reagan
   C: ○ John Kennedy
   D: ○ Helmut Kohl

2. "Speech was given to man to disguise his thoughts."
   A: ○ Hugo Black
   B: ○ Heywood Broun
   C: ○ Charles de Talleyrand
   D: ○ T.S. Eliot

3. "I walk on untrodden ground. There is scarcely any part of my conduct which may not hereafter be drawn into precedent."
   A: ○ George Washington
   B: ○ Neil Armstrong
   C: ○ Sir Edmund Hillary
   D: ○ Martin Luther King

Figure 10-6:
Do you
know the
correct
answer?

Don't be surprised if your browser can't find a Web address you type. It's not your fault; and it's probably not our fault either! Blame it on the World Wide Web itself: Web addresses (and sites themselves) can be pretty fickle. Try looking for a "missing" site with a search engine. And try shortening the address by deleting everything after the `.com` (or `.org` or `.edu`).

Here are some sites for older kids (okay — for parents, too!):

✔ **Rulers:** Who's the president of Djibouti? Kids can get the answer fast by surfing to the alphabetical listings at `http://www.ehu.es/~ziaorarr/00now.html`. See Chapter 9 if you don't know what or where Djibouti is!

✔ **Presidential pearls:** What did George Washington say after he took the oath of office for a second time? (No, that's not the start of a joke!) Now kids can easily find out at the Inaugural Addresses of the Presidents site. Beside being a good homework resource for middle and high school students, these collected speeches give parents an interesting historical perspective on political hot air! (`http://www.columbia.edu/acis/bartleby/inaugural/`)

✔ **Your name in hieroglyphs:** Great fun for 6th- or 7th-graders studying ancient Egypt. They just type their name as it would be spelled phonetically, click a button, and back comes the hieroglyphic equivalent. If kids are interested, this site (which has text in both French and English) can take them deep into information on hieroglyphics. (`http://knety.iut.univ-paris8.fr/~rosmord/nomhiero.html`)

Chapter 11
Doing Science On-Screen

• •

• •

*T*here's no kid alive who doesn't love science — especially when science is digging worms, dissolving baby teeth in cola, examining animal droppings, changing the color of carnations, making baking soda and vinegar volcanoes, or concocting invisible ink.

Our challenge as parents is to tap into that natural curiosity and keep kids all fired up about exploring the world around them as they grow.

Family Science

But suppose your kids don't get their science lessons from Ms. Frizzle, that wacky, beloved teacher from the Magic Schoolbus books? Suppose you're not as inventive as television's Beakman and Jax or as entertaining as that other TV star, Bill Nye the Science Guy? Suppose, just suppose, you're not a rocket scientist. How do "just plain parents" find — and encourage — fun family science?

Here's a list of suggestions to get you started:

___ *Turn your kitchen into a science lab.*

Once a month, invite your kids to pick a drawer or a cupboard. Then, together, design an investigation. If it's the bread drawer, sacrifice two slices of bread to science. Dampen one and see which goes moldy first. If it's the condiment cupboard, let kids learn about density by mixing oils, vinegars, ketchup, soy sauce. Or investigate which household acids (vinegar, lemon juice, or cola, for example) clean old pennies best. Books on kitchen, bathtub, and backyard science abound; check your library.

___ *Check out a children's museum.*

Many communities have discovery centers or science museums where kids can create giant bubbles, stroke a starfish, experience a simulated earthquake, find out what they weigh on Jupiter, unearth pretend fossils, disassemble household appliances, or discover exactly what happens when the toilet flushes. Check the workshops, day camps, and special events these places offer, too.

___ *See what's up at Park & Rec.*

Many local parks departments conduct nature hikes, kite-flying contests, moonlight walks, recycling drives, birding and wildflower expeditions, or soap-box derby races. And there's science in all those things!

___ *Visit the zoo.*

Even if your kids do nothing more than run at top speed from the aardvarks to the zebras (and everything in between), they're absorbing the sights and sounds of wildlife. And that's a good beginning for natural science.

___ *Subscribe to a kids' magazine.*

Kids love getting mail. And magazines like *Your Big Backyard, Ranger Rick, 321 Contact, Kids Discover, Kids World, National Geographic, Family Fun,* and others blaze a natural trail to at-home science ventures.

___ *Surf the World Wide Web.*

The Web is such a rich resource for science that we've devoted a whole section to it later in this chapter!

___ *Try on-screen science.*

When you don't want the kids to make a mess, launch a CD-ROM. There are lots of CD-ROMs that give kids an up-close look at anatomy, biology, chemistry, electronics, oceanography, physics, zoology, and just about every other branch of science.

Science Really Can Happen on Software

Sitting in front of the computer is nothing like firing up a Bunsen burner or inhaling a whiff of formaldehyde. But science really can happen on the computer — especially with CD-ROMs that let kids of all ages poke around, experiment, and experience the "Ah ha!" of scientific discovery for themselves.

How can you spot really good science software for older kids? With all the software on the shelves, it's often hard. But a recipe for smart fun will usually feature some or all of these four ingredients:

___ *Hands on*

On-screen science (and every other kind of science, too) isn't science at all unless kids are doing it — not just viewing it. Software that merely tells kids about an experiment, leads them through a procedure, shows them a video clip, or pops up explanatory text is not good enough. Kids learn better — and have more fun — if software drafts them for "active duty." With hands-on software, it's up to the kids to search for facts, manipulate variables, observe reactions and interactions, test theories, analyze evidence, and more. In short, they get experience *before* they get explanations. And because they have to work at it, they understand things a whole lot better.

Science software for the very young

Here are some little-kid programs that introduce science skills.

✔ Virtually every activity in *Sammy's Science House* lets kids as young as 3 play scientist. Kids can make discoveries about habitats, natural phenomena, animals, plants, minerals, and more. See Chapter 3. (Edmark, Ages 3-6)

✔ The Travel Center in *Paint, Write & Play!* takes kids to ten on-screen destinations, where they can make discoveries about the animals, terrain, and climate in the different habitats. See Chapter 3. (The Learning Company, Ages 4-7)

✔ After you help them learn to "drive" the bus, kids as young as 4 can join Ms. Frizzle's multimedia tours of the human body, the solar system, dinosaurs, and the ocean in the *Magic Schoolbus* series. (Microsoft, Ages 6-10)

✔ The Fripples and Feathered Friends in *Thinkin' Things Collection 1* are fun critters that encourage children to observe and compare attributes, deduce rules, and test a hypothesis. See Chapter 6. (Edmark, Ages 3-8)

✔ With your help, even preschoolers can explore the 16 different ecosystems in *Explorapedia: The World of Nature* and pick up lots of information about the flora and fauna in each habitat. (Microsoft, Ages 6-10)

___ *Weird, yucky, and real*

What does it take to pique a kid's curiosity? Weird challenges, something yucky (since kids, little kids especially, love to be grossed out), or a real-life scenario are great ways to readily involve kids in on-screen science.

___ *Great gameplay*

A hands-on approach, a weird challenge, *plus* a compelling game is a dynamite combination for on-screen science. For lots of software staying power, look for a story line, a sense of humor, a fun character, a quest for kids to pursue, or a mystery to solve.

___ *Off-the-computer fun*

A computer scientist at MIT once told us that good computer programs make kids want to get *off* the computer! With our favorite science titles, kids are so jazzed that they start looking at the world around them with a fresh eye. And the best programs always suggest "recipes" for off-the-computer variations of on-screen activities.

Watch out for bogus science CD-ROMs! Most science programs don't measure up to our four criteria. And unless you try the programs, you can't tell which ones are good. They may look good, and they probably pack a lot of information. But chances are, they're click-and-watch science: CD-ROMs with lots of clicking, lots of looking, lots of listening, but not much thinking. Using them is like handing a teacher the equipment and materials and never getting to run the experiment yourself.

The titles we profile in this chapter, by contrast, blend the preceding four kid-friendly ingredients together into experiences that are the next best thing to doing real science. The programs fall roughly into four categories: on-screen experiments, science gameplay, online science, plus a few essential CD-ROM science references. You can find more ideas for older kids in *TakeCharge Computing For Teens & Parents,* published by IDG Books Worldwide.

Experimenting On-Screen

Our favorite science software gives kids a real feel for doing and enjoying science. It lets them think like scientists, and act like them too, posing questions and discovering answers for themselves. And the surprising part is that kids don't have to be in traditional science settings to do science on-screen. Forget the classroom or the lab. With the computer, real science can happen in "virtual" settings, like an artist's basement, a taxicab, the woodlands of Australia! You'll see what we mean in the following software profiles.

Big Science Comics (ages 8–12)

Big Science Comics (from Theatrix Interactive) is equal parts on-screen science experimentation and comic adventure. Hooked by the story, kids willingly become physicists, exploring and applying concepts like mass, force, and energy.

It's got a wacky adventure

Big Science Comics is the story of a wayward band of aliens known as the Bumptz who inadvertently push their spaceship's panic button and crash land on Earth. Before they know it, their craft is mysteriously dragged away, and they wind up trapped in a basement. Enter a pack rat named Mo, who takes a shine to the confused creatures. ("They were nice kids," Mo observes, "but about as bright as burnt-out flashlights.") The ship, she explains, has been appropriated by an artist named Bette. And unless they get to her *fast*, the ship will be sculpture, and they'll be shipwrecked for life. Your kids' mission: help the Bumptz make their way out of Bette's house and into her studio while there's still a ship to save.

Off-the-wall as this scenario may seem to parents, it's a real kid-pleaser. As the story unfolds comic book style, panel by panel, kids can't wait to find out what happens next. And what happens next involves doing science.

And it's got real-life science

Even though the story is fantasy — even though its heroes are colorful round aliens with goofy smiles — the science is real. It's science that kids may encounter at school, science they can replicate at home. To help the Bumptz reach Bette, kids have to bail the Bumptz out of difficulties, such as traversing open spaces, climbing stairs, pulling companions out of Bette's fresh-baked pies, and opening a window latch. These problems are actually scientific in nature. In each case, a simple machine will do the trick. And kids have to experiment with concepts of mass, balance, force, and energy to devise a solution.

Bumptz Bridge: One of many experiments

Take Bumptz Bridge, for example, pictured in Figure 11-1. Our heroes are too small to jump from a ledge to a box in the basement. But using a nearby hanger, kids discover that it's possible to get them across. Lots of experimentation comes first. The Bumptz come in three colors and three sizes, and kids have to figure out which ones are lighter, heavier, or equal in weight. Then kids have to balance pairs of Bumptz on the hanger so one Bumptz can drop to safety.

Figure 11-1:
The first of many experiments in *Big Science Comics* involves mass and balance.

It's possible to do this solely by trial and error. But wisely, the software shows kids the logic of what they've done, both graphically (a table pictures small red Bumptz at the same weight as three medium blue Bumptz) and with notation (1srB=3mbB). Some kids grasp the numeric representation; for others, the visual shorthand makes more sense. Either way, kids soon have Bumptz whizzing across the basement like miniature Tarzans!

The science in *Big Science Comics* matches up pretty well with the topics covered in 4th- and 5th-grade classrooms. Those are years when kids learn about simple machines and explore the principles of force, energy, friction, harmonic motion, and static equilibrium.

Big Science Comics comes with excellent "recipes" for off-the-computer versions of its activities. Got any empty film canisters around? Your kids (and you) will have fun turning them into Bumptz and seeing what it's like to balance, swing, pull, or sink them in experiments that are the real-life equivalents of their on-screen activities.

The Science Sleuths series (ages 10 & up)

What hooks kids on the *Science Sleuths* series (from VideoDiscovery/MECC) is its realistic, subtly humorous science mysteries. What's the strange blob that washes up on the beach? (Is it poisonous? Is it dangerous? Or is it just plain ugly?) Why are suburban lawns suddenly riddled by explosions? (Did the developer build atop an old cemetery?) Why does everyone from the annual company picnic turn up violently sick at the emergency room? (Could a corporate rival be at fault?) What's the truth behind those skid marks?

A smart-talking Sleuth Extraordinaire sends kids off to the lab and later grills them about the evidence they gather, the tests they conduct, and the conclusion they reach. As the product's name suggests, careful detective work is as much a part of the solution as laboratory analysis and scientific formulas. (That in itself is a valuable lesson for kids.) It pays, for example, to check newspaper "reports" and "interview" witnesses and experts before running tests and taking measurements. Plus, these mock documents and video clips are the source of much of the product's humor — not to mention red herrings planted to throw kids off the track!

The science part of *Science Sleuths* is a set of 24 interactive tools — from the mundane (scale, tape measure, and Bunsen burner) to the sophisticated (Geiger counter, mass spectrometer, and gas chromatograph) — that kids use to develop a data profile of the mystery substance or event. This information alone, however, won't solve the mystery. Kids have to work with the information, plug it into equations, formulate a hypothesis, draw inferences supported both by laboratory data and news reports, test their guesses, and *finally* defend their solution under intense questioning!

Originally developed for the classroom, the *Science Sleuth* series can be great fun at home — if you make it a social thing. Used solo, it's very quiet software, without the bells, whistles, and entertainment kids are used to in software designed for home use. But if they play with a friend, a sibling, or you, kids can have a lot of smart fun with *Science Sleuths*.

Other On-Screen Experiments

What's the Secret?

There's no adventure or story line in this thoughtful, low-key series. But there's lots of fun on-screen experimentation drawn from the Newton's Apple PBS shows. *What's the Secret?* works best, we find, in tandem with school activities. Our suggestion is to get the skinny on your child's science syllabus at back-to-school

▶▶

◀◀ night. Check *What's the Secret?* for similarities. Then explore the CD-ROM together whenever schoolwork coincides with the software.

Here are some topics in Volume 1: "Do bees talk to each other?" "What keeps a roller coaster going?" "Why does the sound change when a train passes by?" "Why does my heart beat?" "How do bats use the Doppler Effect?" Volume 2 features these topics: "How do people in the Arctic keep from freezing?" "Why do I get headaches?" "Why do I forget things?" "What keeps a kite in the air?" "What makes my ears pop?" "How do I smell smells?" "Why does glue stick?" "If a jumbo jet is bigger than a whale, how does it ever get off the ground?" "Why do I shiver?" (3M Interactive, Ages 8-12)

Bumptz Science Carnival

Same goofy characters as *Big Science Comics,* same silly problem: They've crash-landed. Kids help the Bumptz by experimenting with mirrors, color filters, lenses, prisms, the properties of light, magnetism, force, gravity, and more. Nice touches include Viewscope animations of how the "real-world" properties of light, magnetism, and buoyancy work and an Experiment button that lets kids print more than a dozen off-the-computer activities. (Theatrix Interactive, Ages 6-10)

Science Gameplay — with a Purpose

With today's multimedia, it's possible to pack a virtual destination onto a CD-ROM, such as the sights and sounds of a coral reef or a rain forest. The programs in this section do a great job of immersing kids in exceptionally realistic science environments. But these programs go beyond that "being there" feeling. They invite kids to prowl around with a purpose, giving them places to go and games to play.

The World Walker series (ages 9–13)

Programs from Soleil are hard to pigeonhole. They're science, but not exclusively. They're also geography, reading, writing, Spanish, and French! To retailers (who prefer single-subject titles because they're easier to shelve!), Soleil's wide-ranging content is troublesome. But to us (and to teachers), it's a hallmark of truly excellent software.

Classroom teachers increasingly try to teach *thematically.* That means they turn a single topic (like a neighborhood park, a local tide pool, a fairy tale) into a springboard for related lessons in reading, science, history, math, art, geography, writing, music. Why? Because it's artificial to keep all those subjects separate! Learning to read and write go hand in hand; doing science and math takes a similar turn of mind; art offers great insights into history; history is often inseparable from geography; there's a kinship between music and math, and so on. When kids see a web of connections, rather than discrete sets of facts, their studies make so much more sense. And what they learn sticks with them better, too. Soleil's software takes a similar approach.

Because its primary focus is natural science, we've put the *World Walker* series in this chapter. (Its other forté is foreign-language acquisition. In fact, it's got the most innovative, refreshing approach to Spanish and French we've seen! We tell you even more about it in Chapter 13.)

Each *World Walker* title casts kids as explorers of on-screen habitats in places such as Australia and China. In *Destination: Australia,* for example, players find themselves surrounded by the flora and fauna native to the desert, the woodlands, or a swamp. Sometimes it's rainy, sometimes dry. (The game begins differently each time kids play.) Drawn by hand, the panoramic settings are beautiful and instantly invite exploration.

Ecosystem know-how fuels gameplay

But clicking pictures (no matter how pretty) and pop-up facts (no matter how informative) is no guarantee that kids will learn. Not to worry! In *World Walker,* kids prowl around with a purpose. Wherever they roam, kids encounter riddles that prompt exploration: "Find an insect that spends most of its life hanging upside down from branches trying to look like a twig." Or "Find a monotreme whose spikes make it very hard to catch or eat." (Find a what?! It's okay; we didn't know about monotremes either until our kids played this program.)

For every answer they ferret out, kids earn a "battery" for an on-screen flashlight. Collect enough batteries, and kids can go spelunking in an underground maze. Solving riddles also helps kids as they try their hand at a tricky variation on solitaire. And wouldn't you know it? Those two genres — maze games and solitaire — are among the most popular types of computer-based gameplay!

The Cave Game

Spelunkers find themselves in a pitch-dark maze of 3-D caverns, illuminated by a single flashlight (powered by those hard-earned batteries). The goal: navigate the passageways. Search the aborigine cave art for clues that lead to a room with fossil remains. And reassemble the skeleton. If kids wander too long in the maze, they find themselves retracing their steps in total darkness — so they can earn more batteries. With four levels for each riddle, riddles for more than three dozen animals, 50 cave paintings to scour for clues, and a network of 13 different caverns, the Spelunker game is hours and hours of smart fun.

Food-Chain Solitaire

Playing Food-Chain Solitaire takes gameplay smarts, skill with puzzles, and a knowledge of predators and prey in Australian ecosystems. Instead of ordinary cards, the game is played with picture cards of Aussie mammals, birds, reptiles, insects, amphibians, and plants. The idea is to place cards so they complete a pattern linking the "eaters" to the "eaten." It's easy enough with a three-card food chain (bird-insect-leaf, for example). But when there's an eight- or nine-animal pattern like the one you see in Figure 11-2, it's really fiendish. Kids simply cannot play this game mindlessly, the way adults often deal out hand after hand of solitaire! They have to puzzle out and test connections among the eaters and the eaten — in short, conduct on-screen experiments.

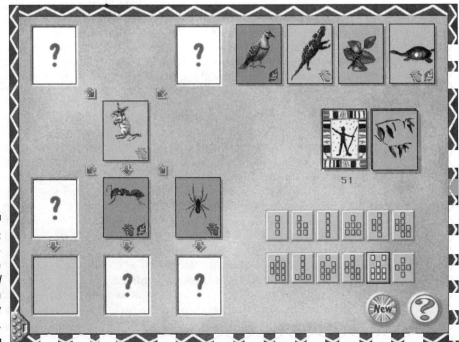

Figure 11-2:
The food-chain game in *World Walker* can get pretty complex.

Print and cut out the critters in Food-Chain Solitaire (see Chapter 17 for tips on screen captures), and you'll have great-looking cards for memory games. Kids can try to match animals of the same class, or the same habitat, or they can try to match predators and prey.

Ever play 20 Questions with little kids only to discover that they know only one fact about their chosen animal? Or that they've answered all your questions in the belief that a platypus is a fish or a polar bear is native to the Antarctic? Hunting for *World Walker* riddles with your 6- to 8-year-olds is a great way to encourage them to soak up real facts. And examining each riddle's carefully structured set of clues provides a subtle lesson in how to ask pertinent questions. The know-how kids need to play *World Walker* is found both in the answers to its riddles and in the Info Cards that pop up whenever kids click an animal. Besides improving kids' chances of on-screen success, both are handy resources for off-the-computer activities like memory games or 20 Questions.

Planetary Taxi (ages 7-12)

Thanks to NASA's planetary probes, space launches, and orbiting telescope, you find an astronomical amount of information about the solar system available on CD-ROM and the World Wide Web. But how do you choose? Where do you begin? We think *Planetary Taxi* (from Voyager) is a great starting point for kids and families because it's got great gameplay, cool characters, and subtle guidance, all at the same time.

Here's the story: Kids drive a futuristic taxi cab (shown in the figure in this sidebar) through the solar system, picking up passengers, figuring out their destinations, and getting them there fast. The passengers are fun and funky. And their destinations range from fairly obvious (for rookie players) to downright tricky (at the expert level). Here's a typical rookie question, from a quirky hayseed with a Midwestern twang: "I'm raising my prize pig Wilbur for 4-H Club, and I want him to win first place as the heaviest pig ever. He already weighs 100 pounds on Earth. But that's not enough, so I'm thinking, 'Why not get Wilbur weighed on another planet?' Take me to the planet where Wilbur will weigh the most."

So you knew the answer was Jupiter? Well try this one: "Whenever I want to go to Disneyland or get in-line skates or do almost anything fun, my parents always say, 'We'll talk about it tomorrow.' Well, I'm getting tired of having to wait a whole day. But now I have a plan so I don't have to wait so long. Take me to the planet that has the shortest day."

As the requests get more challenging, players can dip into the title's vast fund of information — some of it written, some narrated, some in the form of photos, video clips, animations, and charts and graphs. Getting to the right places fast means better tips, a higher score, and more fun.

If playing *Planetary Taxi* whets your kids' appetites for astronomy, consider exploring *Nine Worlds* (Palladium, all ages) together. This great-looking astronomy reference features

(continued)

(continued)

narration by Patrick Stewart (a big hit with fans of Captain Picard of *Star Trek: The Next Generation*) and three intelligently designed ways to get solar-system smarts. Clicking a planet produces an informative multimedia show that includes video footage, photographs, computer-simulated fly-overs, and more. (Each mini-documentary lasts so long that your screen saver might kick in! So jiggle your mouse occasionally.)

Our favorite part of the CD-ROM is called Mankind's View. It's a scrollable, beautifully illustrated timeline, ranging from the ancients to Newtonian England to the Age of Exploration. Besides informative but kid-friendly text, many entries feature video interviews with real astronomers, dramatic readings, and more.

The product's Resource Explorer is a grab bag of information for astronomy lovers: tips on buying or building a telescope; lists of publications, organizations, and observatories; descriptions of shareware astronomy products; multiple choice quizzes; and best of all, an online link to astronomy sites on the World Wide Web.

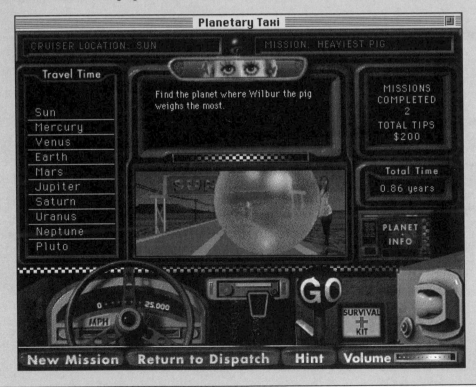

Exploring Science Online

Some of the best science adventures we've found are not on CD-ROMs at all. They're on the World Wide Web. The longer you look, the more you'll find, for little kids, big kids, and kids at heart (that's you). Want to isolate DNA in the kitchen? There's a Web site with easy instructions! Want to stump friends with optical illusions? There's a Web site full of them! Want to know why feet smell? There's a Web site with the answer (but, thankfully, no odor).

But before we tell you about our favorite sites, here are some ideas about finding favorites of your own:

- ✔ Click through the listings you find at Insanely Great Science Websites. (`http://www.eskimo.com/~billb/amateur/coolsci.html`)

- ✔ Search the Yahooligans listings for Science & Oddities. (`http://www.yahooligans.com/Science_and_Oddities/`)

- ✔ Explore the Cool Sites listed in the Exploratorium's Learning Studio (`http://www.exploratorium.edu/learning_studio/sciencesites.html`)

- ✔ Check Kids Web at `http://www.npac.syr.edu/textbook/kidsweb/index.html`. It's a library of Web sites for kids, covering the arts, sciences, social studies, sports, fun, and more.

- ✔ Visit the home pages of the companies that publish your kids' favorite science CD-ROMs. Software publishers often list cool links that relate to their educational products. We've linked to good science sites from Voyager, Theatrix, MECC, 3M, Palladium, and others.

Don't be surprised if your browser can't find a Web address you type. It's not your fault; and it's probably not our fault either! Blame it on the World Wide Web itself: Web addresses (and sites themselves) can be pretty fickle. Try looking for a "missing" site with a search engine. And try shortening the address by deleting everything after the `.com` (or `.org` or `.edu`).

Good starting points

These five sites make great jumping-off points for families, spanning sites with very young children in mind, plus some that are excellent for teens and preteens (for more ideas for teens, see *TakeCharge Computing For Teens & Parents,* published by IDG Books Worldwide):

✔ **Helping your child learn about science:** Make this common sense site from the U.S. Office of Educational Research the first stop on your Web science *surfari*. Besides good explanations of science basics for kids, it suggests great at-home activities plus lots of resources. (http://www.ed.gov/pubs/parents/Science/)

✔ **Ask a scientist:** Can't answer that question about "subduction" or "nebulae"? Let the kids post a question to an expert. You'll find experts of every stripe online. There's an Ask-A-Geologist site (http://walrus.wr.usgs.gov/docs/ask-a-ge.html), Ask-A-Volcanologist site (http://volcano.und.nodak.edu/vwdocs/ask_a.html), Ask-An-Astronomer site (http://syborg.ucolink.org/~mountain/AAA/), and more.

✔ **Two-minute science:** Now available on the Web, the broadcasts from the Earth & Sky radio program make excellent science reading for kids. The Web site is nothing fancy, but the short reports are easy to read and intriguing, ranging from why the sea is salty to Groundhog Day, jellyfish, and Saturn's rings. (http://www.earthsky.com)

✔ **What do you think?:** NPR's Science Friday Kids Connection site presents fun and informative activities and, best of all, an open forum for kids to share ideas. A new topic is added every week. If kids are fired up by a particular topic — "Which of the emerging diseases do you think is most dangerous to the middle school student and why?" "Do dreams have a purpose?" "Would you want to know if the foods you eat have been produced through genetic engineering?" — they just click, write a response, and read what other kids have been saying. (http://www.npr.org/sfkids/)

✔ **Test your knowledge:** You can find some fun quizzes on the Explorit Science Center's site, which covers general science knowledge as well as astronomy, biology, earth science, math, physics, and technology. (http://www.dcn.davis.ca.us/go/explorit/)

It's science fair season!

Why is it that every year, when science fair season rolls around, every single book of project ideas disappears from every library and every book store? With the Web, you never run into that problem. Basically there are two types of sites, the kind with how-to advice and those with project ideas.

How-to advice

These sites tell kids everything they need to know about science fair projects (but were probably too lazy to ask). They include hints for getting started, tips for coming up with projects, timetables and to-do lists, and more. Even if your kids check out only one of these sites, you won't believe how much more organized they'll be!

✔ **Hints for getting started:** Kids will find practical pointers from the Cyberspace Middle School. (`http://www.scri.fsu.edu/~dennis1/CMS/sf/sf.html`)

✔ **What makes a good project:** Kids often undertake projects that end up being far more complex than they first imagined. They can avoid that problem by reading up on "doable" projects. (`http://www.isd77.k12.mn.us/resources/cf/goodproject.html`)

✔ **Developing project ideas:** Kids can use a fun fill-in-the-blank form for fleshing out their science-project ideas. (`http://www.isd77.k12.mn.us/resources/cf/ideas.html`)

✔ **Taking it step-by-step:** Kids will find an eight-step checklist covering what to do and in what order. (`http://www.isd77.k12.mn.us/resources/cf/steps.html`)

✔ **An easy-to-follow process for 3rd-5th graders:** This site helps kids come up with a hypothesis, design experimental procedures, conduct experiments, and more. (`http://www.isd77.k12.mn.us/resources/cf/SciProjIntro.html`)

✔ **Advice for middle and high school students:** Older kids can get help tackling more challenging science projects. (`http://www.isd77.k12.mn.us/resources/cf/SciProjInter.html`)

Project ideas

After kids understand the procedure for conducting a science fair experiment, it's time to choose an experiment to conduct. Project ideas abound on the Web. In fact, the ideas we found are too good for once-a-year projects! We hope you and your kids will be inspired to try some once a month at home.

✔ **Newton's Apple:** This site showcases lessons from the award-winning public television show of the same name and includes dozens and dozens of Science Try Its. One of these is sure to inspire your kids. For explanations of what's going on in these activities, make sure to explore the Science behind the Science Try Its section. (`http://ericir.syr.edu/Projects/Newton/index.html`)

✔ **50 Questions:** This area of the You Can with Beakman and Jax site features kids' science questions. (Why does my hair get curly when the humidity goes up? Why do feet smell?) And many of the answers include fun activities that kids can easily turn into science fair experiments. (`http://www.nbn.com/youcan/questionlist.html`)

✔ **Thinking Fountain:** Here kids will find an A to Z listing of activities from the Science Museum of Minnesota, each with nifty graphics, a material list, step-by-step instructions, plus related questions to think about and links to explore. (`http://www.sci.mus.mn.us/sln/tf/nav/tfatoz.html`)

Science museums online

Some museums do little more than list their exhibits on their Web sites. And what fun is that for kids? Others treat the Web as an exhibit space, a place where kids can do hands-on science. Those are the ones we like best. Here's a sampling of our favorites:

✔ **Exploratorium:** Some of the best science "interactivities" on the Web are at this site. You find mini-experiments in visual perception, memory, sound, optical illusions, and more. Common Cents, pictured in Figure 11-3, is a fun one for young children. (`http://www.exploratorium.learning_studio/lsexhibits.html`)

Figure 11-3:
We all know what a penny looks like, right? Try these Exploratorium challenges to test your visual memory.

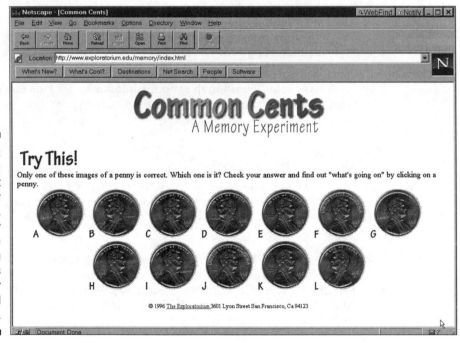

✔ **Yuckiest Site on the Internet:** Who can resist a site with a name like that? Created by Liberty Science Center, it features wonderfully gross and fascinating stuff. Try the Cockroach World area (`http://www.nj.com/yucky/roaches/index.html`), with roach facts, hilarious quizzes (like the one pictured in Figure 11-4), and kitchen experiments. The Worm World area (`http://www.nj.com/yucky/worm/index.html`) features mini-movies of beating worm hearts, worm mad libs, worm jokes, and more.

✔ **Techno-Challenges:** The activities on The Computer Museum Network site (`http://www.tcm.org/`) invite kids to work together — across cyberspace — to solve a Networked Puzzle. Make sure to try Design Your Own Robot.

✔ **DNA in your kitchen!:** For 10-year-olds and up, the Utah Museum of Natural History's Web site suggests intriguing genetic science activities. Its most popular experiment is a procedure for extracting DNA from everyday foods like peas and onions (`http://raven.umnh.utah.edu/new/projects/kitchenDNA.html`)

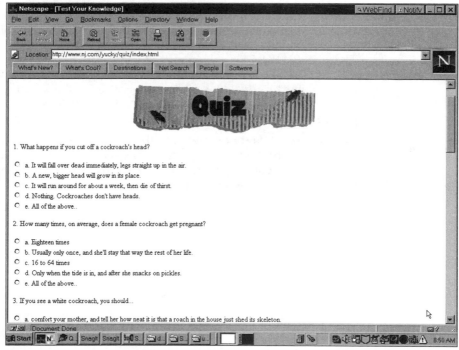

Figure 11-4:
If you think you know the answer, check your guess on the Yuckiest Site on the Internet.

Essential References for Science

It's useful to have a few science references in your family software library. These references won't get the everyday use that on-screen experiments or science games will. But they're a handy starting place when your kid suddenly remembers that two paragraphs (plus diagram) on the greenhouse effect are due tomorrow morning. Here's a strategy for rounding out your software library with science reference CD-ROMs that make sense for your kids.

✔ **Keep at least one all-purpose reference on hand:** Our favorite is *Microsoft Encarta.* A good supplement is the *Eyewitness Encyclopedia of Science,* with more than 200 entries in mathematics, physics, chemistry, and life sciences. No science homework this week? Use the Quiz Master feature with your kids. It tosses out intriguing, random questions: Will the Earth be swallowed up by the sun? What kind of carbon molecule looks like a soccer ball? How do penguins keep warm? Click the Look Up button beneath a question, and the program charts an efficient path through its vast database, showing step-by-step how to reach the answer. (DK Multimedia, Ages 11 & up)

✔ **Go with your kids' interests:** Has your 7-year-old taken up bird watching? Is the 10-year-old's passion for go-carts wrecking your garage? There's a CD-ROM for aficionados of every stripe — we guarantee it. Even if the topic is a passing fancy, spending time with a reference CD-ROM has its advantages: Your kids will get a lot of reading practice. They'll learn how to look things up. And they'll have something informative to share at the supper table!

✔ **Choose CD-ROMs that dovetail with your kids' school work:** At back-to-school night, find out what the year's science curriculum covers. That way, you can play matchmaker effectively. And don't forget to ask the teacher for recommendations.

Chapter 12

Stimulating the Brain — with Simulation Software

*I*n the preceding three chapters, we talk about real things, places, and time periods that kids can explore via computer software: the Australian outback, the planets, ancient Greece, the continents, the westward expansion. You name it, kids can explore it.

Chapter 12 is about explorations, too. But with a twist. The programs in this chapter are called *simulations*. This kind of software casts kids in roles and lets them do *things they could never, ever do in real life*. Ever heard of a 12-year-old big-city mayor? An 8-year-old fighter pilot? A 10-year-old genetic engineer? A 9-year-old park ranger?

Simulations are incredibly sophisticated "let's pretend" games, aimed at double-digit kids (with a few for 8- to 12-year-olds). They mimic real-life situations, and put kids in charge. But don't be fooled by the word *game*. It's hard to find computer adventures that give kids more mental exercise and more insight into real-life situations than simulations do.

Just What's So Stimulating about Simulations?

We once saw a wonderful typo, the kind that brings a smile to your face. The word was supposed to *simulation,* the type of program that's the focus of this chapter. And instead, it appeared as *stimulation*.

But that misplaced *T* got us thinking. Although the extra letter got there by accident, there's a very real connection between programs that *simulate* reality and activities that *stimulate* kids to think. In fact, the more we thought about it, the more we realized just how stimulating simulations can be. Good simulation software offers these three hallmark features:

- ✔ Invigorates thinking
- ✔ Excites imagination
- ✔ Inspires a personal stake

Here's what we mean by these qualities.

Simulations are thinking games

Sometimes we worry that software makes things too easy for kids. They point, they click, they watch. But are they really thinking? Well, the good news is that simulations are a terrific antidote to that all-too-common tendency among kids to "glaze over" in front of electronic devices. Kids can't point and click their way through a simulation. They've got to think, and think hard.

What kind of thinking?

Simulations model complex systems of many sorts: marine life in the Great Barrier Reef, urban development, the stock market, battlefield tactics, circus acts, and more. And whatever the subject, kids have to figure out the rules and tools that make a particular simulation run. They have to think about interactions, cause and effect, interrelationships. And after they grapple with how the system works, they have to figure out how to take control.

What about off-the-computer?

Obviously kids can't hire out as city planners on the strength of their prowess with a program like *SimCity 2000,* which you read about later in this chapter. (At least not right away!) But the mental exercise of a simulation has real off-the-computer value for kids. Good simulations can help kids become more adept at analytic thinking, weighing choices, planning ahead, strategizing.

Because they give kids a hands-on feel for the interplay among economics and environment, exploration and conquest, simulations are a good counterpart to social studies textbooks for 5th graders on up. Best of all, simulations can inspire kids to look with fresh eyes at real-world systems, to look beyond the game and see some of the interdependencies in real life.

Simulations make demands on kids' imaginations

Our favorite simulations don't have that you-are-there aura of reality that kids (and parents) often expect in multimedia software. They're not picture-perfect. In fact, what kids see on the computer screen sometimes looks as abstract as their kid brother's *Kid Pix* scribbles!

What appears on the screen is a kind of *shorthand* — scores of symbols, grids, maps, graphs, diagrams, charts — for the workings of a simulated environment. This shorthand leaves a lot to the imagination. Kids must interpret all those attributes. And once they do, they begin to "see" the screen differently in their minds' eye. The screen takes on a life beyond the symbols, with qualities that kids have imagined into it.

In short, simulation software doesn't hand kids a photorealistic experience on a platter. It doesn't re-create reality for them — it gives them the tools and the inspiration to *envision* for themselves.

Simulations give kids a personal stake in events

Kids are in the hot seat when they play simulations. It's a tricky business balancing the varied forces and objectives at work in a simulated slice of life. And it's daunting, too, because each choice and each consequence — from their first decision to its most distant trickle-down effect — is their responsibility, and theirs alone.

If cockroaches invade an apartment tower they've constructed, kids are to blame. But if they resuscitate a languishing community, kids are the heroes. This personal power can sometimes make kids a bit fanatical. But this capability can also encourage them to be thoughtful and persistent. (And who knows? Maybe one day it'll carry over into real life, and you can quit lecturing them about the consequences of their actions!)

What's Your Pleasure? Parks, Towns, Golf Links?

You can find many kinds of simulations: flight simulators, sports simula-tions, simulation games about the legislative process, reenactments of the Civil War, pinball game simulators. But the ones we like best have some educational underpinnings. One of the best known makers of simulation games is Maxis, and its recent introductions are great for kids as young as 8. One of our favorites — *SimPark* — combines the design-it-and-see-if-it-works fun of a simulation with a wealth of underlying information about the animals, habitats, and plants of North America. You can find more ideas for older kids in *TakeCharge Computing For Teens & Parents,* published by IDG Books Worldwide.

SimPark (ages 8–12)

SimPark (Windows CD-ROM only) casts kids as junior rangers in charge of designing a park and striking a healthy balance among wildlife, plants, climates, and people and the problems they bring. With nine North American climate zones as settings and 132 plant and animals species as "building blocks," kids can create an urban pocket park, an expanse of wilderness, or anything in between.

As soon as kids see *SimPark*'s array of birds, flowers, mammals, shrubs, reptiles, and trees (some shown in Figure 12-1), there's no stopping them. Their instinct is to literally paint the screen by clicking plants and animals, just the way kids do with stamps in an art program. Why? Because the animals move. The wolves stalk the hares, the hawks circle in search of prey. And there's a tapestry of natural sounds as kids click animals into their park.

Figure 12-1: As kids decide what to click next, the bear lumbers past, the mallard quacks, and the seasons advance!

Don't discourage them! In fact, this wild abandon is a great way for kids to get started with *SimPark*. In the following sections, we suggest a process for first-time play that lets you encourage your kids' exuberance — while introducing some of the product's educational features. Best of all, this approach really surprises kids with the power of the product's simulator.

Phase 1: Go with the flow

Encourage kids to click every single icon they see on the left side of the screen. Figure 12-2 shows the buttons they see for mammals, trees, shrubs, grasses, flowers, birds, reptiles, amphibians, and human elements (such as park benches, hot-dog stands, foot bridges, gazebos, and tents).

After two minutes of pointing and clicking, your kids will notice some changes. Plants that started out small have grown. That's good. But suddenly, the flora has turned brown. That's bad. No, it's just winter. In *SimPark*, seasons pass in a minute. So when kids click around for another minute, they find it's spring again.

Phase 2: Go exploring

Once kids have their fill of clicking, suggest that they go exploring and meanwhile let nature take its course in their park. Now's the time for them to check out the icons pictured in Figure 12-2 on the right side of the screen.

Figure 12-2: *SimPark* gives kids an array of choices (represented by icons on the left side of the screen) for "populating" their parks and five kinds of tools (represented by icons on the right) for managing growth.

The microphone icon is a fun one. Kids click it, and a frog named Rizzo hops onto the screen. His job is to check on the park animals' well-being and relay their feedback to kids. If their comments are worrisome — "I'm too cold," "I'm starving," "I'm being eaten" — then it's back to the icons on the left side of the screen for some corrective clicking.

The computer icon on the lower right is your kids' gateway to *SimPark*'s wealth of park-management and natural-science information. Click the icon, and several tools appear at the top of the screen. Kids can check their funds with the Budget tool. (A park gets $10,000 a year from tax revenue, but kids can earn more by renting gazebos for weddings, among other tactics.) They can check for messages from the head ranger and others with the E-Mail tool. To earn commendations from their boss, kids can try their hand with the Identa-Species tool. This tool displays a plant or animal and then steps kids through a series of questions that helps them zero in on its exact identity. The Species Checklist tool shows what's living in the park. And the Charts & Graphs tool lets kids analyze different populations.

Most important is the Field Guide tool, with information on the product's 132 species. Remind your kids that they'll have a strategic advantage if they spend time with this good-looking resource. They can populate their park more wisely if they know what different animals like to eat and what habitats they prefer.

Once your kids become accomplished *SimPark* players, let them check out the *SimPark* Web site. They'll be able to download new species from the Web for their parks and link to other sites about ecology, wildlife, and parks.

Phase 3: Go back — but be prepared for a surprise!

By now kids have probably had enough of all this information stuff. So switch back to the park. And get ready for a surprise. All that willy-nilly stamping has probably produced an ecological disaster of some sort!

The first time we played *SimPark,* the place was overrun with squirrels. The next time, all the trees had died out. And the time after that, the bobcat population went sky high.

During the time we were off exploring the park-management tools, the park simulator was doing its thing. There weren't enough predators to keep the rodent population down. Lots of big animals starved through lack of appropriate prey. Desert shrubs died off because they were planted in temperate zones. Our mistakes were outrageous and obvious.

That's why it's fun to start out with random clicking. The ridiculous results really underscore the power of the simulation. And that makes kids want to get a lot smarter, a lot faster with their next park.

SimPark comes with an excellent off-the-computer activity guide. This guide suggests more than a dozen ways kids can carry their interest in plants into their own backyards, their neighborhoods, and local parks. Some suggestions are good for younger children ("Find a food chain"). Some can easily be turned into science projects ("Observe a tree transpiring"). And others make good club or scouting activities ("Create a wildlife map" or "Go on a photojournalist mission").

Other Sims

You can find lots of other Maxis simulations. Here's a run-down of our favorites:

SimTown

Visual pizzazz, designer characters, and easy-to-understand symbols make this an especially friendly simulation for 8- to 12-year-olds. The idea is to develop a community — either from scratch, from one of several Starter Towns, or from Fixer-Upper Towns — and keep a healthy balance among its people, buildings, terrain, and natural resources. Kids like the look of the things they can put in their towns: Chinese restaurants that resemble take-out cartons, adobe homes, book-shaped libraries, haunted houses, video arcades, and the like. They enjoy peeking into the homes to see what the Sims are up to. And they love creating their own special Sim by clicking options shown in Figure 12-3. (How about a pizza fanatic who skateboards around town, keeps a pet penguin, and says "Oh, botheration!" when he's sad?) After *SimPark,* this is our favorite *Sim* title for preteens. (Maxis, Ages 8-12)

SimCity 2000

As mayors and city planners, kids design, build, and manage cities from the ground up. And we mean that literally. Kids can start by *editing* the landscape: raising and lowering sea level, digging streams, carving mountains, and the like. Next comes city building, starting with big-picture considerations like power, transportation infrastructure, and zoning; moving on to

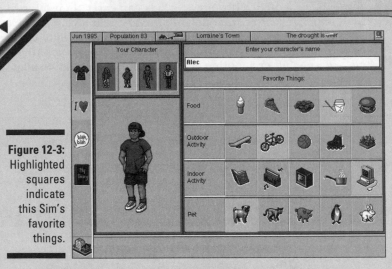

Figure 12-3:
Highlighted squares indicate this Sim's favorite things.

education, city services, and recreation; and going all the way down to street signs. Once the city is powered up and has a network of roads, Sims begin to move in. And then the municipality begins to grow and take on a life of its own. A host of indicators tells kids about their city's finances, politics, industries, and demographics. And of course, there are tools for controlling those elements. Want to encourage tourism? Then lower the tax rate for the hospitality industry. Want to hear the sounds of a happy populace? Then lower property taxes. (The Sims literally do cheer!) But be prepared for the domino effect that less income inevitably produces. And encourage your kids to keep their police and fire funding as high as possible so they can cope with random disasters like fire, floods, tornadoes, airplane crashes, earthquakes, and monster attacks. For information about software on the *Great Software For Kids & Parents* CD-ROM, see Appendix C. (Maxis, Ages 12 & up)

SimCity fanatics can post their creations, download ready-made cities, share tips and strategies, and find Easter eggs on a variety of online sites. What the heck's an *Easter egg*? It's a cheat code — a combination of keystrokes or a word that kids type — to make things happen. There's one for doubling your money at the start of *SimTower,* another for stopping a flood in *SimCity,* and hundreds more.

Here are some Web sites to get your kids started:

- *Maxis* at `http://www.maxis.com`

- *SimForum* at `http://www.geocities.com/Silicon Valley/Park/7618/`

- *ClubOpolis* at `http://www.eskimo.com/~pcoston/co/`

- *Yahoo!*'s SimCity sites at `http://www.yahoo.com/recreation/games/Genres/Simulation/Titles/Simcity/`

SimIsle

Kids play a provincial ruler juggling ecological concerns and economic growth as they develop a Southeast Asian island. *SimIsle* boasts some terrific predesigned scenarios, from nurturing and exporting rare animal species to turning the island into a tourist haven. It also adds a new element — 24 agents, each with a special talent — to the player's strategic arsenal. If kids employ the most suitable agents for the job, they may have an edge in managing native populations, attracting tourists, introducing industry, protecting wildlife, or whatever their particular goal happens to be. (Maxis, Ages 12 & up)

SimTower

As the owner and general manager of a modern skyscraper, kids get to build condos, offices, fast-food joints, shops, movie theaters, hotels, medical facilities, recycling centers, parking garages, subway stations — even a cathedral if they play smart. But their edifice will never get off the ground (at least not much higher than a few stories) if the Sims are unhappy. And they can get pretty ornery if the elevators, escalators, and staircases are not to their liking. Keep them waiting too long, put a noisy tenant nearby, or let the cockroaches get out of hand, and they see red (kids can literally watch their stress level inch into the red) and move out. Complex, but worth the learning curve. (Maxis, Ages 12 & up)

◄◄

SimCity Classic

This program is great for *SimCity* aficionados who want to take on some really fiendish prebuilt conditions — with the clock ticking. In *SimCity Classic,* kids grapple with real (or ridiculous) scenarios like getting San Francisco on the road to recovery after the 1906 earthquake, rebuilding Tokyo following an attack by a huge reptilian monster in 1957, reducing crime and rebuilding industry in Detroit circa 1972, and more. (Maxis, Ages 12 & up)

SimCopter

Kids who save their creations from *SimCity 2000* can fly into their own cities with *SimCopter.* Or they can fly 3-D missions between skyscrapers and over the roads of 30 prebuilt cities. (Maxis, Ages 12 & up, Windows 95 CD-ROM only)

■

Getting real-life lessons out of simulations

Despite their obvious relevance to real-world issues, the true lure of most simulation titles is the gameplay. No question they've got useful lessons in them. But truth is, they're not teaching tools. So it's up to parents (and teachers, if they can set aside enough time) to encourage kids to make connections between "sim" situations and real life. If your kids are open to suggestion, see if they take to these ideas:

✔ **Re-create a familiar park with *SimPark*.** Take kids on a fact-finding mission before they launch the program so they can design something realistic. What kinds of plants and animals are native to the park? Are there ponds, streams? How many play structures and recreation areas are in the park? How many people use it? Do the police patrol the area? Help kids keep up with the local news ("Injured swan taken to zoo," "Windstorm fells a dozen trees") so they can adjust their simulation accordingly.

✔ **Replicate your neighborhood with *SimTown*.** This is a good way to get kids to take a closer-than-usual look at people and places they may take for granted. They'll need to take an inventory of their neighborhood: the exact placement and number of houses, kinds of restaurants, playgrounds, street signs and stop lights, and the like. They'll also have to find out how their neighbors are employed and include businesses in their simulation. (Their simulated town will die a quick death without jobs.) And like it or not, they'll have to include a school. Since it's one of the program's underlying assumptions that kids go to school, a simulated town won't flourish without one (or more).

✔ **Build the city you live in with *SimCity*.** Best for older kids or social studies classes, this project also begins with considerable research. To create an accurate model, kids need to find out about local terrain and resources, population, tax rates, industrial mix, zoning, transportation infrastructure, power plants. If your child is friends with a *Sim* fanatic, try suggesting that they both model their home town on their own computers. Then see who comes closest to reality.

✔ **Can kids build Maui with *SimIsle*?** Ask your kids to pick a tropical island they'd like to visit and bring it to life on the computer screen. Can they build the Galapagos? Or a Pacific atoll slowly coming back to life after nuclear testing?

Besides underscoring real-world issues for kids, these projects are a good way of showing them what simulation programs *can't* do. Sooner or later, kids' creative plans may run up against the constraints of the program they're using. Here are some examples. Kids can't make their own rules for a fish's behavior in *Odell Down Under;* they can choose only among the behaviors the program supplies. They can't create a retirement community with *SimTown* because one of its underlying rules is that people must have jobs. Another underlying rule prevents kids from having success with a food-fanatics town where Sims eat only pizza.

Other simulations

The *Sim* titles are not the only simulations around. In fact, you find our favorite history simulations in Chapter 10. Other titles with reasonably sound educational underpinnings include:

✔ ***Odell Down Under*:** In this marine-life simulation, kids take on the role of a fish in Australia's Great Barrier Reef. Survival depends on finding out what to eat and what to avoid, how to escape and how to get defensive. Kids who "live" long enough become Reef Ruler. (MECC, Ages 8-12, Macintosh or DOS floppy only)

▶▶

◀◀

✔ **SMG2000:** Aimed at students in grades 4-12, the *Stock Market Game* is an online simulation that challenges teams of kids to invest $100,000 (don't worry, it's hypothetical!) in common stocks and see how high they can boost the equity in their portfolio by semester's end. Look into it for your kids' class at school or for an after-school club. (`http://www.smg2000.org/top.shtml`) For similar games, virtual investors young and old should check Yahoo!'s listing of stock market simulations.

✔ **Civilization II:** Kids who conquer the world or colonize space are the winners in this popular empire-building game. Be prepared for lots of military action; but the game also challenges kids to use exploration, diplomacy, economics, research, and politics as means of advancing through a vast historical canvas. (MicroProse, Ages 12 & up, Windows CD-ROM only)

Constructing Your Own Simulations

What to do if your kids get frustrated by the limits a program imposes on their imagination? Then it's time to get really creative — with software that lets kids design *every single thing* that shows up on the computer screen.

You're headed for uncharted territory here! Some of the programs that let kids really take charge work better in a classroom setting than at home. Others are usable at home but are still in the development stages. And they're not for everyone. To get a sense of whether your family is a good candidate for simulation-building, ask yourself these questions:

✔ Do your kids want to create scenarios that their programs won't let them create?

✔ Are you comfortable with experimentation?

✔ Do you have time to invest in a really open-ended project?

If the answers are "yes," read on.

One of the most accessible, build-it-yourself simulation kits we've found is a program called *Cocoa*, developed by the Apple Computer Advanced Technology Group, that you can download from the World Wide Web. (`http://cocoa.apple.com/cocoa`)

Cocoa works identically on both Macintosh and Windows systems. The Web page gives you a choice of versions to download. Just click the one that's right for your computer; then follow the instructions that appear on-screen for installing it on your hard drive. Then launch *Cocoa* as you would any other kids' software program.

Cocoa (ages 10 & up)

Cocoa lets kids make interactive creations, like simulations, games, animations, and more, without any special commands. Using *Cocoa*, for example, kids can:

- ✔ Devise a simulation that mimicks a natural process
- ✔ Invent an interactive world with characters kids draw and animate
- ✔ Create an animated picture book that's different every time kids read it

For even more fun, kids can publish their creations on the World Wide Web, swap characters and scenarios they create with other kids, and share tips.

What kind of simulations?

Anything's possible with *Cocoa*. But we'll let kids speak for themselves. Here are some kid-created examples:

Frisky

An 8-year-old friend (with her mother's help) created some on-screen adventures for her pet hamster, Frisky. She started by drawing a hamster. Then she taught it to run. Next she drew a tube for it to run through. Then came edible treats, scattered around the screen, that the hamster would stop and eat. Future plans for Frisky's on-screen existence include giving it a hiding place like a house or a log and teaching it to poop.

Bubble World

This creation by two 11-year-old girls starts out peacefully enough, with bubbles drifting randomly around the screen. Then comes trouble. "Acid" raindrops begin to fall from above. And when a droplet hits a bubble, the bubble pops. The random movement makes Bubble World fun to watch. Some bubbles manage to escape their fate for a long time, and occasionally two bubbles spawn a new one. You'll find yourself rooting for the bubbles as you watch.

How do kids do it?

To get started, we suggest that you take a look at the samples and tutorials that are available on the *Cocoa* Web page. The link titled Cocoa Hall of Fame takes you to simulations other people have created with *Cocoa*. The Tutorials link takes you to an excellent step-by-step introduction to creating with *Cocoa*.

Or you can try the first-time approach we sketch out next. It produces a *very basic* simulation. But because it's fast and easy, we guarantee that this process will get your kids jazzed about creating simulations and eager to explore more complex possibilities.

Step 1: Envisioning a scenario

Encourage your kids to pick something simple for their first *Cocoa* simulation, *not* the kind of complex system they're accustomed to in the *Sim* titles. For ideas, check the Hall of Fame section of the *Cocoa* Web site. Its sampler of *Cocoa* creations includes the animated life cycle of a flower, an adventure game, a science kit, a probability game, and more.

Step 2: Drawing objects

Once kids have a situation in mind, they need to create some objects. If, for example, kids want to make a frog jump on a log — how's that for simple! — they need to draw two objects.

First they click the paint-tube icon, shown at the bottom left of Figure 12-4. This squeezes a colorful blob onto the screen. Click the paintbrush icon, and kids are whisked into a mini-art program, shown in the center of Figure 12-4. Now don't laugh at us, but that object you see is our (admittedly inept) attempt at a frog!

When kids are satisfied with their artwork, they click the Done button, and the object they drew appears on *Cocoa*'s game board, the area where the action will take place.

To draw a log for our frog, we clicked the paint tube and paintbrush icons again. When we clicked Done, we had a frog next to a log on the game board. And we were ready to assign an amphibian behavior.

Step 3: Directing the action

Ordinarily, the only way to define actions in a simulation (or any kind of software) is with a particular computer programming language. But not in *Cocoa*. Kids can make that frog jump by moving a series of pictures (or "graphical rules") that simply shows the computer what they want to happen. Here's how kids do it:

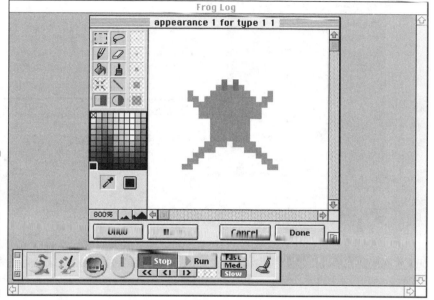

Figure 12-4:
Drawing objects in *Cocoa* is much like using a kids' art program.

1. **Select the frog.**

   To do this, kids first click the movie-camera icon at the bottom of the screen. This action "attaches" the movie-camera to the cursor. Next they click the frog. This click makes three things happen simultaneously. The game board becomes a grid. The frog lights up and little "handles" appear on the sides of the square it's sitting on. And a Rule window opens so kids can show the frog what to do next.

2. **Include the log.**

   In the Rule window, kids see two identical pictures of the frog (see Figure 12-5). One is labeled *Before,* the other *After.* To make the log appear, kids click and drag the handle to the right of the frog. Next they click and drag the handle above the frog. That creates empty squares above the frog and log, giving the frog a space to jump into.

   Now comes the fun part.

3. **Move the frog.**

   Kids click the frog in the *After* picture and drag the frog into the empty space on top of the log. Figure 12-6 shows the resulting change in the Rule window: In the *Before* picture, the frog is *next to* the log; in the *After* picture, it's *on top of* the log.

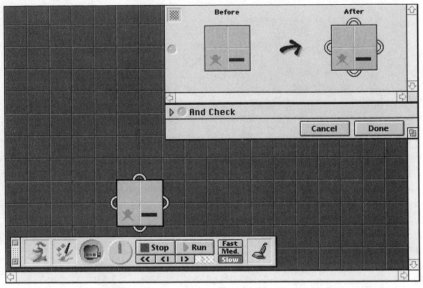

Figure 12-5:
Here's the frog alongside the log, awaiting kids' instructions for where to go next.

Now's the time for kids to "tell" the software to "remember" the change in the frog's position.

4. **Record the action.**

Clicking the Record button tells the software to remember how to make the frog do its thing.

5. **Click the Done button.**

This click closes the Rule window and takes kids back to the game board — with the frog back in its original spot, sitting next to the log. And now for the final click . . .

6. **Make it happen!**

When kids click the Run button at the bottom of the screen, the software follows the instructions kids recorded for the frog. And as it does so, the frog becomes the star of a little animation and jumps onto the log.

You'll find many step-by-step examples — all more interesting than our frog-log animation but still relatively simple — on the *Cocoa* Web site.

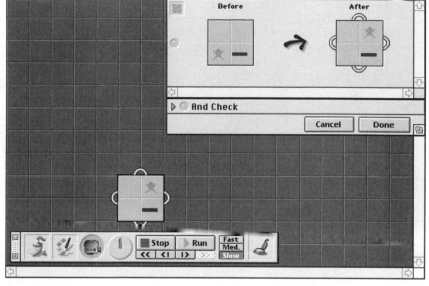

Figure 12-6:
By
changing
the frog's
position,
kids are in
effect
programming
it to jump.

What's so educational about this?

Pretty different from playing *SimPark* or *Oregon Trail,* isn't it? You won't find any of the implicit lessons in ecology or economy or history that other simulations titles in this chapter (and elsewhere in the book) contain. But learning is going on — the self-taught variety. Help your kids play with a construction kit like *Cocoa,* and they'll have an opportunity to:

✔ **See themselves as designers and inventors:** With *Cocoa,* they gain confidence to experiment and express themselves in new ways, on and off the computer.

✔ **Act like a scientist — but without a lab!** The process of creating, trying out, and refining behavioral rules with *Cocoa* is much like the scientific method of posing, testing, and reformulating a hypothesis.

✔ **Solve problems by creating models:** Building models is a powerful way of understanding how and why things work, and *Cocoa* gets kids in the habit of doing this with its simple, pictorial procedures.

✔ **Improve at procedural thinking:** It takes clear, step-by-step thinking to make things happen in *Cocoa.* And that's a skill that can help kids with *everything* they do, on and off the computer.

✔ **Develop an understanding of programming concepts:** Although kids don't use conventional programming language in *Cocoa,* they are in fact writing programs when they create rules. Experimenting with a tool like *Cocoa* may make it easier for kids to use the computer to express and explore ideas.

Follow the links (words or images you can click to go other places on the Web) on the *Cocoa* Web site to find other kits for building simulations and animations. If your kids are really into it, consider trying some programs designed for school use, including *Logo* and *MicroWorlds Project Builder,* both from Logo Computer Systems Inc. With adult assistance to get them started, kids can use *MicroWorlds* as a design and learning environment where they can create animations, simulations, and games.

Chapter 13

Using the Computer to Learn Foreign Languages

¿*H*abla español? Parlez-vous français? Sprechen sie deutsche?

You don't? Well, never mind. Your computer does! And it can be a great help if your kids are learning a new language. Your computer can immerse your kids in the sights and sounds of foreign countries. It can tutor and test them. It can tempt them to explore new words, new people, new places. And it can translate all (well, not quite all) the hard work into fun.

How can you help your kids gain fluency in a new language? Here are some suggestions for both off- and on-the-computer strategies that you might want to check off your list:

Off the computer:

✔ **Talk to their instructor.** Many instructors will be happy to suggest language activities that nonspeakers (parents) and speakers (kids) can enjoy together. Some will even teach you a useful phrase or two! Get their recommendations for software, too.

With kids in the early grades, find out from the regular classroom teacher what they're reading in class; then get a foreign-language version. Hunt for words your kids know; try to "read" them together; let your kids correct your pronunciation!

✔ **Look and listen.** Our vocabulary and our place names owe a lot to other languages: cafeteria, plaza, marina, barbecue, tornado, boulevard, Des Moines, Los Angeles, Orlando, Montpelier, and the like. Make a game of guessing word derivations. And listen for words that are pretty much the same in native and target languages (telephone, animal, organization).

✔ **Mix and match.** As your kids' vocabularies grow, mix foreign words into everyday English. It's the kind of silliness — Set *la mesa* for dinner; *por favor espera;* Did you brush your *dentes*? — that encourages kids to master those weekly word lists.

✔ **Order take-out.** We're all multilingual when it comes to food: tacos and burritos, crêpes and soufflés, pizza and spaghetti, chow mein and sushi. Collect some take-out menus and practice ordering. Then let your kids order take-out by phone — in their target language!

On the computer:

✔ **Play with your kids' software.** It won't hurt you to learn some of the vocabulary your kids are practicing! But more important, you'll get a feel for how long your kids are likely to stick with different programs. That way, you'll know when it's realistic to nag them to practice longer! And you'll know when it's more sensible to call it quits.

✔ **Testing, testing, 1-2-3.** Buy a microphone, or test the one you have to make sure it works. Good foreign-language software gives kids spoken practice. Kids record themselves and then listen to their pronunciation; some products even assess their accent.

✔ **Say something silly.** While there's no alternative to memorization and practice, you can cheer your kids on by mastering some words and phrases of your own like *Vieni per dare un forte abbraccio a mamma!* (Come give Mom a great big hug!) or *Ausgezeichnet!* (Fabulous!). We show you where to find comments like these in the "Getting Wired" section of this chapter.

✔ **Take them surfing!** The foreign-language resources on the World Wide Web are great both for practicing and playing. Where else can kids sample jokes from French 5th graders? Learn how to say "Space — the final frontier" in Spanish? Hear the greetings that Voyager carried into space — in 55 languages?

You have several options when it comes to foreign-language software. For starters, you can use regular kids' programs that just so happen to have a second-language component to them. Most don't teach the language. But they do provide kid-friendly exposure. We tell you about them in the "Getting Started" section later in this chapter.

Next build your kids' enthusiasm with some language adventures. These programs do teach the language — but in highly unusual and inventive settings. You'll see what we mean in the "Getting Excited" section. The most conventional programs are in the "Getting Practice" section. And for Web adventures with foreign languages, check the "Getting Wired" section. You can find more ideas for older kids in *TakeCharge Computing For Teens & Parents,* published by IDG Books Worldwide.

PARENT TIP

Ready to add a foreign-language program or two to the family software library? ¡Muy bien! Klasse! Formidable! Bene! When it comes to picking out kid-pleasers, we like a combination of these features:

✔ **People, places, and experiences that matter to kids:** Learning a language is easier when the lessons focus on things kids care about. That way, kids can apply what they learn to their lives, right away. Programs with a focus on friends and family, school and home, sports and hobbies, vacations and birthdays, emotions and even some mild expletives(!) are good bets.

✔ **Kids' voices:** Whose voices do kids hear in their other software? Talking cows, perky rabbits, colorful aliens, globe-trotting crooks, cartoon kids. Almost *never* a grown-up. With foreign-language software, kids need to hear native speakers, enunciating carefully, speaking slowly. Usually they're adults. But not always. And it really boosts the fun factor when kids do the talking!

✔ **Lots of multimedia cues:** Even if they don't quite "get" what's being said, kids can often puzzle out the meaning — if there's a picture. Animations help, too. So do sound effects. For beginners in particular, look for great graphics and multimedia touches. For intermediate learners, "talk back" technology is important so they can practice speaking.

✔ **Gameplay that intrigues *your* kids:** Computer games can be a surefire path to learning. So let kids gain fluency while solving a mystery, exploring the rain forest, playing concentration, surfing the Web.

✔ **Plenty of practice:** Only practice can turn kids into confident, competent speakers. And software, while it can't take the place of real-life learning, can help enormously by giving kids opportunities to memorize vocabulary and grammatical constructs, imitate native speakers, take part in "virtual" conversations, and work at comprehension, both aural and reading.

Getting Started

Before you rush out to hunt up some great foreign-language programs, take a closer look at the software your kids already have. Many children's programs have a foreign-language component. You simply may not have noticed — because you didn't need it before.

The Living Books series (ages 3 & up)

This terrific series of interactive storybooks (also profiled in Chapter 4) is *the* best starting point for foreign-language exposure via computer.

If your kids are above the age of 8, however, be prepared for a mixed reaction at first. For starters, they'll protest that picture books are too babyish. Just ignore them! Launch a *Living Books* CD-ROM, and in the opening screen, choose the Spanish option (or Japanese, in *Just Grandma and Me*). As soon as your kids see the text in Spanish and hear the characters' rapid-fire conversations, the program won't seem so babyish after all!

Pretty soon, they'll be delighted. After all, these are the titles they perhaps loved and played incessantly not so long ago. The familiar stories and characters are a real advantage, too. They help make kids feel at home with a new language — even if kids can't quite understand the language yet.

Familiarity breeds . . . language smarts

Living Books are inviting for beginners because they focus on everyday topics that are important to kids:

- Squabbling with siblings
- Planning birthday parties
- Playing with friends, toys, and pets
- Going to school
- Tackling homework, and more

The vocabulary, the expressions, and the conversations in the text all relate to these kid-focused issues. And they're worth learning because kids can actually use them in real life!

Multimedia clues help learners

Hearing real kids talk in *Living Books* titles makes learning a new language more fun. Listening to the correct pronunciation and tone of voice by clicking words (again and again) is a big help. And the sound effects and hot-spot animations (clickable spots that trigger fun stuff) are *more* than mere fun. They serve a very real purpose for language learners: They give kids important clues about meaning.

Sound effects

Watch the opening scene in *Arthur's Teacher Trouble,* for example. The voice-over says, "La campana sonó." Then comes a sound effect: a dismissal bell. And guess what? Whether or not they learned it in class, kids immediately know that *campana* is bell and *sonó* means ring.

Animation

Take a look at Page 1 of *Arthur's Birthday,* shown in Figure 13-1, to see how animation can help.

Figure 13-1: Animations — and language learning opportunities — are hidden behind characters throughout this page.

In Figure 13-1, Arthur's sister DW is feeding the baby breakfast. Click the spoon, and kids hear DW say something that's not anywhere on the screen. The baby responds by wiggling and jiggling, opening wide, and gulping down a mouthful of cereal. It doesn't take long for kids to realize that when DW says *Ablar la bocita*, she means "Open your mouth." Chances are, they learned *boca* in school. Now they discover — on their own — that *bocita* is mouth, too.

Getting more mileage out of Living Books

Because no lessons *per se* are in these interactive stories, parents can find it hard to make language discoveries like these *stick* with kids. After all, if you don't speak Spanish, you can't incorporate new words into conversation. And you can't test the kids. (Well, you could try; but no self-respecting child would put up with that!) So other than simply playing the story in Spanish (and asking kids what the words mean), what else can you do with a *Living Books* CD-ROM?

- ✔ **Let kids turn the books that come with each CD-ROM into personalized picture dictionaries.** Show the book to the teacher and find out which words your kids are learning. Stick little white labels next to the appropriate pictures. Then encourage kids to fill in the Spanish words as they play the software.

- ✔ **Play I Spy.** Once the pages are labeled, you can use them to play "I Spy" at the computer. If the picture of "children" has a label, you say "I spy the children." But your kids should point, click, and respond in Spanish: "*Yo veo los niños.*" Chances are, their reward will be a fun animation.

- ✔ **Track down the hidden extras.** Lots of extra, unwritten dialogue is in *Living Books*. Click around together to find some of these special hot spots on each page. (Usually you can find them by clicking characters, but not always.) Then ask your kids to figure out what the characters said, writing it down first in Spanish and then translating it into English.

   Now play the CD-ROM in English together. Click the same hot spots, and see how close your kids come to being correct. They'll feel great when they're right. But being wrong can be fun, too — kind of like a game of telephone where the phrase gets pretty badly garbled.

Not all *Living Books* have a foreign-language option. The following titles all feature Spanish: *Arthur's Birthday, Arthur's Teacher Trouble, The Berenstain Bears Get in a Fight, Harry and the Haunted House, Just Grandma and Me, Little Monster at School, The Tortoise and the Hare,* and *Sheila Rae the Brave. Just Grandma and Me* also has Japanese.

OPEN

It's Not Foreign-Language Software, but You Can Learn a Lot From It!

You'll find fun and informative foreign-language activities in other kids' titles, too. But bear in mind: They're not designed as language lessons. It's up to you to encourage kids to explore their language options. Here's what *they* do — and what *you* can do with them:

Word Stuff

When played in English, this program is for *very* young kids. But played in Spanish, this interactive picture dictionary provides an excellent click-look-and-listen introduction to nouns, adjectives, and verbs.

In its I Spy mode of play, the program displays and pronounces words (in kids' voices) when kids click pictures. In the I Play mode, clicking triggers animated definitions of opposite words, noisy words, and action words. Click the baby carriage in the fair scene, for example, and a special window appears with three words below the carriage: *llovar, arrullar, reirse.* Click the first word, the baby bursts into tears, and kids learn that *llovar* means "to cry." After more clicking and more sound effects, kids discover the Spanish for coo and giggle. Scores of words are awaiting discovery in four settings: a farm, a campground, a snow scene, and a fair.

Encourage your kids to search those scenes for words they're learning in class and to click the print icon every time they find one. Pretty soon, they'll have a printed picture dictionary for use at homework time or in class. The pictures (along with their Spanish names) appear as line drawings that kids can color. Stick to one-word pictures for beginners — *unos patos* (ducks), for example. Later on, they can print the same picture with more detail: *las plumas de la cola* (tail feathers), *un ala* (wing), *un pico* (beak), and *un patito* (duckling). Figure 13-2 shows what you'll see on the computer screen before you print a page of "duck" words. (Sanctuary Woods, Ages 3 & up)

▶▶

Figure 13-2:
When you print this scene, Spanish vocabulary words replace the little rectangles with arrows, creating a labeled coloring book.

Kid Pix

By clicking the Spanish option in this paint program (profiled in Chapter 15), kids can hear the ABCs in Spanish, including *ch, ll* and *ñ* sounds, when they're using letter stamps. They can also hear the Spanish for numerals 0–9 and symbols like plus, minus, and equals. (Broderbund, Ages 3 & up)

The Gigglebone Gang World Tour

This lively geography title provides a wealth of fun facts about people and customs in ten different countries around the world. And when kids "visit" Mexico, they can play a game that teaches dozens of words in Spanish. (Headbone/Broderbund, Ages 4-8)

Mieko

This storybook introduces kids to five different languages: English, French, Spanish, German, and Japanese. Kids can listen to the story in one language and see the text in another. They can hear the alphabet and numbers 1-10 in all five languages. And for introducing vocabulary, the software displays scenes from the story with a blinking outline around the picture associated with each new word.

This CD-ROM is best, however, for kids who are learning Japanese. The story about a Nisei girl (an American child of naturalized parents who were born in Japan) and her encounters with her family's heritage provides kid-friendly explanations of Japanese beliefs, drama, clothing, music, architecture, customs, and more. And for hands-on fun, the title has a design-a-garden activity (pictured in Figure 13-3) and step-by-step origami (paper folding) instructions. (Digital Productions/Broderbund, Ages 5 & up)

Figure 13-3: Familiar click-and-drag art elements let kids create a simple garden.

Zurk's Rainforest Lab

Because Spanish is the language spoken in the rain forests of Central and South America, it's only fitting that kids can hear, read, and write Spanish in *Zurk's Rainforest Lab*. The heart of the program is Jungle Discovery, an interactive watercolor depicting scores of rain forest dwellers. As kids scroll from the understory to the floor to the canopy (play the game, and you'll learn what those terms mean), they can hear animals' names and realistic sound effects, read about them, or hear text read aloud. One click, and the language they hear and see is Spanish, as shown in Figure 13-4. Another click, and it's French!

Figure 13-4: Kids can try to read this passage themselves, or they can click the Ear icon to hear it read.

> **Rana venenosa**
>
> Los colores brillantes de la rana son una advertencia para sus enemigos. Tiene un veneno muy poderoso en su piel que puede matar a pájaros y animales pequeños. Los indios usan este veneno para untar las puntas de sus flechas y dardos, pero deben tener mucho cuidado al agarrar estas ranas.

As they explore, kids can snap pictures and make log entries for an on-screen photo album. For kids just beginning Spanish or French, those entries can be as simple as "I saw a toucan," the first two words familiar from class, the last word a term they can copy from the software. As their vocabulary grows, so can their descriptions: "It has colors I like: yellow, red, and green." Intermediate and advanced students can try to complete the story starters that pop up whenever they open the Photo Album. (Soleil/Maxis, Ages 5-9)

Copying can be a useful exercise. That's because writing (or typing) is a kind of repetition. And repetition is what helps kids remember. While some of the vocabulary in *Zurk's* pop-up text is fairly exotic, kids can find plenty of ordinary words, grammatical constructs, and expressions to copy for practice.

◄◄

Zurk's Alaskan Trek

Spanish and French in the 49th state? It's surprising, we admit! But we're always on the lookout for foreign-language activities that go beyond vocabulary drills. And *Zurk's Alaskan Trek* does just that. Playing to kids' interest in animals, it focuses on real-life scenarios in the Alaskan tundra, the Denali region, and the ice floes. And it lets kids use their foreign-language skills to script an animated wildlife adventure. (Soleil/Maxis, Ages 6-10)

■

Getting Excited

Language adventures are a great new way to keep up your kids' enthusiasm as they progress with their lessons. We profile two language adventures in this section. One is for kids who are still in the early stages of learning a new language, the other for intermediate students, kids, and adults alike. Because both are quite unlike any other language software available, we got really excited about them. (Hence the name of this section!) And we think your kids will, too.

Language Explorer (ages 7 & up)

The Language Explorer activity within the *World Walker Destination: Australia* (from Soleil/Maxis) CD-ROM does something exceptional: It creates an environment where kids really do seem to learn by osmosis. Language Explorer doesn't give kids vocabulary to memorize or drills to complete. And yet kids come away from it knowing the meaning of more than 350 words in French or Spanish, how to pronounce them, and how to put them together (correctly!) into meaningful sentences. (For information about software on the *Great Software For Kids & Parents* CD-ROM, see Appendix C.)

Here's how it happens.

Kids start by choosing among eight watercolor settings depicting food, sports, the body, seasons, city, bedroom/bathroom, kitchen/living room, and transportation. The scene they clicked now reappears, along with a colorful array of stylized pictures, symbols, words, and blank boxes. But there are no instructions about what to do; kids simply have to click, see what happens, and figure out what to do next. Here's a typical discovery process in the City setting, pictured in Figure 13-5.

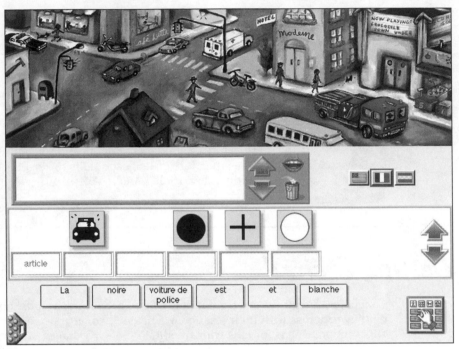

Figure 13-5:
Persistent clicking yields visual and sound clues that help kids drag these French words into a sensible order — and understand their meaning.

✔ Let's assume your kids are beginning students of French. When they opt to play in French by clicking the appropriate flag, what *they* see next is what *you* see in Figure 13-5.

✔ Now comes some experimental clicking. Nothing happens if they click the street scene; nothing happens if they click the mouth icon, the trash can, the empty boxes. (Not at this point, at least.)

✔ But when kids click the picture of the police car, a voice says, *La voiture de police*. Click the black circle, and they hear *noire*. The white circle says *blanche*. The result: They discover what the French words for police car, black, and white *sound* like.

✔ By now they've probably guessed that the words at the bottom of the screen belong under the pictures. So they test that assumption by clicking a word, dragging it beneath a picture, and releasing it. If they're lucky, they get a match the first time! And they quickly start dragging all the other words into place.

✔ But suppose they drag the word *blanche* under the black circle? As they watch it bounce back to the word bank below, they learn that *blanche* is not black.

✔ By the end of the click-drag-and-drop process, they've discovered what the French words for police car, black, and white sound like and what they look like. And thanks to the little pictures, they also realize that *La voiture de police est noire et blanche* probably means "The police car is black and white."

✔ Once the words are correctly assembled into a sentence, the software reads it aloud, and a new set of icons, blanks, and words appears.

Kids can build more than 200 sentences in Language Explorer, some as short as two words, others as long as eight. In doing so, they can teach themselves more than 350 words. Better still, they get hands-on experience with the parts of speech and sentence structure. Here are some of the grammatical rules kids can pick up by building sentences:

✔ Sentences can include pronouns, nouns, adjectives, adverbs, verbs, articles, prepositions, and conjunctions.

✔ Adjectives follow the nouns they modify in Spanish and French.

✔ Nouns have gender in French and Spanish.

✔ Adjectives "agree" with the gender of the noun they modify.

✔ The subject is sometimes understood as part of the verb in Spanish.

PARENT TIP

Urge your child *not* to click the American flag for a translation; with a little persistence they can probably figure out a sentence's meaning on their own. But occasionally it is instructive to toggle between English and French or Spanish. Take the sentence, "The man walks," for example. In French, it shrinks to *L'homme marche.* Seeing the sentence change from three to two words may help kids remember what the teacher said in class about articles and nouns that start with a vowel or the letter *H!*

Language Explorer also features a Concentration card game that uses the vocabulary words from the sentence-builder scenes. The words on the face-down cards can be in English and French, English and Spanish, or French and Spanish. Kids can play at three levels of difficulty, ranging from 10 to 36 cards. Success earns kids certificates for exceptional performance.

Kids can also opt to play the product's ecosystem activities in Spanish or French. And they can practice aural and reading comprehension with the multilingual reference cards that display information about 40 animals that are native to Australia. For a profile of *World Walker*'s natural science activities, refer to Chapter 11.

Who Is Oscar Lake? (ages 12 & up)

Who Is Oscar Lake? (from Language Publications Interactive) is a suspenseful adventure that has all the hallmarks of an intense, intriguing computer game. It gives kids a role to play, characters to meet, a mystery to solve, clues to track — and three different endings to discover. Oh, and by the way, it takes place *entirely* in Spanish, French, German, or Italian!

Language immersion on the computer doesn't get more fun than this.

The story

The scene opens in a train station. A telephone is ringing. Click the receiver, and a woman's voice says, "*Habla la Sra. Velasquez. Compra un billete. Toma el tren de las 5:45 para la Cuidad de Mexico.*"

Didn't quite get that? Click again for a repetition. Luckily, the words also appear on the screen. And even if your kids' Spanish is pretty basic, they'll probably recognize *el tren* and realize that they're supposed to take a train to somewhere in Mexico. Logic says they should go to the ticket booth (and so does the Spanish). A few clicks around this virtual environment, and they're at the ticket booth, conversing with the agent.

Whenever characters make comments or ask questions, kids get a choice of dialogue they can use in reply. Sometimes the choices are merely different ways of saying the same thing. Either of the replies pictured in Figure 13-6, for example, suffice in answer to the ticket clerk. But in other encounters, different replies can affect the outcome of the adventure.

After they're in Mexico City, with a few clicks and conversations, kids discover that their character is a diamond expert! Seems like fun until a notorious thief named Oscar Lake tries to frame you-know-who for the theft of a famous gem.

Kids can get pretty far along in the story on sheer gameplay smarts — click everywhere, explore everything, take notes — and basic language skills. But as the plot thickens, the language gets more complex. So before kids get frustrated, point out these two features, if they haven't already discovered them:

- **Starburst cursor:** Whenever the cursor turns into a starburst, kids can click to see the name of an on-screen object.

- **Translation button:** At the lower-right corner of the screen is a cluster of three buttons, pictured in Figure 13-6. Click the top one (showing three *a*'s, with accent marks), and translations appear beneath all the text on screen.

Figure 13-6:
Click one
of the two
possible
replies that
appear on-
screen, and
the dialogue
continues.

Urge kids to click *every* starburst they come across. By "meeting" as much vocabulary as they can, they're more likely to recognize those words when they come up in dialogue. But encourage them to use the Translation button sparingly. It's tempting to click for instant answers. But it's much better if kids try to make sense of a new expression or unfamiliar word on their own at first by using context clues and what they already know.

Language-learning activities

When trying to prove their innocence gets too intense, kids can take a break from the adventure and try some language-practice activities. At least they won't wind up in jail if they slip up on one of these exercises!

From the Activity menu, kids can choose among three types of activities set in six locations (train station, hotel, gallery, police station, street, or cafe). Some activities focus on following instructions, such as clicking certain objects or dragging them to a particular location. Other activities stress vocabulary and reading comprehension by asking kids to make the correct choice between two possible responses. And still others encourage kids to practice speaking by recording their answers to questions. All told, the activities provide focused exercises with some 1,200 words and topics, such as greetings, numbers, dates, telling time, colors, weather, clothing, food and drink, plural and singular constructs, directions, and more. Answer ten questions, and the software sends kids back into the adventure.

Try using *Who Is Oscar Lake?* to help reinforce what your kids are learning at school. Start by finding out from your kids exactly what's going on in class. Now pull down the Activities menu for a complete listing of practice exercises. Encourage your kids to spend time with the activities that best correspond to their classroom work.

Getting Practice

If you're looking for drill software, here's the good news. You have quite a few choices. Practice programs offer carefully paced, well-structured lessons. They have good explanations of the whys and wherefores of grammar and idioms. They provide lots of opportunities for learners to participate in conversations by recording their voices, typing dialog, or choosing among multiple-choice responses. And some drills even have voice-recognition technology that can assess a speaker's accuracy and accent.

Now for the bad news. Most drills are aimed at adults and business travelers. Very few are expressly for youngsters; that is, they don't feature kids' voices, situations, expressions, or graphics with kid-appeal. They focus mainly on situations that children aren't likely to encounter: finding a place to live, working with the maid, getting a taxi. The dialog is not particularly pertinent to kids: *Queiro encargar unos cheques de viaje. Cinco mil pesos, pero en sucres, de ser posible.* (I want to get some traveler's checks. Five thousand pesos, but in sucres, if that's possible.) Their "games" are not enough fun for kids, either.

But in some situations, adult-oriented language software *might* work for your kids:

- **If learning a new language is a family endeavor:** In this case, the whole family uses the software. That way, adults can help kids over the boring parts!

- **If particular lessons dovetail with classroom work:** It can be very helpful to practice the *same* vocabulary and expressions that kids encounter in class in a *different* way.

- **If your kids are bored by kid-oriented programs:** Adult titles are often more technically sophisticated, and often kids enjoy that.

- **If you're planning a trip abroad and your kids are the designated translators:** (Just a joke!)

Good choices at the adult end of the spectrum are available from The Learning Company and Syracuse Language Systems. The Learning Company offers two lines of language programs: the *Berlitz Think & Talk* series (in Spanish, French, German, and Italian) and the *Learn to Speak* series (Spanish, French, German, and Japanese). The skill-builder program *Practice Makes Perfect* can be used with either series. Syracuse Language Systems has three product lines for adults: the *Your Way* series (Spanish and French), the *Let's Talk* series (Spanish, French, German, Italian, and English), and the *TriplePlay Plus!* series (Spanish, French, German, Japanese, Hebrew, Italian, and English).

For *kid-friendly practice* software, we think your best bets are titles from Syracuse Language Systems. Our favorite is a collection of games called *All-in-One Language Fun* (from Syracuse Language Systems) that introduces more than 200 words and expressions in Spanish, French, German, Japanese, or English.

All-in-One Language Fun (all ages)

Kids start by clicking the language they're learning and then choosing among dozens of practice-makes-perfect games.

Kid-friendly features

Here's what we like about this product:

- ✔ **Foreign language only:** Once kids choose a language, that's the only language they hear. There are no translations. But kids take this in stride. From the pictures on the screen or by a little trial-and-error clicking, they can almost always figure out what to do.

- ✔ **Free play:** *All-in-One Language Fun* lets kids choose any learning game, at any level, any time they play. Because there's no carefully paced sequence of lessons, using the program "feels" more like play and less like practice (although it is, in fact, practice).

- ✔ **Explore mode:** Many of the title's games open with a Practice/Explore screen filled with objects and scenes. By clicking around for hot spots, kids can hear vocabulary and expressions *before* they click Go to start the game. Some kids like the opportunity to "meet" new words first. Others prefer to jump right into a game. But don't worry; they'll go exploring later to learn the words they couldn't guess.

- ✔ **Good topics for beginners:** The basics get a lot of reinforcement with this product because the words and expressions are pretty much the same ones kids learn in class. Topics include colors, shapes, sizes, numbers, parts of face and body, clothing, animals, classroom objects, fruit, vegetables, tableware, food and drink, household objects, preposi-tions, time, and the like.

✔ **Fun games:** The games in *All-in-One Language Fun* are standard kid fare: concentration, jigsaw puzzles, Simon Says, bingo, two-player contests, memory sequencing challenges, and lots more.

Turn up the volume on your computer speakers, and transform Simon Says into a game with family or friends. Station one person at the keyboard, and have the others gather at the far end of the room. Now follow Simon's directions. Every time kids follow an instruction correctly, they get to advance one step toward the computer. Players who make a mistake stay put. The first one to reach the computer wins — and trades places with the person at the keyboard.

Beginners only

All-in-One Language Fun is best for beginners. (It's also good for parents who want to keep up — or catch up — with their kids!) For intermediate stu-dents, however, the program has some drawbacks. There's no reading or writing. This limitation is OK initially because kids are focused on honing their aural comprehension skills. On the other hand, it doesn't give kids any practice with reading comprehension. They also don't have an opportunity to "talk back." The bottom line is that *All-in-One Language Fun* can take kids only so far. Once they've mastered its 200-word vocabulary, it's time to search out the kid-friendliest portions of adult-oriented products — or explore the Web-based options presented later in this chapter.

ᵒᴾᴱᴺ *TriplePlay Plus!*

After kids master the 200 vocabulary words and expressions in *All-in-One Language Fun,* the *TriplePlay Plus!* series is a good next step. It includes many of the aural comprehension games from *All-in-One Language Fun.* And it adds reading comprehension games and speech-recognition technology, so kids can work on pronunciation and conversational exchanges.

Before your kids choose a subject and a game, make sure they click the Child button in the upper-right corner of the main screen. This choice tells the computer to factor kids' voice characteristics — a beginner's less-than-perfect accent and slower-than-normal talking speed — into its evaluation.

▶▶

> *TriplePlay Plus!* covers six subjects: food, numbers, home and office, places and transportation, people and clothing, and activities. Although the 12 conversation games are adult-oriented, several are reasonably interesting for kids: At the Baseball Game, Moving In, At the Market, and Going on Vacation, among others. Kids may get a giggle out of some "adult" conversations, like this exchange in the At the Library scene: *What are you studying? I'm studying nuclear physics, and you?* The conversation ultimately leads to a spur-of-the-moment date at the movies! (Syracuse Language Systems, All ages)

Getting Wired

The World Wide Web is fast becoming one of the best resources for kids (and adults) who are learning a new language. We show you some all-purpose sites that serve as gateways to more information, sites where you and your kids can go for basics, and sites that are just plain fun.

Don't be surprised if your browser can't find a Web address you type. It's not your fault; and it's probably not our fault either! Blame it on the World Wide Web itself: Web addresses (and sites themselves) can be pretty fickle. Try looking for a "missing" site with a search engine. And try shortening the address by deleting everything after the `.com` (or `.org` or `.edu`).

Languages A to Z

These sites list other sites that list still more sites or provide lessons, dictionaries, and other online resources.

The Human-Languages Page

Our favorite gateway, organized alphabetically by language (from Aboriginal languages to Welsh), makes it easy to start searching for resources that are right for *your* kids. Type the following URL, and then click the first of the many categories listed. (`http://www.hardlink.com/~chambers/`)

Foreign Language Resources on the Web

This extensive list suggests useful sites where parents and kids can learn about more than a dozen languages, including Latin and Yiddish. (`http://www.itp.berkeley.edu/~thorne/HumanResources.html`)

Virtual language lessons

Do kids need lessons on the Web if they're studying a language at school? No, but using the Web is fun for kids. So it can be an appealing kind of "sugar-coating" for after-school practice. Besides, it can be helpful to tackle school topics in an unschool-like setting.

International language development

An excellent series of interactive language lessons in French, German, Japanese, Korean, Russian, and Spanish. Each lesson covers vocabulary, grammar, dialogues, and exercises. You also find information on the culture of the countries where those languages are spoken. Use `http://www.ild.com` to get to the home page, and then choose a language.

Foreign languages for travelers

Slick looking, easy to use, and not for travelers only! Kids start by selecting the language they speak. Next they choose the language they want to learn from a colorful menu of maps.

Finally they choose among seven lessons — basic words, numbers, shopping and dining, travel, directions, places, and time and dates — and get down to work. At intervals, kids can click the Take a Quick Quiz button and test their vocabulary smarts.

Taking quizzes like the one shown in Figure 13-7 is a good way for kids to study for tests at school. For one thing, the vocabulary in many of the lessons is similar to the words they're learning in class. For another, the tests are short. And the technology makes them kind of fun. So kids are often tempted to click New Quiz for another set of questions!

The URL for Foreign Languages for Travelers is `http://www.travlang.com/languages/`.

Fun stuff

Whenever conjugations get your kids down, venture onto some foreign language sites like these:

Star Trek Spanish

Don't ask us why, but the *Basic Spanish for the Virtual Student* Web site has a page featuring phrases from Star Trek III — In Search of Spock! Our kids took to saying ¡*Alerta roja!, ¡alerta roja!* (red alert) whenever they detected a parent in a bad mood. And memorizing the opening voice-over — *El Espacio, la última frontera. Son los viajes continuos de la astronave Enterprise* — helped their pronunciation! (`http://www.umr.edu/~amigos/Peliculas/Spock.html`)

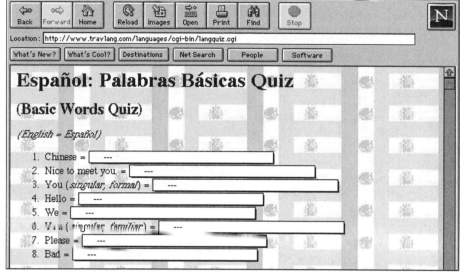

Figure 13-7:
A typical vocabulary quiz for students of Spanish.

Greetings to the Universe

If spacefaring aliens ever come in contact with the Voyager spacecraft, they can hear spoken greetings from Earth people in 55 languages. Your kids can hear them, too, at http://vraptor.jpl.nasa.gov/voyager/lang.html.

Inane Italian

Created by the makers of Ragu sauces (!), this site has a wonderfully funny collection of Italian phrases kids *won't* learn in school. It also gives parents a supply of remarks to use with the kids: *Hai già fatto it tuo compito per casa?* (Have you done your homework yet?); *Chi ne vuole ancora?* (Who wants a second helping?); *Abbiamo la famiglia piu bella del mondo* (We have the best family in the universe). (http://www.eat.com/learn-italian/index.html)

Japan Window

This site is the best-looking, kid-friendliest place on the Web for youngsters who are learning Japanese or studying Japanese culture. It lets kids begin learning Hiragana and Katakana, explore Kanji, play interactive storybooks, and explore cultural activities. (Kids can also find a restaurant section where they can practice phrases as they look at mouth-watering pictures!) Especially good for beginners is its multimedia picture dictionary, with a fun activity on every page. In the animal page pictured in Figure 13-8, for example, kids click to hear the sounds animals make in Japanese. Did you know that cats say *meow* in English but *nyaa* in Japanese? (http://jw.stanford.edu:80/KIDS/SCHOOL/LANG)

Figure 13-8:
Besides
animal
sounds, this
activity
contrasts
English and
Japanese
sound
effects
such as a
car horn
blaring or a
telephone
ringing.

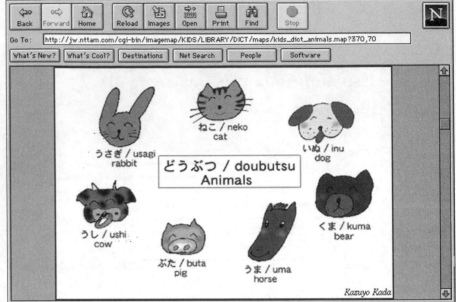

Just kidding

Kids (and parents) are really at home in a new language when they know
enough to understand jokes. You can find joke sites via many gateways
(listed in the preceding "Languages A to Z" section). One of our favorites is
Jokes in French at `http://www.jde.fr/jde5.html` from Les Journal des
Enfants.

Part VI
Creative Pursuits

The 5th Wave   By Rich Tennant

"I APPRECIATE YOUR COMPUTER HAS 256 COLORS. I JUST DON'T THINK THEY ALL HAD TO BE USED IN ONE BOOK REPORT."

In this part . . .

Make room on your refrigerator door and pull up extra chairs around the computer! The software in Part VI will inspire your kids to express themselves — and present their creations — in new ways, both on the computer and off.

More than any other kind of software, creativity programs let kids take total charge. Beginning with an empty screen, kids construct whatever they want to see (and hear). Equipped with an amazing array of creative tools, kids are free to explore the possibilities of computer graphics, sound, and animation in their own way, at their own pace.

If kids' creative explorations seem more like play than work, don't worry! Creativity programs provide subtle encouragement for kids to learn. Learn what? To envision an idea and follow it through, to try new things, to recover from mistakes, and to have confidence in their choices and point of view.

Part VI is filled with great creative software for kids of all ages. In Chapter 14, you find "cool tools" that really rev up kids ages 8-14. Chapter 15 covers must-have, general-purpose programs that spark the imaginations of kids of all ages (and parents, too).

Chapter 14

Cool Tools for Cool Kids

*W*hat happens when you put sophisticated technology in the hands of kids? Amazing things. Like pictures that play music. Photos that look like oil paintings. Animated 3-D stories. Web sites created for kids by kids. In this chapter, we introduce you to software that gets kids jazzed and helps them create remarkable things. It doesn't matter if your kids can't carry a tune, shoot a photo, or draw a straight line. All they need is an active imagination, a computer, and cool tools.

What exactly is a cool tool? It's a software program that lets kids create something extraordinary on-screen. Something they couldn't have done when they were little. Something they could never do at all without the computer. Here's how you can tell a cool tool when you see one:

___ *The Wow factor*

Cool tools wow kids! They're powerful, they're slick, and they let kids create something that's possible *only* on the computer.

___ *The Grown-Up factor*

At a certain age, kids begin to lose their interest in "kid stuff" software. But cool tools have the allure of the adult world; they're not just for kids.

___ *The Creativity factor*

Cool tools offer intriguing possibilities and rapid results. Because kids get so jazzed, they don't stop to ask: "Can I do it?" Suddenly, kids who can't read notes are creating music. And reluctant writers are typing up a storm.

Cool tools don't teach kids academic skills like grammar rules, math facts, or geography. But that doesn't mean kids aren't learning. On the contrary, cool tools immerse kids in creative ferment. And as they work, kids practice important skills:

- Focusing on a goal
- Organizing information
- Envisioning and testing ideas
- Seeking imaginative solutions
- Making decisions
- Learning from mess-ups

Cool tools are great to share with friends. Working in tandem, kids are less likely to get stuck. They feed each other ideas, work through problems, propose new approaches — often pushing their creative ideas further when they work together.

Your active interest can also help when your kids work with cool tools. What if you don't have a clue about musical composition or image editing? Don't worry! You'll help the most by taking an interest in their creations. Ask them to show you how they do it. These tools are so much fun you might even want to try yourself.

Making Music

It's easy to get kids started with art. A box of crayons, some markers, and a pad of paper, and they're off. But making music is not so easy. Kids need an instrument to play and lessons to learn how to play it before the fun can begin. So oftentimes, kids just listen to music rather than create it. But with *SimTunes* (from Maxis), composing music is as easy as painting colors on the computer screen. A combination music software, painting program, simulation and computer game, *SimTunes* is unlike anything your kids have ever seen. Using *SimTunes*' ingenious art and music tools, kids can add music to pictures, attach pictures to music, or experiment with the interactions between them.

SimTunes (ages 8 & up)

At first blush, *SimTunes* looks like an art program. Click on a color tool, and it paints the screen with tiny dots of color. Click on an eraser, and it wipes the dots away. But when four video-gamelike creatures waddle into the computer screen, things start to get more interesting. The computer creates wild bursts of sound and color every time one of these little creatures, known as the *SimTunes* bugz, bumps into a dot of paint.

And the sound bursts are always changing because each dot of paint plays a different musical pitch. Yellow is low C, for example. Sky blue is low G. Pink is D. Red is E, and so on. Paint a line of yellow, chartreuse, lime green, turquoise, light blue, sky blue, periwinkle, and purple dots, and kids have a musical scale. Paint blue, periwinkle, purple, pink, and they start chopsticks. But that's not all. Each of the bugz represents a different instrument family, so kids can hear their painted dots played as an oboe, a piano, a steel drum, an electric guitar, and more.

Playing with bugz

SimTunes features 40 different bugz (some shown in Figure 14-1), each with its own sound, shape, color burst, and name. (Adults especially will appreciate the pun-filled names.)

- ✔ High-pitched instruments are played by yellow bugz with names like Toot (the flute), Benny (clarinet), and Plucks (violin)

- ✔ Medium-pitched instruments are played by green bugz like Xylo (marimba), Ace (electric guitar), and Jo (banjo).

- ✔ Low-pitched instruments are played by blue bugz like Yo Yo Pa (cello) and Octavius (organ).

- ✔ Percussion instruments are played by red bugz like Tapper (conga), Zoundz (animal sounds), and Boomer (Latin drums).

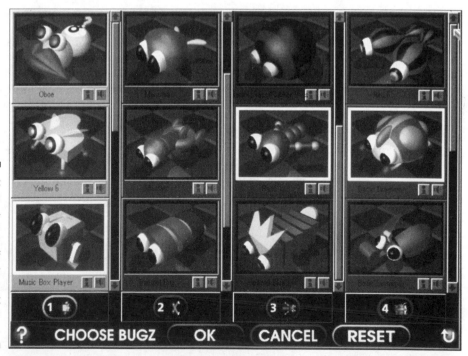

Figure 14-1: In *SimTunes,* kids can create a tapestry of sound by mixing colored art tools and 40 zany bugz.

Our favorites are the "loop" bugz, who sound off in chords or riffs or vocalize like an electronic Aretha Franklin or James Brown.

Learning about music

In *SimTunes,* the fundamentals of music — notes, rhythm, tempo, scales — come alive as kids noodle around with shapes, colors, sounds, and bugz. Absolutely no music training is required to create a Sim tune. And kids don't have to pay attention to the musical lessons implicit in the color dots or bugs — unless they're interested.

But suppose you'd like your kids to get interested in music. What's the best way to encourage their interest? Join your kids in an exploration of the tutorials in the *Bugmaster's Guide* that comes in the *SimTunes* package. As they step kids through the process of creating a Sim tune, the tutorials also introduce music concepts. For example, kids learn how to recognize different instruments, identify different musical scales, understand pitch, tempo, and rhythm, detect inverted patterns of notes, and much more.

Exploring the possibilities

As with all good creativity programs, kids can play *SimTunes* any way they want. And, initially, that's what they should do — simply paint the screen and experiment with the bugz to see (and hear) what happens. But at some point, kids may want some help. Then it's time to visit *SimTunes'* tutorial and gallery.

The Tutorial

This short interactive lesson introduces kids to *SimTunes'* unusual art tools, such as a rainbow pen that paints notes in a scale or the spray can that creates a cacophony of random notes. Kids will also find bug management tools, such as the tweezers, useful for moving bugz or changing the direction in which they travel.

The Bugmaster's Guide

Filled with information and tips, the *Guide* is a useful reference for kids who want to re-create familiar melodies in *SimTunes.* There's information about the Bugz instruments, instructions for using the advanced paint tools, plus special tips and fun things for kids to try.

The Gallery

Need inspiration? Watch and listen to a few of the more than 40 finished tunes in the gallery. One looks like a birthday card, and guess what it plays? An abstract painting plays rock and roll; a world map plays world music. If kids like a special effect, they can use the magnifying glass to take a closer look at how the effect was created.

Don't worry! If beeping, pinging, singing bugz are driving you crazy, show kids how to turn off the noise. You find the instructions for lowering or turning off bug sounds in the *Bugmaster's Guide*.

Advanced Bugmasters

Once they're comfortable picking out melodies with *SimTunes'* color dots, encourage kids to explore the program's advanced tools. They provide all sorts of visual and aural ways to elaborate on a simple tune. Kids love the cool effects they can create, like controlling a bug's direction and speed to create rhythm and tempo or making their bugz skip and dance around the screen.

It's show time! Sim tunes deserve an audience. Set a date and invite some friends or relatives over for a performance. An especially nice feature: Anyone can open and play a *SimTunes* file, even if they don't own the software. So kids can also surprise grandparents and friends with a *SimTunes* e-mail greeting.

Other Music Programs

We like music programs that transform the abstract structure of music (notes, scales, chords, and the like) into something concrete that kids can manipulate and explore. Just as math teachers use manipulatives to introduce kids to math concepts (see "Math Explorations" software in Chapter 6), music software helps kids learn about the fundamentals of music by playing with patterns, puzzles, and color blocks.

Juilliard Music Adventure

Here's the game: Nasty Gnoise has stolen all the music from the Queen's castle. Kids must figure out how to collect keys to open the doors to the throne room, free the Queen, and return music to the land. To claim the keys, kids must solve the many puzzles layered throughout this adventure game. What's this got to do with music? Each of the puzzles is carefully constructed to introduce a basic element of music like melody, rhythm, orchestration, or musical style. As kids throw themselves

▶▶

into the process of solving a puzzle to gain a much-needed key, they're learning about the structure of music. Kids can also use the program's rhythm and melody tools to create their own music. The software was developed in collaboration with educators at the Juilliard School of Music. (Theatrix Interactive, Ages 9 & up)

Thinkin' Things Collection 1 and 2

They're not music programs per se, but *Thinkin' Things Collection 1 and 2* both feature excellent games involving rhythm, sound, and melody. Spending time with Oranga Banga on the drums and Toony Loon on the xylophone helps kids sharpen their listening skills, their auditory memory, and their ear for rhythmic and musical patterns.

In *Thinkin' Things Collection 1* (ages 3-8), Oranga Banga plays rhythmic patterns for kids to recognize, remember, and play back. Toony Loon plays short musical patterns and then longer more complex ones for kids to repeat. Kids can also create rhythmic patterns and tunes of their own with percussion or xylophone. For the most fun of all, encourage your kids to click the Dark button. That makes the screen go dark, which means kids have to rely on their ears alone to play back rhythms or notes. In *Thinkin' Things Collection 2* (ages 6-12), Oranga Banga is joined by two other musicians who challenge kids to explore one-, two-, and three-part rhythms. Still playing solo, Toony Loon invites kids to create melodies or learn more than a dozen well-known songs. (Edmark, Ages 3-12)

Writing for the (Wired) World to Read

Creating a Web site is hot stuff for kids these days. But it takes far more careful thinking — and sustained effort — than other forms of online communication. By contrast, joining a kids' chat forum, sending an e-mail message, or clicking through other people's sites is kid stuff. To develop a Web site, kids not only need to ponder *what* they want to say, but also need to pay close attention to *how* they say it in order to craft their presentation so that it's interesting to other kids.

What's all this talk about the Web?

Just like computers, the Internet has its own set of buzz words. If you're new to the online world, you may not have encountered its vocabulary. As you read this section, if you run into an unfamiliar term, check this list for a quick definition.

✔ **Browser:** Special software you need to move around the Web. Most people use either *Netscape Navigator* or *Microsoft Internet Explorer* as their browser.

✔ **Home page:** The first page of a Web site.

✔ **HTML:** Short for HyperText Markup Language. This language is used to format Web pages so that they support hypertext links and can be read by Web browser.

✔ **Hypertext:** A cool technology that links one location on the Web to another. Click on a link on one Web page (it can be a highlighted word, a button, or a picture), and it jumps you directly to a different Web page. A hypertext link may take you to another page in the same Web site or to another Web site altogether.

✔ **ISP:** An Internet Service Provider. Your ISP leases you a connection to the Internet just like the phone company leases you access to the phone network. There are

many ISPs, both local and national, including companies like AT&T, Netcom, and Pipeline.

✔ **Modem:** Translates your computer's data so that it can be transmitted over the phone lines. In order for a modem to work, your computer must have special communication software installed on it. Chances are that a modem and communication software were already installed in your computer when you purchased it.

✔ **Server:** A computer that holds content (in the form of Web sites) that can be accessed by other computers on the Internet.

✔ **URL:** Every Web page has its own address called a URL or Uniform Resource Locator. A Web address is that string of letters and numbers you see sprinkled throughout the pages of this book whenever we refer to a Web site.

✔ **Web site:** A location on the Web. Sites are composed of one or more pages. A page is the visual equivalent of what you see on your computer screen.

✔ **World Wide Web:** The best way to access the Internet. The Web delivers a multimedia experience with text, pictures, animation, and sound.

Kids on the Web

There's a growing community of kids contributing to the Web, some through school projects, others as part of family pages, and still others with their own Web sites. Surf with your kids through the kids' sites on Kids on the Net (http://www.kidsonthenet.com) to see what kid sites are like. Kids mostly write about themselves (surprise, surprise), filling their page with details of everyday life, school, hobbies, friends, favorite TV shows, or computer games. They share jokes, riddles, stories, art, movie reviews, favorite Web sites. They ask other kids to send them e-mail. For a more original approach, take a look at David's Grab Bag Page, pictured in Figure 14-2. At this site, a 7 ¹/₂-year-old named David illustrates interesting facts about things he likes: the ocean, space, summer vacation. (`http://www.chas-source.com/sawchak/beach.htm`)

Getting started

Encourage your kids to spend time getting acquainted with the Web's distinctive environment *before* they begin work on their own page. Visit the sites noted in this book's WebVenture icons to get a feel for how pages are designed and information is organized. Then when they're ready, here's what they'll need to create a site:

___ *An online connection*

With a computer modem, families can connect to the Web via an online service like America Online or through an ISP.

___ *Web "real estate"*

Every Web site must be housed on a server. Server space is often available through the ISP that connects your family's computer to the Internet.

Figure 14-2:
On this Web site, a young author shares information about things he likes.

___ HTML translations

To be "viewable," Web pages must be formatted in a special language, called *HTML*. Kids can either learn to program in HTML or create their site with Web design software like *Adobe PageMill* or *HTML Web Weaver* that handles the HTML formatting for them.

___ A Web design tool

New Web design software tools make it easy to lay out text, graphics, and hypertext links — the basic elements of a Web page.

For more in-depth information about connecting to the World Wide Web, take a look at *The Internet For Dummies,* 3rd Edition, or *The World Wide Web For Kids & Parents,* both published by IDG Books Worldwide. If you and your kids want to venture into HTML programming, the *HTML For Dummies Quick Reference,* also published by IDG Books Worldwide, will help you get started.

Web Workshop (ages 8–14)

Web Workshop (from Vividus) is a Web design tool designed just for kids. This software program has several things going for it. It gives kids a step-by-step approach to creating Web pages. It handles the technicalities of HTML translation. It helps establish the necessary "real estate" with the family's ISP. Plus, its publisher offers many ways to help kids connect with other kids publishing on the Web. (For information about the software on the *Great Software For Kids & Parents* CD-ROM, see Appendix C.)

Web Workshop comes with everything kids need to create a simple Web site. It has the friendly look and feel of a kids' art program and an approach to Web page design so intuitive that even parents can do it! Here's how:

Step 1: Open a home page

A home page is the first page of any Web site and functions like a colorful, enticing book cover and table of contents rolled into one. From this page, readers learn who authored this site and what kind of information they'll find there. In *Web Workshop,* kids define their home page by saving it under the name Index. They should give any subsequent pages different names, such as Page 2, Page 3, and so on.

Step 2: Create a look

Web Workshop provides lots of ways to add visual pizzazz to a page. Kids start with the Add Graphics button to select artwork. Then they choose from a library of backgrounds, page dividers, and clip art or create original graphics with *Web Workshop*'s basic drawing and painting tools. The possibilities expand when kids copy and paste pictures or text from other programs or purchase additional *Web Workshop* art packs.

Step 3: Add words

To add words, kids click on the Type & Paint button. Choosing Text opens a box, like the one shown in Figure 14-3, that expands to hold text as kids type. When they're finished typing, kids click the mouse, and their text becomes an "object" that can be moved anywhere on a page. In *Web Workshop,* kids can easily move any design element — text boxes, clip art, dividers, graphics — by clicking and dragging the element to a new position on the page.

In *Web Workshop,* constructing a page is so simple that it's easy for kids to skip the hard part: thinking things through. This is where you come in. Talk with your kids about what they want to say. Encourage them to think about their audience. What will make their site interesting enough for other kids to want to read? And make sure they understand the rules of the Web:

- ✔ *Never* give out any personal information like your phone number or address.

- ✔ Be mature and responsible about what you say.

- ✔ Tell your family about any e-mail from strangers.

- ✔ Tell your family if you encounter anything on the Web that makes you feel uncomfortable.

For an excellent overview of Web safety for both kids and parents, check Kids on the Net. (http://www.kidsonthenet.com)

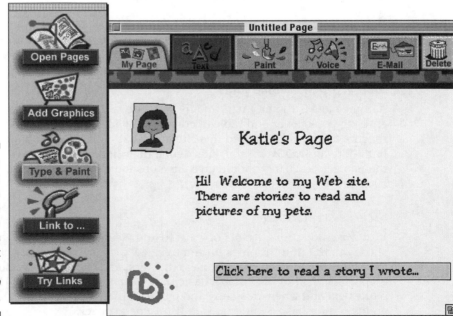

Figure 14-3: To design her Web page, Katie used the graphics and text tools in *Web Workshop* .

Step 4: Create links

One of the Web's coolest features is *hypertext,* a linking technology that lets readers click on a word or picture and jump instantly to a different spot on the Web. In *Web Workshop,* clicking on the Create Links button lets kids add *hypertext links* to their site. What's more, it encourages kids to link to kid-appropriate sites by providing a library of instant links, including the following:

- ✔ **Yahooligans!:** The Yahoo! directory of recommended Web sites for kids

- ✔ **Cool Sites:** Kid sites selected by the program's publisher

- ✔ **Kids Clubs:** Collections of kid-created sites organized around topics like music, sports, and cartoons

Kids can also create links to *any* site on the Web as long as they know its URL. To help kids connect with other kids, be sure they add a link to Kids Clubs and Kids on the Net, another collection of kid-authored sites.

If you feel uncomfortable (as we do) giving your kids free range on the Web, look into a parental control program to block material you may not want them to see. You'll find more information about these programs on the Kids on the Net Web site. (http://www.kidsonthenet.com)

Step 5: Publish

Before kids publish their work online, consider adopting a family "Web oversight" policy to review *how* and *what* they're presenting.

- ✔ Proofread your kids' pages to help them get in the habit of checking their own work. (*Web Workshop* does not include a spell checker.)

- ✔ Discuss whether the information they've chosen to share and the manner they've chosen to present it are appropriate for a public audience.

- ✔ Asking other kids online for their experiences with sibling spats, for example, is an OK way to cope with big-kid–little-kid troubles. But it's not OK to name names and trash a sibling online, for all the world to see! Work with your kids to make changes. But make it clear that *you* are the final arbiter of what goes online.

- ✔ Finally, test the links kids put in their site, double-checking to see that they take kids to the sites they intended.

Before a site can go online, it needs a "home" on an Internet server. Your best bet for server space is with your ISP. Before you can publish a *Web Workshop* file, you need to contact your service provider to learn the address of the directory for Web files on your account. You can also contact Vividus, the developers of *Web Workshop,* at http://www.vividus.com, to learn more about their hosting service for kids' sites.

OPEN

Other Web Publishing Programs for Kids

Web page design tools — for adults as well as kids — is a new and growing category of software. As more of these programs emerge, more kids will produce their own pages, and the community of kids communicating on the Web will grow. Here are two other programs that also offer Web publishing tools for kids.

Net Explorations with Web Workshop

A good choice for families new to the Web, *Net Explorations* combines all *Web Workshop*'s Web page-design tools with a set of "tours" introducing kids to the Web's resources. Organized around educational themes, the tours include Web sites to visit, questions to explore, and off-the-computer projects that build on the information kids collected online. One tour, for example, takes kids to the White House Web site for kids and then encourages them to send e-mail to the president. As with most Web activities, these explorations are best for kids and parents together.

Net Explorations also offers free server space for children's Web sites. The program's publisher will host Web sites free for 30 days and at minimal cost thereafter. And for families who aren't Web connected, *Net Explorations* comes with all the software and connections families need to go online. (Sunburst Communications, Ages 8-14)

Creative Writer 2

Chock full of art and publishing tools, *Creative Writer 2* also provides a set of page layouts to help kids design Web pages. The program's construction process is not as intuitive as *Web Workshop,* so check the tips in "Creating a World Wide Web Page" under the Help button's list of How-Tos. But the upside is more clip art, sound effects, and music to embellish kids' sites. (Microsoft, Ages 8 & up)

Playing with Pictures

As kids reach the double-digit age, they begin to look for "bigger" computer challenges — like the kind they find in "not just for kids" programs. Oftentimes this means games, with their sophisticated graphics and "action" story lines (and no classroom connection whatsoever!). But it can also mean adult "tools," too. Give imaginative kids an adult creativity program like *Adobe PhotoDeluxe,* and some very cool things can happen.

Adobe PhotoDeluxe (ages 10 & up)

Since the introduction of *Adobe Photoshop* over a decade ago, this software tool has changed the way designers, artists, and photographers work with photo images. Now with *Adobe PhotoDeluxe,* a kind of junior *Photoshop* for everyday users, kids (and families) can experiment with many of these same powerful photo-editing techniques. In *Adobe PhotoDeluxe,* kids can make a new photo look old, fracture a familiar image into a kaleidoscopelike abstraction, or put the cat's head on the body of their pesky little brother! For kids who like to make things, *Adobe PhotoDeluxe* also presents a series of well-organized lessons on producing cards, posters, calendars, report covers, and more — all illustrated with personal photographs. (See the sample report cover in Figure 14-4.)

Figure 14-4: *Adobe PhotoDeluxe* includes step-by-step tutorials for adding photo images to school report covers, cards, calendars, and more.

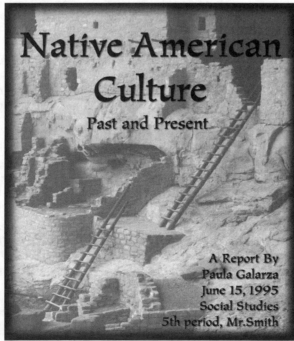

Working with photographs on the computer

In order for the computer to work with a photographic image, the photograph must first be *digitized*. To digitize an image means to convert the picture to a *digital image,* a set of bits that can be processed by the computer. Here are three ways to digitize your photographs.

✔ **Digital camera:** This camera works like any other, except instead of capturing images on film, the pictures are stored in the camera's memory as digital images. The camera can then be attached to the computer to transfer the images to the computer's hard disk.

✔ **Flat-bed scanner:** A flat-bed scanner looks and works much like a small copy machine, except that it's connected to your computer. When the scanner takes a picture of your photograph, it converts your photograph into a digital image and stores it in your computer.

✔ **Photo CD:** With a Photo CD, you can use your plain old film camera to produce digital images. You take pictures by using standard film. Then when it's time to process the film, ask for a Photo CD disc along with your prints. With your standard glossy photos, you get a CD-ROM disc filled with digital images of your photographs. You then can put the CD-ROM into your computer and read the photos by using software like *Adobe PhotoDeluxe.* Best of all, this option lets you create digitized images without buying any more computer equipment.

✔ **Photo scanner:** Smaller than this book, a photo scanner is optimized to convert standard-sized photographs to digital images. Because it costs less than a flat-bed scanner and takes up less room next to your computer, a photo-scanner is well suited for home and school use.

Using family photographs

Personal is the operative word here. While *Adobe PhotoDeluxe* includes a library of stock photos, the real fun comes when kids manipulate images from their own lives — assembling a collage of pictures from summer camp, building a screen-saver from family snapshots, or illustrating a card with a picture of a favorite pet.

Before *Adobe PhotoDeluxe* can work with personal photographs, however, each photo must first be converted into a digital image that the computer can read. Your family can accomplish this in several ways: Use a scanner or photo reader, take pictures with a digital camera, or develop regular film as digital images on a floppy disk or photo CD.

If you don't own a scanner, see whether your local copy shop offers a photo scanning service. And check with your local film developer to learn about developing film or transferring negatives onto a CD-ROM, which can store as many as one hundred photos in a computer-ready file format.

On the computer, image files are real space hogs. One 4 x 6-inch photograph may take up 2MB or more on your hard drive! Because you can't give up lots of space to photo files, it's important to help kids manage their images. Encourage them to work with one image at a time, storing others on a floppy disk or external hard drive.

Photo-editing fun

For adults, *Adobe PhotoDeluxe* has a practical side: You can remove those flash-induced red eyes! You also can resize photos for family newsletters, adjust a photo's color contrast for your annual Christmas card, and the like. But for kids, the razzmatazz effects that can transform a photo into something entirely different are where the real fun is. Just watch them blur an image with a visual gust of wind, stretch a cheek-to-cheek smile into a shoulder-to-shoulder grin, disguise friends or relatives with a pair of glasses and a funny hat, twist their brother's face till he's all out of shape, or put their best friend's face on a one hundred dollar bill (see Figure 14-5).

Adobe PhotoDeluxe shows kids how to use its sophisticated tools in a series of simple step-by-step tutorials. Who said the grass had to be green? Turn it blue or black by following the Tint tutorial's four steps. First get a photo — from the samples included with the program, from a photo CD, from a set of digitized family photos. Next select the area of the image to be altered. Then click on the Hue/Saturation button that's right there in the tutorial. Three scales — hue, saturation, and lightness — appear on the screen. As kids slide a button along each scale, they can watch how the color changes from green to blue. When they're happy with the change, they click on OK. *Adobe PhotoDeluxe* even prompts kids through those all-important, final steps — saving and printing their tinted image.

Want to know more about hue and saturation? Do your kids ever wonder why apples are red and the grass is green? Families can learn about the science of color with a visit to "Make a Splash with Color," the online exhibit at The Tech Museum of Innovation of San Jose, California. (`http://color.thetech.org/hyper/color/intro/`)

Publishing their work

Besides experimenting with photo transformations simply to see what happens, here are ways kids can use *Adobe PhotoDeluxe* for more polished productions, both on and off the computer:

- Print edited images on cards, invitations, book covers, or as stand-alone artwork.
- Export images to a word-processing or publishing program for use as illustrations in reports or newsletters.
- Publish images on World Wide Web sites.

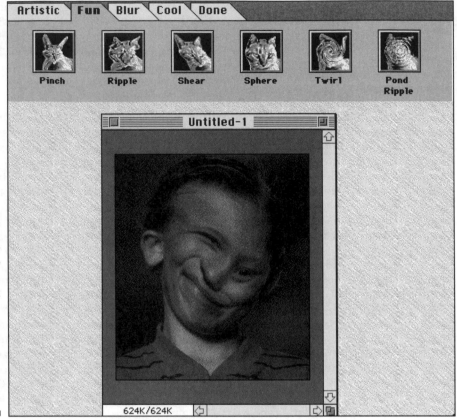

Figure 14-5:
Adobe PhotoDeluxe lets kids experiment with photo-editing effects like twisting, shearing, rippling, and smudging.

For picture-perfect publishing, consult the advice about formatting and sizing photographs for the Web in the *Adobe PhotoDeluxe* user's guide. And be sure kids credit the source of any photographs that are not their own.

EasyPhoto Reader (all ages)

Adding photographs to computer creations is great fun, but extra trips to the photo or copy store to turn pictures into computer files are not. That's why we like photo scanners made just for family snapshots.

Take *EasyPhoto Reader* (from Storm Technology), for example. This handy
little box, which plugs right into the back of your computer, scans standard
photographs (print sizes up to 5 x 7-inches) one by one and stores the
digital images in a "gallery," illustrated in Figure 14-6. Because you can set
up as many galleries as you like, you'll find they are a useful (and visual)
way to organize your images. *EasyPhoto Reader* also comes with a CD-ROM
filled with more than 450 stock photos, another reason why it's a nice add-
on for *PhotoDeluxe* users.

Once images are stored in a gallery, kids can easily move them to another
program for editing and illustrating cards, a Web site, or school report, or
what have you. *EasyPhoto DesignWorks,* packaged with the *EasyPhoto
Reader,* also offers design and layout tools for family projects like slide
shows, photo collages, albums, and newsletters.

Figure 14-6:
The
galleries in
*EasyPhoto
Reader*
are a
convenient
way to
store photo
images.

OPEN

More Cool Tools

Here are some more cool special effects and animation software for kids (and parents) to try. Kids can use the tools and techniques in these programs to create their own versions of popular media images they've encountered in movies, magazines, TV shows, and computer games.

Morph

When kids "morph" something, it changes into something different right before their eyes. Your kids have probably seen this visual technique in TV ads and movies, and now they can try it for themselves. Watch their eyes light up as they transform the family cat into a fire-breathing dragon or a sibling into Homer Simpson. For kids excited by the techniques in *Adobe PhotoDeluxe,* the animations in *Morph* are a good next step. (Gryphon, Ages 10 & up)

Kai's Power Goo

For kids who are enamored with special effects, *Kai's Power Goo* creates fabulous caricatures by smearing, stretching, shrinking, and distorting images in lots of imaginative ways. The software includes lots of photos of people and animal faces to play with. Plus ambitious kids can animate their effects. (MetaTools, Ages 10 & up)

Amazing Animation

This multimedia tool kit is good half-way product for kids who've outgrown the animated stamps in *Kid Pix Studio* but aren't quite ready for the discipline of *3D Movie Maker.* The basic animation is so simple a 3-year-old can do it. Kids choose a stamp and move it around the screen. The software remembers the path they chart and replays it as an animation. For added variety, kids can use the paint tools to create — and animate — original art.

▶▶

Later they can experiment with more advanced animation controls like rotating or resizing. They can also create a "movie" by linking a series of animated screens, complete with wipes, pauses, and other special effects. You also find a collection of sound effects. Or kids can add their own with a microphone. (Claris, Ages 5-12)

3D Movie Maker

While these productions aren't quite ready for the big screen, they do give kids a realistic feel for what's involved in creating an animation — and kids love the 3-D effects. Kids begin in the Project Room where a 3-D wizard named Melanie explains all the decisions kids need to make. Kids pick a set; choose camera angles; select characters and determine their movements and dialogue; add props, sound effects, and a soundtrack; and then synchronize all the elements — scene by scene. Mastering the process requires persistence. But once kids get the idea, they can have a lot of fun creating their own kooky flicks. (Microsoft, Ages 10 & up)

Chapter 15

Painting, Publishing, and Perusing Art

• •

• •

*I*f you've got kids, you've got art! If you're lucky, it's on paper, a black board, an easel, or the sidewalk. But chances are, it's on their hands and overalls, and your kitchen floor, too. For children, drawing and painting are as natural as walking and talking. It's one of the ways they interpret the world around them and express their thoughts and feelings. And it's one of our jobs as parents to encourage that creativity.

But what if you can't even draw a recognizable stick figure or tell a Picasso from an O'Keeffe?

Don't worry. Parents — even artistically challenged parents — can do some simple things to encourage kids' artistic pursuits.

____ *Fill your home with art supplies kids can use anytime.*

The supplies don't have to be expensive: crayons, markers, paper, scissors, glue, and glitter are great for starters. As kids grow, provide new tools to encourage new skills.

____ *Show an interest in what your kids create.*

Be their audience. Create a "gallery" for displaying their work.

_____ *Help your kids discover the elements of design.*

Look for lines, light, shapes, colors, sizes, and patterns in the world around you — and point them out in your kids' artwork.

_____ *Look at art together.*

Plenty of art books are designed especially for kids. But your dusty art history textbook, old magazines, and library books are fine, too.

_____ *Make an art program one of the first additions to your software library.*

Because kids can make something different every time they play, they'll use creativity programs for years.

Do Kids Really Need Art Software?

We know what you're thinking: My kids already have hundreds of crayons, six kinds of paint, a barrel of chalk, plenty of modeling clay, not to mention art projects at school. Do they really need art on the computer, too?

Our answer: Yes! Art on the computer is an innovative addition to your supply cupboard, exciting for art enthusiasts, and encouraging for reluctant artists. Here's why:

- ✔ **It's filled with possibilities.** In just one art program, kids find hundreds of tools, techniques, and activities to explore.

- ✔ **It's funny.** With silly sounds and lots of animated surprises, art software brings a special brand of playfulness to the creative process. It gives kids a chance to express their own brand of humor, too.

- ✔ **It's forgiving.** Creativity software encourages kids to try new things. Starting over is easy if they don't like something. Just click the Undo button, and the offending artwork disappears. Plus, there's no clean up!

Different kinds of art and creativity software appeal to kids of different ages. In Chapter 14, we spotlight creativity programs that put a new spin on music, photography, and writing. This chapter looks at three different ways to experience art with a computer: painting, publishing, and appreciating.

We talk about creativity programs in other chapters of this book, too. For little kids, read about *Paint, Write & Play!* in Chapter 3. For all ages, check out the writing programs in Chapter 5 since they also include illustration and printing capabilities.

Painting and Producing

In the real world, paint is for painting. But on the computer, paint programs do a whole lot more. Like an enormous box of art supplies, the software in this section is bursting with goodies. Some are on-screen variations of familiar stuff: tubes of paint, markers, stamps, erasers, and stencils. Others are unique to the computer: brushes that paint plaids or sparkles or numbers and letters; footprints that stomp noisily across the screen; and pencils that draw rainbow-colored lines.

With the screen as their canvas, kids can doodle, explore subtle gradations of color, assemble a collage. Kids can color inside the lines, if that's what they want to do. But they don't have to. The grass can be purple, if they want. Or the sun can set in the East. Anything goes with paint programs. Best of all, they never run out of anything!

Kid Pix Studio (ages 3–12)

Kid Pix Studio is one of our all-time favorites. It's got a zany kid kind of humor. It's got a one-of-a-kind look. And it's got tons of inventive art tools and activities that can keep kids (and parents) happy for years.

Kid Pix is a great example of a classic kids' program. Originally created by an art professor for his young son, *Kid Pix* was introduced well over a decade ago. But through the years, Broderbund, the program's publisher, has continued to improve and expand the program to take advantage of new technology. The latest version, called *Kid Pix Studio,* adds animation, music and sound to the program's whimsical art tools. The happy result: *Kid Pix Studio* is actually two studios in one: an incredibly well-stocked, on-screen studio for creating colorful, noisy artwork and a wild multimedia studio for creating simple animations.

An art studio

For little kids, exploring *Kid Pix Studio* is a great adventure in itself, whether or not they even get around to making a picture. Start them in the art studio. Even toddlers who can't really draw with the mouse find plenty to do just by clicking around.

As kids try each tool, they encounter the basic building blocks of visual design: lines, geometric shapes, colors, and patterns. And they have a special brand of fun.

They can blast a picture to smithereens with a stick of dynamite. They can "erase" a seemingly blank screen to reveal a hidden picture. They can power up the Electric Mixer to turn a picture into kaleidoscope fragments or another zany transformation. And they can stamp their scenes with genies, princesses, dinosaurs, fire engines, dragons, pagodas, windmills, stars, teacups — more than a thousand stamps in all.

Kid Pix Studio is filled with fun surprises for kids of all ages. Take its wacky paint brushes, for example. Clicking the paint brush tool summons an array of 84 different ways to paint the screen. Choose one brush, and paint drips down the page; click another, and hugs and kisses (in the form of Xs and Os) appear everywhere. Other choices produce a spattering of rainbow-colored dots, a sprinkling of buttons and bows, or a line of brightly colored bugs that squeak across the screen. Figure 15-1 shows a screen filled with some of the wonderful patterns and special effects kids can create with a wacky brush.

Stick around when very young children use *Kid Pix Studio*. The tool box and color palette that pop up on the screen are small, so it's sometimes hard for little kids to aim the cursor and select exactly what they want. They may also need your help with pull-down menus to open and save files.

Figure 15-1:
In *Kid Pix Studio,* kids can use wacky brushes to make follow-the-dot pictures, spray clouds, and rainbows on the screen, or create cartoons.

An animation studio

In the animation studio, kids add sound and movement to their *Kid Pix* artwork. In Moopies, the wacky brushes paint moving images like falling raindrops, somersaulting letters or color spots that shimmer their way across the page. In Digital Puppets, kids choose a puppet — an Egyptian princess, a space alien, an elf, or a dragon, for example — and direct its movements by pressing letters on the computer keyboard. Each letter creates a different action — a wink, a kick, a wave. When kids combine the movements and push the first button in the control panel (see Figure 15-2), the software records the sequence as 30-second animation.

Figure 15-2: In *Kid Pix Studio,* kids can make Doofus the elf dance by tapping keys on the keyboard.

Older kids can turn their imaginations loose producing animated scenes. Say that your kids decide to make a pink elephant dance up the Leaning Tower of Pisa, like the picture in Figure 15-3. They can do this in, literally, a 1-2-3 process. Here's what they do:

1. **Open the Stampimator, and select the Leaning Tower from the background menu.**

2. **Choose the pink elephant stamp.**

3. **Hold down the mouse button and drag the elephant around the screen.**

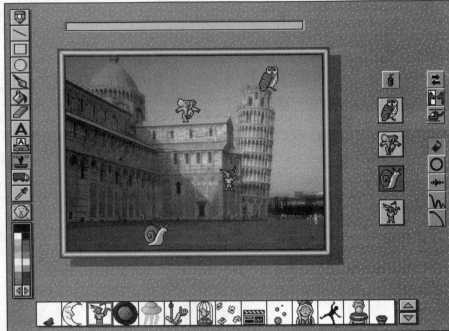

Figure 15-3:
In *Kid Pix Studio,* kids create animated scenes with simple point, click, and drag movements.

The software remembers that zig-zag motion and repeats it again and again. If that's not silly enough, kids can click the Pick a Sound menu and select a trumpet fanfare or an African drumbeat to play as the pachyderm pirouettes. Need mood music? Kids can attach a song clip — a tango, perhaps, or a carnival rhumba — to the scene.

In the slide show, kids can bring together every element of *Kid Pix Studio* and assemble pictures, animated scenes, digital puppets, music, and their own recorded voices in a multimedia creation to share with family and friends.

If your kids love to produce multimedia shows on the computer, consider a program with more sophisticated animation tools. Look for some recommendations in the "More Cool Tools" section of Chapter 14.

For kids who really love computer art, consider investing in a graphics tablet like *kidDraw* (from kidBoard) or the *Wacom Art Pad* (from Wacom). Kids of all ages can use a special pen to draw on the tablet that transmits the image to the computer screen. The result: far more control than they can get with a mouse.

Other Paint Programs for Kids

Borrowing features from high-end paint programs used by professional artists, these programs offer digital tools that replicate the look and feel of real art materials like oil paints, watercolors, or pastels.

Art Explorer

A good choice for kids 7 and older with a Macintosh computer, *Art Explorer* combines sophisticated painting tools with fun activities. In addition to the usual paint brushes and pencils, kids can create with calligraphy pens, charcoal, magic markers, and finger paints and use special electronic effects like twisting or smearing. The program offers a huge selection of colors that kids can alter with intriguing techniques such as glazing or tinting. For kids who like to build pictures with stamps, *Art Explorer*'s extensive stamp collection, organized around themes like Aqua World, Superhero World, Prehistoric World, or Fashion World, comes in three variations: Stamp Itz, where kids arrange stamps on a background; Color Itz, where kids paint their stamps; and Build Itz, where kids assemble stamp parts to create their own sea creatures, aliens, or funky cave men. (Adobe, Ages 8-12, Macintosh only)

Dabbler

Dabbler is for kids who take their art seriously. Working in an electronic sketchbook, kids experiment with traditional art media, such as oil paints, chalk, or pen and ink. *Dabbler*'s tools look and act like the real thing. Markers bleed, chalk smudges, crayons leave a waxy trail, and the effect of each tool changes depending on which of the program's 100 plus paper textures kids select. Instead of stamps or wacky brushes, *Dabbler* emphasizes a more grown-up approach to computer art. It offers features like 16 different color palettes (plus a color wheel so kids can create their own palette), stencil shapes, special digital effects such as blur and distort, tracing paper for crafting frame-by-frame cartoon animation, and two multimedia tutorials that demonstrate how to draw and animate cartoons. (Fractal Design, Ages 8 & up)

Orly's Draw-A-Story (Ages 5–9)

Here's a paint program (from Broderbund) with personality! Meet Orly (short for Orlando), a spunky kid who lives on the island of Jamaica with her family and her pet frog, Lancelot. Blessed with an active imagination and a penchant for storytelling, Orly invites kids to join her stories by creating pictures that she weaves into her tales.

And what tall tales they are. There's the story about the strange princess who's distraught when her kisses transform frogs into handsome princes, or the one about the little Explorer bug whose ship is capsized by a huge sea monster, or the troll girl who begs the magic dragon to make her the ugliest girl in the world. As Orly tells each story, she pauses to involve kids: "OK, man. We need a picture of a frightening sea monster . . . a beautiful princess . . . an ugly troll girl." Each story transports kids to the Drawing Pad where they can draw their pictures from scratch or select an already-started line drawing to color and paint.

3-D painting

Orly's Drawing Pad, pictured in Figure 15-4, is simple, but immensely satisfying. The paint pots have the look (and almost the feel) of real paints. The 3-D textures range from realistic (bricks, basket weave) to radical (cheetah fur, Swiss cheese). When kids paint, the colors always stay in the lines. Orly cheers kids on with encouraging comments like "I can't wait to see what you're going to draw!" or "You sure made that scary looking." But best of all, kids see the creations they draw and paint come alive in the very next scene of the story.

Storytelling fun

Orly also invites kids to spin their own tales.

In the program's Make Your Own Storybook section, kids find all the tools they need to write a story, illustrate it, add sounds, and play it back on the computer. They can use background scenes, characters, and props from Orly's stories or create their own. And Orly's there to inspire them with story starters ("That story is about when Lancelot and me ran away from home." "That story is about when me and Lance found that magic potion inside the old pirate's chest.") Kids continue writing the story in the text window, which works like a simple word processor.

Orly's creativity tools are great, but it's Orly and her vivid imagination that distinguish this program from other art software. A funky, funny presence, Orly's an ever-present companion, sharing her wild stories, talking to kids as if they were right by her side, encouraging their participation, cheering on their drawings, and making them laugh.

Figure 15-4:
In *Orly's Draw-A-Story*, kids can paint with 3-D textures like raffia, leather, and psychedelic swirls.

If your kids love Orly's jammin' Jamaican tunes as much as ours do, you'll be glad to know that you can play the software CD-ROM on your audio CD player, too. Just place it in the player, and select Track 1 (if you have a newer CD player) or Track 2 (if you don't).

Designing and Publishing

As kids get older, they begin to use art programs not just for self-expression but as a form of communication, too. Besides dabbling, drawing, painting, and playing, kids become interested in producing things on the computer for off-the-computer purposes. They love to make cards, add pictures to thank-you notes, print illustrated covers for school reports, produce comic strips, create flip books. In short, they're into publishing!

That's where publishing programs come in. Their powerful design tools and huge collection of graphics help kids create polished, professional-looking results.

Publishing programs aren't just for kids. In one computer-savvy family we know, the kids produce party invitations, birthday cards, and thank-you notes; the mom tackles their annual Christmas letter, gift tags, and Brownie newsletters; and the dad handles Little League standings and garage sale posters.

The Print Shop (ages 9 & up)

Because they're so versatile and easy to use, publishing titles like *The Print Shop* (from Broderbund) are great additions to any family software library. Here's a quick look at how your kids can put *The Print Shop* to work.

Pick a project

What do your kids need today? A Halloween party invitation, a birthday card for a best friend, a sign to keep little brothers (or sisters) out of their rooms, a cover for the big social studies report? Step one: Kids click on a project choice in *The Print Shop* menu pictured in Figure 15-5.

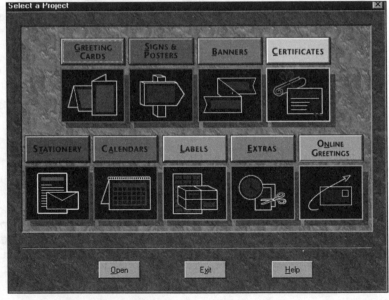

Figure 15-5:
In *The Print Shop,* kids get instant design choices for cards, signs, banners, stationery, and more.

Select a design

The next decision: Do your kids want to customize a ready-made design or start from scratch? For fast results, they can peruse the sample designs like the one shown in Figure 15-6, find one they like, fill in the details, print, and their project is done.

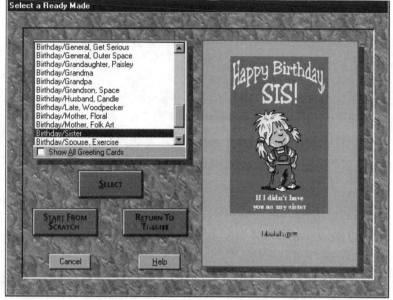

Figure 15-6:
The Print Shop lets kids produce a predesigned card or create one of their own.

Starting from scratch, on the other hand, opens a blank page where kids paste their own text and graphics selections. The software offers layout suggestions, but kids can always modify a layout or create their own. As kids place art and text on a page, the software immediately shows them how it looks. If they don't like something, they simply press the Undo button and try again.

Glorious graphics

Publishing programs are loaded with fonts and graphics — thousands of graphics. In *The Print Shop*, kids find graphics for every holiday, from New Year's to Christmas, and for every event — a sister's birthday, a brother's graduation, a cousin's new baby. What kids can't do in a publishing program is create something from scratch because unlike art software, most publishing programs don't include painting and drawing tools.

Every month families can download new *Print Shop* graphics, designs, and project ideas from The Print Shop Connection. It's all free at `http://www.broder.com/PrintShop/home.html`.

Time to print

Family publishing programs give a whole new meaning to the term "home made." With a color printer, you and your kids can produce great looking pieces with a personal touch. Or you can print a black and white design on colored paper. Stop by your local stationery store to check out special paper supplies for home publishers such as innovative laser papers and ink-jet greeting cards.

OPEN

Other Home Publishing Programs

Home publishing is a popular software category, so you'll see many variations on *The Print Shop* approach. Some programs focus on making greeting cards, others on making special projects like buttons or holiday decorations. We think your kids will get more mileage from a program that covers a broad selection of printed creations. Here are some that kids like.

Print Artist

A good choice for kids who love arts and crafts, *Print Artist* includes projects like creating gift boxes, board games, and paper airplanes. It also has clip art, type styles, stock photos, and more than 1,000 predesigned layouts for creating customized cards, signs, banners, calendars, stationery, and certificates. (Sierra, Ages 10 & up)

Creative Writer 2

If you buy only one creativity program for your kids, this one is a good choice. The reason: It's really four programs in one — word-processing, storywriting, art, and publishing, in print or online. For art and publishing projects, you find a collection of backgrounds, borders, kid-pleasing clip art, and painting and drawing tools to create original art. Kids love the cool text effects for stretching and stacking words. And even parents can get some use from the program's many layout suggestions to help create cards, newsletters, posters, banners, tickets, certificates, personal notebook paper, and more. (Microsoft, Ages 8 & up)

Computer cards for little kids

PARENT TIP

Young children love to create their own cards and invitations on the computer, but home publishing programs are too complex for little kids. Instead, consider the easy approach of *Bailey's Book House* or *Kid Cuts*. The Make-A-Card activity in *Bailey's Book House* is just right for kids 3-6 who happily lay out their creations by clicking simple sentiments (Happy Valentine's Day, Happy Birthday, Thank you for the present) and equally simple graphics (hearts, balloons, a birthday cake) into place. (For more about *Bailey's Book House* from Edmark, refer to Chapter 3.) Designing and coloring cards is one of the many crafts activities in *Kid Cuts,* an inexpensive add-on program for kids who use *Kid Pix Studio* (Broderbund, Ages 3-12).

Looking at Art

Ever taken your kids to an art museum? Here's what happens to us. Cautious guards follow us suspiciously, waiting for our kids to reach out and touch something. (Not allowed!) Art patrons glower as the kids loudly announce their opinions to the entire room. (Not appreciated!) And the kids race to the next room (or the bathroom, or the restaurant) when we stop to admire a favorite painting. (Not fun!)

So we were pleased to discover we could introduce our kids to great art right at home: art from Paris, Chicago, New York, or St. Petersburg, art they can "touch," art they can play with. All kids need is a computer and your encouragement to take a closer look.

You can view fine art on a computer in two ways: from a CD-ROM or from the World Wide Web. Both have their pros and cons. A CD-ROM delivers the images to your computer screen more rapidly, but your viewing is limited to what's on the CD-ROM, which is usually artwork from one artist or one collection. There's more diverse viewing on the Web — you can literally hop from museum to museum across the country and around the world — but if your online connection is slow, your kids may lose interest waiting for the artwork to download.

Art — and artists — abound on CD-ROMs. Tour the Barnes Foundation and its extraordinary collection of paintings by Matisse, Cezanne, Renoir, and other masters in *A Passion For Art.* Wander through London's National Gallery in Microsoft's *Art Gallery.* Hear Cezanne reflect on the inspiration and ideas behind his paintings in *Paul Cezanne: Portrait of My World.* And take your kids along on a very special tour of The Art Institute of Chicago in *With Open Eyes.*

With Open Eyes (ages 3–12)

What's so special about *With Open Eyes?* As soon as you open this program (from Voyager), you know it's designed with kids in mind. The art is surrounded by a frame filled with bright, lively buttons, pictured in Figure 15-7:

a plump green frog, a pair of shiny red lips, a couch potato. Kids use these buttons to choose how they want to interact with the art. Clicking the frog, for example, launches a surprise tour where the images jump randomly — from an Egyptian sarcophagus to a Renaissance Madonna, from a Duchamps sculpture to an Amish quilt — through more than 200 works from many different time periods, cultures, and mediums. Clicking the clock, kids plot a historical tour through 5,000 years of art. Clicking the globe gives kids a geographical perspective as they select images continent by continent.

With Open Eyes invites kids to interact with the art in other ways, too. The camera button lets them snap pictures they like and store them in a scrapbook. The game box button opens an activity for each picture. For example, kids reassemble a jigsaw puzzle of an image or test their visual memories by determining what's been changed or what's missing from a painting.

Instead of the silence of an art museum, *With Open Eyes* is filled with sounds that help kids think about what they see. Each image is accompanied by a sound effect (a fragment of a sea shanty, a drum beat, a scream, a child's laugh), or a question ("Is this a painting of a painter or a photo of a photographer?"), or a fact ("This pitcher and basin are adorned with shells like the shore in Italy where they were made.").

You'll find lots of ways to tie *With Open Eyes* into school work. Click the clock icon to show kids a timeline of world art. Click the globe icon to explore art continent by continent. When your kids are learning about ancient Greece, Mayan culture, or the Renaissance, suggest using *With Open Eyes* to create a scrapbook of art from the period they're studying. Make their slide show a family affair. And ask them what the artwork says about the culture that produced it.

Kids need you to join them in their exploration of *With Open Eyes*. Let them decide how they want to wander through the program, and then encourage them to talk about what they see. You'll know your kids are thinking from the questions and comments they pose. "Was that before the dinosaurs?" queried a 5-year-old looking at a statue built 4,000 years ago. Raphael's cherubs prompted this question from a 4-year-old: "Why are angels always babies?" Expect their comments to take a serious turn, too. When viewing great art, kids come face to face with war, religion, birth, death — the universal themes of human existence.

You can use the images in *With Open Eyes* to inspire creative fun on and off the computer. Challenge kids to either imitate a painting with their art supplies or re-create it by using their favorite computer art program. Can they duplicate a Van Gogh brush stroke with a *Kid Pix Studio* wacky brush? The spattered dots of Seurat with an airbrush tool?

Figure 15-7:
With Open Eyes introduces kids to more than 200 works of art from The Art Institute of Chicago.

Art museums online

It's great fun to take your kids to an art museum via the World Wide Web. But a few words of caution first. Image files are large and take time to download to your computer. Depending on your modem speed, be prepared for a wait. And plan your online museum excursions for off-peak hours, like evenings and weekends, when there's less network traffic and so less waiting.

Don't be surprised if your browser can't find a Web address you type. It's not your fault; and it's probably not our fault either! Blame it on the World Wide Web itself: Web addresses (and sites themselves) can be pretty fickle. Try looking for a "missing" site with a search engine. And try shortening the address by deleting everything after the `.com` (or `.org` or `.edu`).

WebMuseum

The best place to view art in cyberspace isn't a museum at all: It's a Web site created by a French technology consultant who presents an impressive collection of paintings from more than one hundred artists. You find art from every major period, plus useful background information from the *Encyclopaedia Britannica*. When you enter this site, be sure to click the WebMuseum network for the fastest connection. (`http://sunsite.unc.edu/wm/`)

The fine arts museums of San Francisco

On the Web, most museums share only a few pieces from their collections. But the deYoung Museum and the Legion of Honor are committed to making their entire collection available to online visitors. Their Art Imagebase already includes more than 60,000 works, and it lets visitors search for particular artists, types of media, or kinds of images. You also find well-designed online tours of some of their current exhibitions. (`http://www.thinker.org/index.html`)

The National Museum of American Art

Here is another generous online collection, with nearly 1,000 images to view including paintings, portraits, and American crafts. Create a tour for your kids by searching for artwork by date, type of media, or themes such as African-American art, art from the American Southwest, and American landscapes. (`http://www.nmaa.si.edu/`)

Museum of Modern Art

Stop by to view some of MOMA's most popular works, such as Van Gogh's Starry Night, Picasso's Les Demoiselles d'Avignon, and Rousseau's The Dream. (`http://moma.org/`)

Eyes on Art

If you want a more structured approach to appreciating art online, visit this collection of Internet art lessons. Organized by San Diego State University's Department of Educational Technology, each lesson is designed to help kids learn to look at a different aspect of art. The Visual Glossary, for example, prompts kids to observe how artists use art elements and design techniques in their paintings. The Rules of Styles lesson explores the historical evolution of art styles. Although the lessons were designed for schools, they're easy to adapt for home use, particularly if you and your kids explore them together. (`http://www.kn.pacbell.com/wired/art/art.html`)

Part VII
The Part of Tens

The 5th Wave   By Rich Tennant

DAD ADDS MULTIMEDIA SOUND AND GRAPHICS TO THE TRADITIONAL CAMPFIRE GHOST STORY.

In this part . . .

We've tried to be pretty organized in this book to make it easy for you to do right by your computer-generation kids. So far, that is.

But as all parents know, some things simply defy organization! That's why *stuff* piles up on kitchen counters, keys go missing, and socks never stay paired. And that's why the *...For Dummies* series came up with The Part of Tens. It's the official grab bag for ideas and advice, lists and activities that don't quite fit anywhere else.

In our Part of Tens, you find list after list of our favorite kids' software — think of them as the blueprints for the family software library. You find step-by-step instructions for printing out screens from software titles, plus ideas for what to do with those *screen captures* once you've printed them! You find cool Web sites especially for girls on the brink of adolescence. And who knows, maybe you'll find that one nugget of advice you've been looking for.

Chapter 16

Ten (well, nine) Lists of Our Favorite Kids' Software

- -

In This Chapter

▶ Must-have software for every family

▶ Must-have software for every age

▶ Must-have software for the middle-school grades

▶ Great fun-and-games titles

- -

*T*here's nothing like a list to make your life easier — unless it's nine lists! Welcome to the mega-list section of *Great Software For Kids & Parents*.

We think of these lists as blueprints to guide the long-term growth of your family software library. But they serve practical, day-to-day needs, too. Consult them when your kids want to give software as a birthday gift. Use them when relatives call and ask what to give the kids. Use them when you're trying to talk your kids out of a software title that they want but you don't!

And if you figure out other nifty uses for these lists, please let us know. You'll find our address in the Feedback! section of the Introduction.

Ten Must-Haves for Every Family

Kid Pix Studio (Broderbund, Ages 3-12). See Chapters 3, 10 and 15.

The Thinkin' Things Collection 1, 2, & 3 (Edmark, Ages 3-13). See Chapter 6.

The Imagination Express series (Edmark, Ages 5-12). See Chapters 5 and 10.

Math Workshop (Broderbund, Ages 5-12). See Chapter 6.

Strategy Challenge Collection 1: Around the World (Edmark, Ages 7-13). See Chapter 6.

Where in the World Is Carmen Sandiego? (Broderbund, Ages 8-12). See Chapter 9.

The Dr. Brain series (Sierra, Ages 9 & up). See Chapter 6.

The Trail series (MECC, Ages 9-16). See Chapter 10.

Print Shop Ensemble (Broderbund, All ages). See Chapter 15.

Microsoft Encarta (Microsoft, 9 & up). See Chapter 8.

Six Picks: Our Favorites for 2- to 3-Year-Olds

Just Grandma and Me (Living Books). See Chapter 4.

Millie's Math House (Edmark). See Chapter 3.

Putt-Putt Saves the Zoo (Humongous). See Chapter 3.

Build-A-Book with Roberto (Theatrix Interactive). See Chapter 3.

Dr. Seuss's ABC (Living Books). See Chapter 4.

Playskool Puzzles (Hasbro). See Chapters 3 and 6.

Six Picks: Our Favorites for 4- to 5-Year-Olds

Arthur's Reading Race (Living Books). See Chapter 4.

AlphaBonk Farm (Headbone Interactive). See Chapter 4.

Paint, Write & Play! (The Learning Company). See Chapter 3.

Mr. Potato Head Saves Veggie Valley (Hasbro). See Chapter 3.

Sammy's Science House (Edmark). See Chapter 3.

Mighty Math Carnival Countdown (Edmark). See Chapter 6.

Six Picks: Our Favorites for 6- to 7-Year-Olds

Orly's Draw-A-Story (Broderbund). See Chapter 15.

Gigglebone Gang World Tour (Headbone Interactive). See Chapter 9.

Pajama Sam In No Need to Hide When It's Dark (Humongous). See Chapter 3.

Where in the World Is Carmen Sandiego? Junior Detective Edition (Broderbund). See Chapter 9.

Microsoft Explorapedia (Microsoft). See Chapter 11.

Interactive Math Journey (The Learning Company). See Chapter 6.

Six Picks: Our Favorites for 8- to 9-Year-Olds

The Amazing Writing Machine (Broderbund). See Chapter 5.

The Logical Journey of the Zoombinis (Broderbund). See Chapter 6.

SimPark (Maxis). See Chapter 12.

Big Science Comics (Theatrix Interactive). See Chapter 11.

World Walker: Destination Australia (Soleil/Maxis). See Chapters 11 and 13.

Oregon Trail II (MECC, Ages 10-16). See Chapter 9.

Six Picks: Our Favorites for 10- to 14-Year-Olds

Web Workshop (Vividus). See Chapter 14.

Hollywood High (Theatrix Interactive). See Chapter 5.

Math Heads (Theatrix Interactive). See Chapter 6.

Where in the World Is Carmen Sandiego? (Broderbund). See Chapter 9.

SimCity 2000 (Maxis). See Chapter 12.

Microsoft Creative Writer 2 (Microsoft). See Chapter 15.

Six Picks: Our Favorites for 5th and 6th Grade

Microsoft Ancient Lands (Microsoft). See Chapter 10.

Mighty Math Cosmic Geometry (Edmark). See Chapter 6.

The Ultimate Writing and Creativity Center (The Learning Company). See Chapter 5.

Oregon Trail II (MECC). See Chapter 9.

SkyTrip America (Discovery Channel Multimedia). See Chapter 10.

Microsoft Bookshelf (Microsoft). See Chapter 8.

Six Picks: Our Favorites for 7th and 8th Grade

MayaQuest (MECC). See Chapter 10.

Mighty Math Astro Algebra (Edmark). See Chapter 6.

Science Sleuths series (MECC). See Chapter 11.

The Eyewitness Encyclopedia series (DK Multimedia). See Chapter 10.

Amazon Trail II (MECC). See Chapter 10.

Let's Talk About ME! (GirlGames/Simon & Schuster). See Chapters 5 and 18.

Six Picks: Our Favorites for Fun and Games

This list is a little different from the others. So we want to say a few words about it.

We're happy to say that kids can think of *all* the programs in this book as games. They're fun and entertaining. Some are competitive, others collaborative. And many call for strategic gameplay.

But they are, first and foremost, *learning games*. And sometimes, particularly as they get into the double-digit ages, kids balk at learning games. So we've come up with a list of *real* games — some with a little learning going on; others with not quite so much — that you can feel good about and kids 10 and up will love.

Myst (Broderbund). Be sure to look for the sequel, too!

The Adventures of Simon Challenger (Maxis)

SimCopter (Maxis)

The Time Warp of Dr. Brain (Sierra)

Crystal Skull (SOME Interactive/Maxis)

Iz & Auggie: Escape from Dimension Q (Headbone Interactive)

Chapter 17

Creating Screen Captures for Off-the-Computer Activities

*E*ver notice how little kids like to stay on certain pages of an interactive storybook *forever,* listening to the same two sentences over and over, clicking the hot spots, and giggling at the animations again and again?

With just a little know-how — and a printer — you can turn those favorite on-screen pages into appealing off-the-computer activity sheets for kids in preschool, kindergarten, and the early grades. Give the printed pages to your kids. Hand over a pencil and some markers. And let them practice letter-recognition, reading, and writing skills by doing some of the following:

- Tracing over the words.
- Circling all the As (or Ds or Ms, and so on) on the page.
- Finding all the letters in their names.
- Identifying capital letters.
- Looking for rhyming words. (For more ideas, look at the very end of this chapter.)

In this chapter, we walk you through an easy process for creating *screen captures* from your kids' software and for printing those images. The procedure is somewhat different for Macintosh and Windows computers, so we provide a separate section on each system. But don't worry, it's easy. All it takes is a few clicks.

Screen Captures on a Macintosh

Here's how to capture and print an image when using a Macintosh:

1. **With the scene you want to capture on the screen, press ⌘+Shift+3.**

   You hear a little click that sounds like the shutter of a camera. And in fact, your Macintosh has just taken a "snapshot" of the image on screen.

   What's more, your Macintosh automatically does some housekeeping for you. It turns the screen image into a graphics file known as a PICT file. It names the file for you: Picture 1 or 2 or 3, depending on how many screens you capture. And it saves the PICT file in the hard disk window.

2. **Click the software's Quit icon or press ⌘+Q to quit the kids' program you're in.**

   Now's the time to locate your screen capture.

3. **Double-click the hard-drive icon — a little rectangular box labeled Macintosh HD (or some other name that you've given it) in the upper-right corner of your screen.**

   A window opens showing the contents of your hard drive.

   You see (among other contents) the PICT file you just created. Figure 17-1 shows you what to look for.

   What you're after is that little rectangular icon with the word Picture 1 beneath it.

4. **Select the PICT file.**

5. **From the main menu, select File and then select Print.**

   Congratulations! You just captured, pasted, and printed a screen capture.

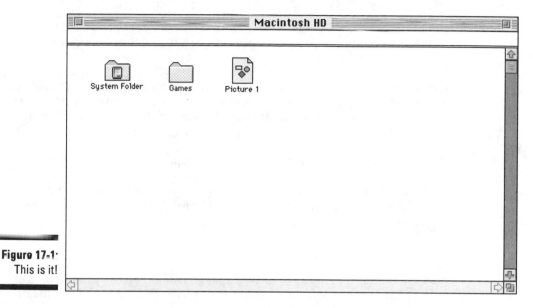

Screen Captures on a PC

Here's how to capture, paste, and print an image when using Windows 95:

1. **With the scene you want to capture on the screen, press the PrintScreen key on your keyboard or press Alt+PrintScreen.**

   Pressing PrintScreen copies the entire screen you see; Alt+PrintScreen copies the active window.

   In order to print the image, you need to paste it into an application. Here's how.

2. **Click the Quit icon or press File⇨Exit to quit the kids' program you're in.**

3. **Open one of the special programs that are part of Windows 95: From Start, select Programs⇨Accessories, and then select, for example, *WordPad* or *Paint*.**

   The program you select opens a new document.

4. **To paste the screen capture into a *WordPad* or *Paint* document, from the Edit menu in *WordPad* or *Paint*, select Paste.**

   The image you captured now appears in your *WordPad* or *Paint* document.

5. Select File➪Print.

Congratulations! You just captured, pasted, and printed a screen capture.

If you think you may want to use your screen capture again, you should name and save it. (You do that in the same way you do with any document you open.) And consider starting a screen capture folder so you can stay organized!

Here are some more ideas for using screen captures with your kids:

✔ Capture a screen that features text in a foreign language. Print it and challenge your kids to write out the translation beneath the picture.

✔ Print a page from a simple storybook and ask beginning readers to cross out three-letter words and write in silly rhymes. Read the results out loud, together.

✔ Encourage older kids to draw a speech balloon on the printed image and, in the balloon, write an original remark that's *not* in the software!

Chapter 18

Using the Computer to Help Raise Great Girls

Statistics tell us some pretty distressing things about girls between 5th and 9th grades. Item: While boys tend to *act out,* girls often *act in* — withdrawing and going "underground" with their interests and abilities. Item: Girls, even girls who have been computer-savvy from early childhood, often drift away from computers in the middle grades and lose their technological edge.

But statistics can change. And we're convinced they will.

We believe it's possible to help girls remain strong learners. And we know it's possible to encourage a continuing interest in the computer, beyond the programs we recommend earlier in this book. This chapter is filled with ideas and resources *for you* — about raising confident, competent girls — and with exciting cyberspace ideas for girls.

Here are some suggestions for both off- and on-the-computer strategies that you might want to consider. And by the way, these pointers are not just for moms and dads. They're for all adults — teachers, stepmothers, stepfathers, grandparents, relatives, friends — who care about the girls in their lives.

If there are boys in your life, we'd like to hear from you. Please let us know at feedback/dummies@idgbooks.com about boys' only sites and advice sites for parents of boys. We'd love to know about them.

Off the computer:

- ✔ **Listen up.** We know that what we're about to say is easier said than done! But if your daughters are 10-14, you're in a "drop-everything-now-and-just-listen" stage. It's important to take time for girls when they need it — not just when it's convenient for you.

- ✔ **Be involved.** That goes for school, for sports, for hobbies, for TV and movies, for shopping, and for the "down" times when girls are just hanging out at home. Get to know who they are *now* — their everyday lives, their hopes and worries, thoughts and feelings — and it'll be easier to keep the connection as they begin to change and grow.

- ✔ **Open up.** Share your own thoughts, feelings, and experiences with your daughters. By showing girls the person inside you, you'll help bridge the gap between generations and encourage your daughters, by example, to share their inner selves, too.

- ✔ **Embrace a wider world.** For both girls and boys, preadolescence and the teen years can be a self-absorbing time. Help kids look beyond themselves by encouraging volunteer activities, clubs, special classes, internships, and community involvement.

On the computer:

- ✔ **Reexamine their software.** Check out all the titles you own that have suggested age ranges reaching into the teens. Do your daughters know them inside out? Have they played every activity and game? Find areas they may have overlooked, and have fun with them together.

- ✔ **Make sure they're having fun.** By the time kids hit middle school, the computer sometimes begins to function more and more as a home-work tool and less and less as a source of creative fun. But it ain't necessarily so.

  Make a joint project of finding fun new software, challenging computer projects, and online adventures. They're out there, we promise. But it takes more work to find them for 10- to 13-year-old girls than for younger kids.

- ✔ **Explore the World Wide Web.** There's great stuff in cyberspace for girls who use computers. In fact, the new profusion of online "destina-tions" for girls is one of the most exciting developments we've seen while researching and writing this book.

The rest of this chapter takes a closer look at cyberspace stuff for girls. We start with sites that are more *for you* than for kids — good sources of advice, gateways to interesting sites for girls, precautions about Web surfing with girls. Then we provide a roundup of our cyberspace favorites for girls.

Don't be surprised if your browser can't find a Web address you type. It's not your fault; and it's probably not our fault either! Blame it on the World Wide Web itself: Web addresses (and sites themselves) can be pretty fickle. Try looking for a "missing" site with a search engine. And try shortening the address by deleting everything after the `.com` (or `.org` or `.edu`).

Finding Advice and Ideas for Parents

As we looked for advice and ideas for families with girls 10 to 13, we were impressed by the intelligence, the inventiveness, and the goodwill of the organizations and individuals developing sites for girls and parents. We chose three "advice sites" to get you started. The first offers the best suggestions we've seen online for how parents can help girls at home and at school. The second is the parents' area of our favorite online girls' club. And the third is a *gateway*, that is, a listing of other sites of interest.

Expect the Best from a Girl and That's What You'll Get. Absolutely the best site to find information about the emotional and educational issues facing girls today, plus advice on how parents can support girls at home and at school. From nearly 100 pointers, here are three typical suggestions to give you the "flavor" of this site:

✔ "Praise girls for their skills, ideas, and successes, not only for their appearance."

✔ "Build your daughter's technological mastery and competence by finding a way for her to use a computer regularly."

✔ "Provide opportunities to develop interests and skills that can lead to careers — agriculture, art, astronomy . . . zoology."

Expect the Best also offers a variety of sensible to-do lists focusing on such things as empowering girls in coed settings and improving schools for girls. There's a revealing fill-in-the-blank form for assessing girls' feelings about math and science. There are research facts. "Girls begin to go 'underground' with their talents and abilities sometime between 5th and 9th grades," for example. Another finding: "Girls and boys have the same range of abilities in reading, writing, and mathematics. Most of the differences we find have more to do with family, social, and cultural experiences and expectations than with capacity."

For adults who want to explore further, *Expect the Best* presents page after page of resources. The information on this site was prepared by the Women's College Coalition in conjunction with the Ad Council; the site itself is maintained by the Office of Communications at Mount Holyoke College. The address is `http://www.academic.org/`.

Raising Healthy Daughters. The pages devoted to this topic are part of *Club Girl Tech,* a terrific site that we recommend later in this chapter for girls. This parent-oriented section features the latest research on girls, ideas about what parents and mentors can do for girls, and a great list of resources. (That list was our first introduction to the Women's Sports Foundation's activities and pamphlets for girls, for example, as well as Science-By-Mail, which pairs 4th-9th graders with pen-pal scientists!)

This site addresses some of its pointers specifically to dads, while others are more mom-oriented. It also invites boys to join its online discussions. Take a look at some of the ongoing discussions in an area called "Boy Talk (It's not What You Think!)," and you'll be impressed by the questions boys and girls raise as well as the answers the experts at this site suggest.

You find parent-oriented information in several locations throughout *Club Girl Tech.* For starters, try clicking the Girl Text icon on the site's main page at http://www.girltech.com.

Women Online. This site is a directory that lists hundreds of sites in dozens of categories, all with special interest for women and girls. Its girl-oriented listing of Web sites is a terrific place for you to start checking out sites for girls to visit. From the site's main page at http://www.wwwomen.com, click the heading that says "Personal/Girls," and you immediately have pages of site names, with brief descriptions, that you can click and visit.

Steering Girls to Absorbing Online Experiences

Stop! Before you read about our favorite sites for girls, there's something you should know.

As with all the products described in this book, we eyed Web sites with some pretty high standards in mind. We went looking for sites that do the following:

- Focus on creative fun through a technological medium
- Provide inventive, appealing ways for girls to communicate among themselves and build a sense of community
- Open new vistas for learning, exploration, and friendship
- Foster high self-esteem and positive attitudes
- And above all, avoid commercialism and sexism

That last point is especially important to us. From an early age, kids in general and girls in particular are easy prey for endless marketing messages: "wear this," "buy that," "act this way." Unfortunately, the World Wide Web is the newest venue for advertising — and for pornographers. But you can help keep your kids safe by doing the following:

___ Checking out (and approving) sites *before* kids visit them

___ Having a frank discussion with your kids — girls and boys — about why you think certain sites are inappropriate

You might even consider looking for a mildly offensive site and asking your kids to view it (briefly) with you. Invite their observations and comments. When kids become critical observers of the ways girls and women are portrayed in our culture — in advertisements, TV shows and commercials, movies, magazines, songs, and on Web sites — they get better at filtering out inappropriate messages.

___ Making spot-checks of their online travels to see that they're visiting preapproved sites and observing family rules for online activity

___ Starting with the sites we suggest next

Club Girl Tech. This site is absolutely the best site for girls to find fun and friendship online. *Club Girl Tech* is filled with activities designed to build girls' self-esteem and sense of community, while encouraging them to have fun and to learn.

The site offers six main areas, each with many "layers," or pages, to explore:

✔ **Chick Chat:** An area where girls can talk to each other and to the personalities that are part of the site.

✔ **Girl's World:** A place for exploring the roles, experiences, activities, and possibilities that are open to today's girls.

✔ **Game Cafe:** An activity zone with games to play online and games to download. Choices include trivia games, fun with pig Latin, word and math puzzles, jokes, science projects, a fill-in-the-blank storymaker, and more.

✔ **Girl Text:** An area with information by and about girls. You find newsletters, opinion polls, book reviews, and more.

✔ **Tech Trips:** A selection of links to fun, smart Web sites for girls.

✔ **Bow-Tique:** A mini-mall online featuring girl-friendly products. (This is the only area of this site that's tinged with commercialism. But it's not bad. And like it or not, many girls do like to shop.)

That's the overview, now for the particulars. One of our *Club Girl Tech* favorites is called Gimme 5. Girls type their name. Then using little pull-down menus, they choose five words that describe themselves. They wind up with a colorful certificate for their bulletin board — plus instructions to say the words out loud five times a day.

Club Girl Tech provides an inventive approach, called the Transformer, for writing first-time letters to overseas pen pals. Girls personalize a chatty, light-hearted fill-in-the-blank letter about their families, homes, school, hobbies, favorite foods. Next they click a French, German, Spanish, or Italian flag. Finally they click a Translate It! button, and in seconds, their letter reappears in a foreign language, ready to print and mail.

Antie Em's advice section is another good area, featuring questions and answers about best friends, fitting in, teasing, siblings, stepparents, and more.

The activities in these areas are constantly updated, so there's a chance that the favorites we describe may be in the site's archives by the time you read these pages. That's the Web for you!

Club Girl Tech was started by a woman who knows how kids like to learn and play — on the computer, and off. Once a teacher, Janese Swanson was part of the team at Broderbund that first produced *Where in the World Is Carmen Sandiego?* She later went on to form a company that designed a popular toy called a Yak-Bak. You can find her latest endeavor at `http://www.girltech.com`.

Girls InterWire. A terrific online newsletter for girls, with new stories, fun facts, interesting quotes, and challenges every month.

It features short articles — about girls' issues, current events, women in the news — each followed by a series of interesting questions and an invitation for girls to share their thoughts by clicking the Tell us! button. Naturally, girls can read what other kids have to say, too.

There's a Mentor of the Month profile; a Check It Out section with short reviews of books, songs, and movies; and monthly challenges like this one: "Born in 1951 in Encino, California, she attended Stanford University and was really good at tennis. She became an astrophysicist, joined NASA, and was the first female in space. Who is she?"

Clicking the Puzzler icon at the bottom of the page whisks kids to an excellent selection of brain teasers, puzzles, quizzes, and mental games. For example: "Sally Saleslady always says that if only people told the truth, she would sell more of her wares. What does she make?" Got that? Then try this: "Peter, Paul, and Mary go collecting aluminum cans for their school's recycling drive. They take a large bag along with them to hold all of the cans for the three of them. Without knowing its dimensions, can you figure out how many cans they can put in the empty bag?"

Girls InterWire is part of a Web site maintained by a CD-ROM developer, GirlGames, Inc. Part of the site is devoted to the company's products (we discuss *Let's Talk About ME!* in Chapter 5), but the site in general does *not* pitch products to its visitors. Visit this site at `http://www.girlgamesinc.com /interwire/index.html`.

Other girls' sites to consider

Here are a few more descriptions, with addresses, that are good for girls:

A Girl's World: Another online clubhouse. Less polished than Club Girl Tech. But the girls who run it, and the cyberpals who visit and chat with them, are a delightful bunch. (`http:// www.agirlsworld.com`)

Girls' Series: A site devoted to "series" books about girls, like Nancy Drew, Little House on the Prairie, the American Girls collection, the Babysitter's Club, and many others. Nostalgic for moms, fun for girls. Excellent links to children's literature sites, as well as a site for boys' series books. (`http://members. aol.com/biblioholc/gseries.html`)

New Moon: A wonderful, advertising-free magazine by and for girls. The quality of the writing — and the flights of imagination — in this publication are exceptional. For a subscription to the print version, call 800-381-4743. Girls can visit the online version, which is not as extensive. (`http://www.newmoon. org/`)

Girls' Homepages: A listing of home pages created by girls. A good place to look when your kids express an interest in creating a page of their own. Note that the rest of this site, produced by CD-ROM developer Her Interactive, has a commercial flavor. But you can go direct to the home page listing. (`http://www.her- online.com/Homepages/ Girls'pages.html`)

Part VIII

Appendixes

In this part . . .

*I*n the last part of this book, we provide lists to help make your pursuit of great kids' software as easy as possible. Want to read about a particular program? Just turn to the list of all the software titles in this book to find the chapters in which they're located. Have a question about a program we recommend? Head to the list of publisher contacts where you can find phone numbers and Web addresses for the publisher of all the programs.

And to try demo versions of some of the software in this book, just open the *Great Software For Kids & Parents* CD-ROM.

Appendix A
Software Titles in This Book

● ●

*H*ere's an alphabetical list of all the programs we recommend in this book. We've also included the publisher's name, our recommended age range, and the chapter to turn to if you want to read more about a program.

Title	Publisher	Age range	Chapter
3D Atlas	Creative Wonders	Ages 8 & up	Chapter 9
3D Movie Maker	Microsoft	Ages 10 & up	Chapter 14
Adobe PhotoDeluxe	Adobe	Ages 10 & up	Chapter 14
The Adventures of Simon Challenger	Maxis	Ages 8 & up	Chapters 9 &16
All-in-One Language Fun	Syracuse Language Systems	Ages 3-12	Chapter 13
AlphaBonk Farm	Headbone Interactive	Ages 3-6	Chapters 4 & 16
Amazing Animation	Claris	Ages 5-12	Chapter 14
The Amazing Writing Machine	Broderbund	Ages 6-12	Chapters 5 &16
Amazon Trail II	MECC	Ages 10-16	Chapters 10 &16
Ancient Lands	Microsoft	Ages 8 & up	Chapters 10 &16
Art Explorer	Adobe	Ages 8-12	Chapter 15
Arthur's Birthday	Living Books	Ages 3-7	Chapter 4
Arthur's Reading Race	Living Books	Ages 3-7	Chapters 4 & 16
Arthur's Teacher Trouble	Living Books	Ages 3-7	Chapter 4
At Ease	Apple Computer	All ages	Chapter 1
Bailey's Book House	Edmark	Ages 2-6	Chapter 3
The Berenstain Bears Get in a Fight	Living Books	Ages 3-6	Chapter 4

(continued)

Title	Publisher	Age Range	Chapter
The Berenstain Bears in the Dark	Living Books	Ages 3-6	Chapter 4
Berlitz Think & Talk	The Learning Company	All ages	Chapter 13
Big Anthony's Mixed Up Magic	MECC	Ages 3-6	Chapter 4
Big Science Comics	Theatrix Interactive	Ages 8-12	Chapters 11 & 16
Build-A-Book with Roberto	Theatrix Interactive	Ages 2-4	Chapters 3 & 16
Bumptz Science Carnival	Theatrix Interactive	Ages 6-10	Chapter 11
Cartopedia	DK Multimedia	Ages 11 & up	Chapter 9
Civilization II	MicroProse	Ages 12 & up	Chapter 12
ClarisWorks	Claris	Ages 9 & up	Chapter 7
Cocoa	Apple	Ages 12 & up	Chapter 12
Cooper McQue Breaks Through!	DreamWorks Interactive	Ages 6-9	Chapter 4
Creative Writer 2	Microsoft	Ages 8 & up	Chapter 15
Crystal Skull	SOME Interactive/ Maxis	Ages 10 & up	Chapter 16
Curious George Comes Home	Houghton Mifflin Interactive	Ages 2-4	Chapter 4
Dabbler	Fractal Design	Ages 8 & up	Chapter 15
Darby the Dragon	Broderbund	Ages 5-9	Chapter 3
Dr. Seuss's ABC	Living Books	Ages 2-6	Chapters 4 & 16
EasyPhoto Reader	Storm Technology	All ages	Chapter 14
Explorapedia: The World of Nature	Microsoft	Ages 6-10	Chapters 11 & 16
Eyewitness Encyclo-pedia of History	DK Multimedia	Ages 11 & up	Chapters 10 & 16
Eyewitness Encyclo-pedia of Science	DK Multimedia	Ages 11 & up	Chapters 11 & 16
Fine Artist	Microsoft	Ages 8-12	Chapter 10

Title	Publisher	Age Range	Chapter
Freddi Fish and the Case of the Missing Kelp Seeds	Humongous Entertainment	Ages 3-6	Chapter 3
Freddi Fish 2 and the Case of the Haunted Schoolhouse	Humongous Entertainment	Ages 3-6	Chapter 3
Geometry Blaster	Davidson	Ages 10 & up	Chapter 6
Gigglebone Gang World Tour	Headbone Interactive	Ages 4-8	Chapters 9 & 16
Green Eggs and Ham	Living Books	Ages 2-6	Chapter 4
Gregory & the Hot Air Balloon	Broderbund	Ages 3-7	Chapter 3
Harry and the Haunted House	Living Books	Ages 3-8	Chapter 13
Hollywood	Theatrix Interactive	Ages 9 & up	Chapter 5
Hollywood High	Theatrix Interactive	Ages 9 & up	Chapters 5 & 16
Imagination Express Destination: Castle	Edmark	Ages 5-12	Chapter 5
Imagination Express Destination: Neighborhood	Edmark	Ages 5-12	Chapter 5
Imagination Express Destination: Ocean	Edmark	Ages 5-12	Chapter 5
Imagination Express Destination: Pyramids	Edmark	Ages 5-12	Chapter 5
Imagination Express Destination: Rain Forest	Edmark	Ages 5-12	Chapters 5 & 16
Imagination Express Destination: Time Trip, USA	Edmark	Ages 5-12	Chapter 5
Interactive Math Journey	The Learning Company	Ages 6-9	Chapters 6 & 16
Iz & Auggie: Escape from Dimension Q	Headbone Interactive	Ages 10 & up	Chapter 16
Juilliard Music Adventure	Theatrix Interactive	Ages 9 & up	Chapter 14

(continued)

Title	Publisher	Age Range	Chapter
JumpStart Preschool	Knowledge Adventure	Ages 2-5	Chapter 3
JumpStart Kindergarten	Knowledge Adventure	Ages 4-6	Chapter 3
Just Grandma and Me	Living Books	Ages 2-5	Chapters 4 & 16
Kai's Power Goo	MetaTools	Ages 10 & up	Chapter 14
KidDesk	Edmark	All ages	Chapter 1
kidDraw	kidBoard	All ages	Chapter 15
Kid Cuts	Broderbund	Ages 3-12	Chapter 15
Kid Pix Studio	Broderbund	Ages 3-12	Chapters 15 & 16
Kid Phonics	Davidson	Ages 4-7	Chapter 4
Kid Phonics 2	Davidson	Ages 6-9	Chapter 4
Launch Pad	Berkeley Systems	All ages	Chapter 1
Learn to Speak Series	The Learning Company	All ages	Chapter 13
Let's Talk About Me!	GirlGames Inc./Simon & Schuster	Ages 10-14	Chapters 5 & 16
Let's Talk Series	Syracuse Language Systems	All ages	Chapter 13
Little Monster at School	Living Books	Ages 2-6	Chapter 4
The Logical Journey of the Zoombinis	Broderbund	Ages 8-12	Chapters 6 & 16
Logo	Logo Computer Systems Inc.		Chapter 12
The Lost Mind of Dr. Brain	Sierra	Ages 9 & up	Chapter 6
Magic Schoolbus Series	Microsoft	Ages 6-10	Chapter 11
Math Blaster: Episode 1: In Search of Spot	Davidson	Ages 6-12	Chapter 6
Math Blaster: Episode 2: Secret of the Lost City	Davidson	Ages 8-12	Chapter 6
Math Blaster Jr.	Davidson	Ages 4-7	Chapter 6

Title	Publisher	Age Range	Chapter
Math Blaster Mystery: The Great Brain Robbery	Davidson	Ages 10 & up	Chapter 6
Math Heads	Theatrix Interactive	Ages 9-13	Chapters 6 & 16
Math Munchers Deluxe	MECC	Ages 8-12	Chapter 6
Math Workshop	Broderbund	Ages 5-12	Chapters 6 & 16
MayaQuest	MECC	Ages 10-16	Chapters 10 & 16
Mega Math Blaster	Davidson	Ages 6-12	Chapter 6
Microsoft Art Gallery	Microsoft	Ages 10 & up	Chapter 15
Microsoft Bookshelf	Microsoft	Ages 9 & up	Chapters 8 & 16
Microsoft Encarta	Microsoft	Ages 9 & up	Chapters 0, 10 & 16
Microsoft Works	Microsoft	Ages 9 & up	Chapter 7
MicroWorlds Project Builder	Logo Computer Systems Inc.		Chapter 12
Mieko	Broderbund	Ages 5 & up	Chapter 13
Mighty Math Astro Algebra	Edmark	Ages 11-14	Chapters 6 & 16
Mighty Math Calculating Crew	Edmark	Ages 8-10	Chapter 6
Mighty Math Carnival Countdown	Edmark	Ages 5-7	Chapters 6 & 16
Mighty Math Cosmic Geometry	Edmark	Ages 11-14	Chapters 6 & 16
Mighty Math Number Heroes	Edmark	Ages 8-10	Chapter 6
Mighty Math Zoo Zillions	Edmark	Ages 5-7	Chapter 6
Millie's Math House	Edmark	Ages 2-6	Chapters 3 & 16
Morgan's Adventures in Ancient Greece	HarperKids	Ages 7-12	Chapter 10
Morgan's Adventures in Colonial America	HarperKids	Ages 7-12	Chapter 10
Morph	Gryphon	Ages 10 & up	Chapter 14

(continued)

Title	Publisher	Age Range	Chapter
Mr. Potato Head Saves Veggie Valley	Hasbro	Ages 3-7	Chapters 3 & 16
My First Amazing World Explorer	DK Multimedia	Ages 4-9	Chapter 9
My Make Believe Castle	Logo Computer Systems Inc.	Ages 4-7	Chapter 6
Myst	Broderbund	Ages 10 & up	Chapter 16
Net Explorations with Web Workshop	Sunburst Communications	Ages 8-14	Chapter 14
The New Kid on the Block	Living Books	Ages 3-7	Chapter 4
Nine Worlds	Palladium	All ages	Chapter 11
Novell PerfectWorks	Novell	Ages 9 & up	Chapter 7
Odell Down Under	MECC	Ages 8-12	Chapter 12
Oregon Trail II	MECC	Ages 10-16	Chapters 10 & 16
Orly's Draw-A-Story	Broderbund	Ages 5-9	Chapters 15 & 16
Paint, Write & Play!	The Learning Company	Ages 4-7	Chapters 3 & 16
Pajama Sam in No Need to Hide When It's Dark Outside	Humongous Entertainment	Ages 3-8	Chapters 3 & 16
A Passion for Art	Corbis	Ages 10 & up	Chapter 15
Paul Cezanne: Portrait of My World	Corbis	Ages 12 & up	Chapter 15
Planetary Taxi	Voyager	Ages 7-12	Chapter 11
Playskool Puzzles	Hasbro	Ages 2-5	Chapters 6 & 16
Print Artist	Sierra	Ages 10 & up	Chapter 15
The Print Shop	Broderbund	Ages 9 & up	Chapter 15
Putt-Putt and Pep's Balloon-O-Rama	Humongous Entertainment	Ages 3-8	Chapter 3
Putt-Putt and Pep's Dog on a Stick	Humongous Entertainment	Ages 3-8	Chapter 3
Putt-Putt Goes to the Moon	Humongous Entertainment	Ages 3-8	Chapter 3

Title	Publisher	Age Range	Chapter
Putt-Putt Joins the Parade	Humongous Entertainment	Ages 3-8	Chapter 3
Putt-Putt Saves the Zoo	Humongous Entertainment	Ages 3-8	Chapters 3 & 16
Practice Makes Perfect	The Learning Company	All ages	Chapter 13
Reader Rabbit 1	The Learning Company	Ages 4-6	Chapter 4
Reader Rabbit 2	The Learning Company	Ages 6-8	Chapter 4
Reader Rabbit's Interactive Reading Journey Volume 1	The Learning Company	Ages 5-8	Chapter 4
Reader Rabbit's Interactive Reading Journey Volume 2	The Learning Company	Ages 4-7	Chapter 4
Reading Blaster Jr.	Davidson	Ages 4-7	Chapter 4
Reading Galaxy	Broderbund	Ages 8-12	Chapter 4
The Reading Lesson	MountCastle	Ages 4 & up	Chapter 4
Sammy's Science House	Edmark	Ages 3-6	Chapters 3 & 16
Science Sleuths	VideoDiscovery/ MECC	Ages 10 & up	Chapters 11 & 16
Sheila Rae the Brave	Living Books	Ages 3-7	Chapter 4
SimCity 2000	Maxis	Ages 12 & up	Chapter 12
SimCity Classic	Maxis	Ages 12 & up	Chapter 12
SimCopter	Maxis	Ages 12 & up	Chapters 12 & 16
SimIsle	Maxis	Ages 12 & up	Chapter 12
SimPark	Maxis	Ages 8-12	Chapter 12
SimTower	Maxis	Ages 12 & up	Chapter 12
SimTown	Maxis	Ages 8-12	Chapter 12
SimTunes	Maxis	Ages 8 & up	Chapter 14
SkyTrip America	Discovery Channel Multimedia	Ages 9 & up	Chapters 10 & 16
Snootz Math Trek	Theatrix Interactive	Ages 5-9	Chapter 6

(continued)

Title	Publisher	Age Range	Chapter
Stanley's Sticker Stories	Edmark	Ages 3-6	Chapter 3
Stellaluna	Living Books	Ages 3-7	Chapter 4
Strategy Challenge Collection 1: Around the World	Edmark	Ages 7-13	Chapters 6 & 16
The Student Writing Center	The Learning Company	Ages 9 & up	Chapter 7
The Student Writing and Research Center	The Learning Company	Ages 9 & up	Chapter 7
SuperSolvers Spellbound	The Learning Company	Ages 7-12	Chapter 4
Thinkin' Things Collection 1	Edmark	Ages 3-8	Chapters 6 & 16
Thinkin' Things Collection 2	Edmark	Ages 6-12	Chapter 6
Thinkin' Things Collection 3	Edmark	Ages 7-13	Chapter 6
The Time Warp of Dr. Brain	Sierra	Ages 10 & up	Chapter 16
Top Secret Decoder	Houghton Mifflin Interactive	Ages 7-14	Chapter 5
The Tortoise and the Hare	Living Books	Ages 3-8	Chapter 13
Travelrama USA	KidSoft	Ages 8-12	Chapter 9
TriplePlay Plus!	Syracuse Language Systems	All ages	Chapter 13
Troggle Trouble Math	MECC	Ages 6-12	Chapter 6
Trudy's Time and Place House	Edmark	Ages 3-6	Chapter 3
Type to Learn	Sunburst Communications	Ages 8-14	Chapter 7
Ultimate Children's Encyclopedia	The Learning Company	Ages 7-9	Chapter 8
The Ultimate Writing & Creativity Center	The Learning Company	Ages 6-10	Chapters 5 & 16
Volcanoes: Life on the Edge	Corbis Corp.	All ages	Chapter 9

Title	Publisher	Age Range	Chapter
Wacom Art Pad	Wacom	All ages	Chapter 15
What's the Secret?	3M Learning Software	Ages 8-12	Chapter 11
Web Workshop	Vividus	Ages 8-14	Chapters 14 & 16
Where in the USA Is Carmen Sandiego?	Broderbund	Ages 8-12	Chapter 9
Where in the World Is Carmen Sandiego?	Broderbund	Ages 8-12	Chapters 9 & 16
Where in the World Is Carmen Sandiego? Junior Detective Edition	Broderbund	Ages 5-8	Chapters 9 & 16
Who Is Uscar Lake?	Language Publications Interactive	Ages 12 & up	Chapter 13
With Open Eyes	Voyager	Ages 3-12	Chapter 15
Word Munchers Deluxe	MECC	Ages 6-11	Chapter 4
Word Stuff	Sanctuary Woods	Ages 3 & up	Chapter 13
World Walker Destination: Australia	Soleil Software	Ages 9-13	Chapters 11 & 16
Wrath of the Gods	SOME Interactive/ Maxis	Ages 9 & up	Chapter 10
Your Way	Syracuse Language Systems	All ages	Chapter 13
The Yukon Trail	MECC	Ages 10-16	Chapter 10
Zurk's Alaskan Trek	Soleil Software	Ages 6-10	Chapter 6
Zurk's Learning Safari	Soleil Software	Ages 2-5	Chapter 4
Zurk's Rainforest Lab	Soleil Software	Ages 5-9	Chapter 5

Appendix B
Publisher Contacts

• •

C an't find a title in the store? Call the publishers at the phone numbers listed in the table below. They'll tell you the location of the closest retailer or sell the program to you directly.

Wonder whether a program will work on your computer? Talk to a publisher's customer service representative. (Don't get stuck in the technical support queue!)

Want to know a title's price? For information about product features and price, the publisher's Web site is a good place to start.

Publisher	Web site address	Telephone number
3M Learning Software		800-219-9022
Adobe	http://www.adobe.com	800-888-6293
Broderbund	http://www.broderbund.com	800-521-6263
Claris	http://www.claris.com	800-325-2747
Corbis	http://www.corbis.com	800-260-0444
Creative Wonders	http://www.cwonders.com	800-KID EXPERT
DK Multimedia	http://www.dk.com	800-225-3362
Davidson	http://www.davd.com	800-545-7677
Digital Productions	http://www.mmdpi.com	909-659-6200
Discovery Channel Multimedia	http://www.multimedia.discovery.com	800-678-3343
Dreamworks Interactive	http://dreamworksgames.com	800-426-9400
Edmark	http://www.edmark.com	800-691-2985
Fractal Design	http://www.fractal.com	800-846-0111
Girl Games	http://girlgamesinc.com	800-475-7785

Publisher	Web site address	Telephone number
Gryphon	http://www.gryphonsw.com	888-8GRYPHON
Hasbro	http://www.hasbro.com	800-638-6927
HarperKids	http://www.harpercollins.com/hci/cats.htm	800-242-7737
Headbone Interactive	http://www.headbone.com	800-267-4709
Houghton Mifflin Interactive	http://www.hmco.com	800-225-3362
Humongous Entertainment	http://www.humongous.com	800-499-8386
kidBoard	http://www.kidBoard.com	800-926-3066
Kidsoft	http://www.kidsoft.com	800-354-6150
Knowledge Adventure	http://www.adventure.com	800-542-4240
Language Publications Interactive	http://languagepub.com	800-416-4555
Living Books	http://www.livingbooks.com	800-776-4724
Logo Computer Systems	http://www.lcsi.ca	800-321-5646
Maxis	http://www.maxis.com	800-526-2947
MECC	http://www.mecc.com	800-685-6322
Microprose	http://www.microprose.com	800-695-4263
Microsoft	http://www.microsoft.com	800-426-9400
Mount Castle		800-585-7323
Palladium Interactive	http://www.palladiumnet.com/palladium.html	800-910-2696
Sanctuary Woods Multimedia	http://www.sanctuary.com	800-872-3518
Sierra	http://www.sierra.com	800-757-7707
Simon and Schuster Interactive	http://www.mcp.com	800-910-0099
Soleil	http://www.soleil.com	800-501-0110
SOME Interactive	http://www.maxis.com/shopping/product.cgi?ProductName=wrath_of_the_gods	800-526-2947

Publisher	Web site address	Telephone number
Storm Technology	http://www.stormsoft.com	800-438-3279
Sunburst Communications	http://www.nysunburst.com	800-321-7511
Syracuse Language Systems	http://www.syrlang.com	800-797-5264
The Learning Company	http://www.learningco.com	800-852-2255
Theatrix Interactive	http://www.theatrix.com	800-955-8749
Voyager	http://www.voyagerco.com	800-446-2001
VideoDiscovery	http://www.videodiscovery.com/vdyweb	800-548-3472
Vividus	http://www.vividus.com	415-321-2221
Wacom Technology	http://www.wacom.com	800-922-6613

Appendix C
About the CD

• •

Now it's time to play! Open this CD-ROM so you can experience firsthand some of the great software we recommend. We've assembled a collection of program demos with something for kids from 2 to 12 to sample. These demos are organized into four categories:

Getting to the Web

All you need to know to connect your family computer to the World Wide Web.

Playing to Learn

The best programs for little kids let them learn through playing.

The 3 'Rs

Lots of great software is available to help kids master essential reading, writing, and math skills.

Exploration and Enrichment

On the computer, kids do things they can't do anywhere else — like go back in time, journey down the Amazon, travel 'round the world, or build (and destroy) entire cities.

Creative Pursuits

With great creativity programs, kids find new tools for expressing themselves visually and in writing.

System Requirements

Your computer should have the following in order to meet the system requirements for using this CD:

- ✔ A PC with an Intel processor or equivalent running Windows 3.1 or Windows 95, or any Macintosh with a 68020 processor or better running System 7.1 or higher (System 7.5 recommended)
- ✔ At least 8MB total RAM

> ✔ A CD-ROM drive — double speed (2x) or faster
>
> ✔ A sound card with speakers (for PCs)
>
> ✔ A monitor capable of displaying at least 256 colors or grayscale

What Do I Do First with the CD?

For Windows 95

1. **Insert the CD in your computer's CD-ROM drive.**

2. **Wait a minute or two to see if the CD's interface starts up automatically.**

   If so, the first thing you see is the IDG license agreement. To use the CD, you need to Accept the terms of this agreement.

   If you then see a picture of a happy Dummies family, the CD is up and running, and you can begin using the software on the CD.

   However, if nothing appears after a minute or two, you need to move on to the next step.

3. **Click the Start button, and choose <u>R</u>un.**

4. **In the Run dialog box, type** D:\INSTALL.EXE.

   Substitute your actual CD-ROM drive letter if it is something other than D.

5. **Click OK.**

   The *Great Software For Kids & Parents* icon is installed in a program group named IDG Books Worldwide, which is located in the Start menu. To run the CD, click Start and choose Programs⇨IDG Books Worldwide⇨Great Software For Kids & Parents.

For Windows 3.1

1. **Insert the CD in your computer's CD-ROM drive.**

2. **In Program Manager, choose <u>F</u>ile⇨<u>R</u>un.**

3. **In the Run dialog box, type** D:\INSTALL.EXE.

   Substitute your actual CD-ROM drive letter if it is something other than D.

4. **Click OK.**

   The *Great Software For Kids & Parents* icon is installed in Program Manager in a program group named IDG Books Worldwide. To run the

CD, from Program Manager double-click the IDG Books Worldwide program group and then double-click the Great Software For Kids & Parents icon.

Note to Windows users: See the section "(Re)Starting the CD Interface in Windows" to actually get the CD up and running.

For Macintosh

1. **Insert the CD in your computer's CD-ROM drive.**
2. **Double-click the *Great Software For Kids & Parents* icon to run the interface.**

(Re)Starting the CD Interface in Windows

Windows 3.1 users can start the CD interface by opening the IDG Books Worldwide program group, which is found in your Program Manager and double-clicking the *Great Software For Kids & Parents* icon.

Windows 95 users without the IDG Books Worldwide group in your Start⇨Programs menu can double-click the My Computer icon and then double-click the CD-ROM icon to restart the interface.

Windows 95 users who have the IDG Books Worldwide group in your Start⇨Programs menu can open that group and select the *Great Software For Kids & Parents* icon to run the interface.

What You'll Find

Here's a summary of the software you'll find on this CD. Running any of the demos is easy, thanks to our CD interface. Start the interface program by clicking its icon from the Program Manager or Start button. Then click the software category you'd like to explore. To open a program demo, click the button with the title of the program you want to see. Follow the instructions in the program's description window on how to run the demo. Have fun!

AT&T WorldNet Service

In the Getting to the Web category
For Windows and Macintosh
From AT&T

We've provided the AT&T WorldNet Service software, which enables you to sign on to the Internet. Depending on the sign-on software version available for your computer, AT&T WorldNet Service offers a customized version of either the Netscape Navigator or the Microsoft Internet Explorer Web browser.

Note: The Windows 3.1 version of AT&T WorldNet Service comes with a customized version of Netscape Navigator 1.22, which doesn't accept plug-in software. You can obtain version 2.0 of Netscape Navigator on the Web. (http://home.netscape.com)

For more information and updates of AT&T WorldNet Service, visit the AT&T WorldNet Web site. (http://www.att.com/worldnet)

If you're an AT&T long distance residential customer, use this registration code when prompted by the account registration program: L5SQIM631.

If you use another long distance phone company, please use this registration code when prompted: L5SQIM632.

If you already have an Internet Service Provider, please note that AT&T WorldNet Service software makes changes to your computer's current Internet configuration and may replace your current provider's settings.

The CD contains exportable versions of AT&T WorldNet Service and Web browers. However, AT&T WorldNet Service is currently supported only in the United States. Future AT&T international access is subject to regional variations.

Trudy's Time and Place House demo

In the Playing to Learn category
For Windows and Macintosh
From the Edmark *House* series (ages 2-6)

If you wonder what we mean by software that lets kids learn by doing, check out this demo for little kids. You'll meet Trudy the friendly crocodile and get a feel for Edmark's wonderful programs for young kids. This demo looks best in 16-bit color or greater.

Find out more about Edmark's children's learning products at their Web site. (http://www.edmark.com)

Pajama Sam and No Need to Hide When It's Dark Outside demo

In the Playing to Learn category
For Windows and Macintosh
From Humongous Entertainment (ages 3-8)

Kids relish the challenge of the Humongous Entertainment *Junior Adventures.* Don't be surprised if you can't pull them away from the demo!

Interested in this or other Humongous Entertainment products? Drop by their Web site. (http://www.humongous.com)

Living Books Sampler

In the 3 'Rs category
For Windows and Macintosh
From Living Books (ages 2-7)

Meet some of our favorite characters from Living Books. Each demo shows a page or two from a Living Books program. Be sure to click here and there in the book's pages to find many surprises. You can enjoy more brief encounters with all the Living Books at the Living Books Web site. (http://www.livingbooks.com)

Reading Blaster Jr. Preview

In the 3 'Rs category
For Windows and Macintosh
From Davidson (ages 4-7)

Introduce your kids to the Blasternauts' fun-loving approach to phonics skills and reading basics. You can find more about this and other programs at Davidson's Web site. (http://www.davd.com)

Mighty Math Number Heroes demo

In the 3 'Rs category
For Windows and Macintosh
From Edmark (ages 8-10)

Let your kids noodle around with essential math concepts. For more information about this new series with programs for kids from 5-14, visit Edmark's Web site. (http://www.edmark.com) This demo looks best in 16-bit color or greater.

The Lost Mind of Dr. Brain demo

In the 3 'Rs category
For Windows and Macintosh
From Sierra (ages 10 & up)

Kids (and parents, too!) will enjoy this introduction to the brain-teasing, mind-bending puzzles they encounter in the *Dr. Brain* series from Sierra. Drop by the Sierra On-Line Web site for more information on this and other Sierra products. (`http://www.sierra.com`)

Problems with Dr. Brain in Windows 3.1?

If you get strange error messages when running the Dr. Brain demo in Program Manager, try this fix:

1. **Insert the CD into your CD-ROM drive.**

2. **In Program Manager, open the Sierra program group, and then click the Dr. Brain icon *once*.**

3. **Choose File⇨Properties.**

4. **In the Command line text box, type** `D:\DRBRAIN\DRBRAIN.EXE` **(substitute your CD-ROM drive letter if different from D).**

5. **Click the Choose Icon button, click the cool-looking brain icon, and click OK.**

6. **Click OK in the Properties window to save your changes.**

You should now be able to run the Dr. Brain demo using the new brain icon. Remember that you must insert the CD in your CD-ROM drive to run this demo.

Thinkin' Things Collection 1-2-3 demo

In the 3 'Rs category
For Windows and Macintosh
From Edmark (ages 3-13)

There's a *Thinkin' Things* program for every kid from 3-13. See how these software activities push kids to really think! See more about Edmark at their Web site. (`http://www.edmark.com`)

My First Amazing World Explorer demo

In the Exploration and Enrichment category
For Windows and Macintosh
From DK Multimedia (ages 4-9)

A fun way to introduce young kids to maps and world geography. More information on programs from DK Multimedia can be found on the Web. (http://www.dk.com) The QuickTime movies for this demo are located on the CD-ROM itself in the DKINC_EX folder.

Oregon Trail II demo

In the Exploration and Enrichment category
For Windows and Macintosh
From MECC (ages 10-16)

Experience one of the most popular educational programs of all time. In this game, kids make decisions that determine whether their wagon train will make it to the trail's end.

Check out the MECC Web site for more information on this and other products. (http://www.mecc.com)

World Walker Destination: Australia demo

In the Exploration and Enrichment category
For Windows and Macintosh
From Soleil Software (ages 9-13)

A combination science program, language learning tool, and spelunking adventure, this World Walker program introduces kids to the wildlife of Australia. On this demo, kids can play some of the games from the program. To learn more about this program, visit Soleil Software on the World Wide Web. (http://www.soleil.com)

SimCity 2000 demo

In the Exploration and Enrichment category
For Windows and Macintosh
From Maxis (ages 12 & up)

Kids and adults can build their own metropolis by placing pieces of the infrastructure — roads, apartment buildings, parks, subway stations, nuclear power plants — on a grid and watching what happens over time. In the full version, kids can create all sorts of disasters, too, such as Godzilla trashing the sports arena!

Look for more information on this and other Maxis products at the Maxis Web site. (http://www.maxis.com)

Web Workshop

In the Creative Pursuits category
For Windows and Macintosh
From Vividus (ages 8-14)

Web Workshop makes it easy for kids to design and build their own Web sites. If you have an Internet connection, your kids can try creating a sample home page — and publish it on the Vividus Web site for free. To publish their pages, you must have a working Internet connection and an e-mail address. Then just click on Publish, and follow the steps in the software.

Note: This is the real program — not just a demo. If your kids want to try it out, be sure to install the program on your computer's hard disk. Once you open the program, kids can use it free for four weeks. (There's one restriction: They can create only four pages.) You can purchase this copy of *Web Workshop* with a credit card. Just contact Vividus on the Web (`http://www.vividus.com`), or call the company at 888-4-VIVIDUS.

Orly's Draw-A-Story demo

In the Creative Pursuits category
For Windows and Macintosh
From Broderbund (ages 5-9)

Open this demo to experience one of the most engaging software characters we've ever met. Making pictures and telling stories with Orly is great fun for kids from 5-9. See more information about this product and others at Broderbund's Web page. (`http://www.broderbund.com`)

Problems with Orly Draw-A-Story demo in Windows 3.1?

If you can't get the Orly Draw-A-Story demo to run from the CD interface, try this:

1. **With the CD in your CD-ROM drive, choose File⇨Run in Program Manager.**

2. **In the text box, type** `D:\ORLYDEMO\ORLYDEMO.EXE` **(substitute your CD-ROM drive letter if different from D), and then click OK.**

Note: If you have a problem while running the programs from the CD that you can't resolve by using the instructions we give, please call the IDG Books Worldwide Customer Service office at 1-800-762-2974.

Index

• P •

Paint, Write & Play! (ages 4-7), 19, 49–50, 81, 133
  art studio, 49
  science and, 197
  travel agency, 49, 164
  word pictures, 50
  writing tools, 50
painting. *See* art; art software
palindromes, 95
A Passion For Art (all ages), 287
passwords, keeping secret, 22
Paul Cezanne: Portrait of My World (all ages), 287
phonics, 73–76
  activities, 76
  Kid Phonics 2 (ages 6-9), 74
  Kid Phonics (ages 4-7), 74
  Reader Rabbit phonics games, 76
  Reading Blaster Jr. (ages 4-7), 75
  See also reading
Photo CD, 268
photographic software
  Adobe PhotoDeluxe (ages 10 & up), 267–270
  EasyPhoto Reader (all ages), 270–271
photographs, 267–271
  digital camera and, 268
  editing, 269
  family, 268–269
  flat-bed scanners and, 268
  photo scanners and, 268
  publishing, 269–270
  working with on computer, 268
Planetary Taxi (ages 7-12), 205–206
  description, 205
  illustrated, 206
  See also science
Playskool Puzzles (ages 2-5), 19, 122
preschool kids. *See* kids (2-5)
Print Artist (ages 10 & up), 286
printers, 43, 299
printing
  artwork, 285
  Encarta articles, 142
  on-screen pages, 299
  stories, 49, 52

The Print Shop (ages 9 & up), 284–285, 294
  designs, 284–285
  graphics, 285
  illustrated, 284, 285
  printing with, 285
  projects, 284
problem-solving adventures, 43–48
programs. *See* software
publisher contacts, 323–325
publishing
  art, 283–287
  photographs, 269–270
  programs, 283–284
  Web, 260–266
  writing and, 89
purchasing. *See* shopping
Putt-Putt and Pep's Balloon-O-Rama (ages 3-8), 46
Putt-Putt and Pep's Dog on a Stick (ages 3-8), 46
Putt-Putt Goes to the Moon (ages 3-8), 45–46
Putt-Putt Joins the Parade (ages 3-8), 45, 164
Putt-Putt Saves the Zoo (ages 3-8), 44–45

• R •

Reader Rabbit 1 (ages 4-6), 76
Reader Rabbit 2 (ages 6-8), 76
Reader Rabbit *Interactive Reading Journey* series, 71–73
  advantages/disadvantages of, 72
  Volume 1, 72–73
  Volume 2, 73
reading, 59–78
  games, 71
  history, 178
  letters, learning, 69–71
  phonics, 73–76
  reluctance, 78
  skill building, 67–76
  spelling and, 77
  storybooks, 60–67
  tips for, 59–60
  on the Web, 68, 78
Reading Blaster Jr. (ages 4-7), 75
Reading Galaxy (ages 8-12), 77

Introducing
AT&T WorldNet^{SM} Service

A World of Possibilities...

With AT&T WorldNet℠ Service, a world of possibilities awaits you. Discover new ways to stay in touch with the people, ideas, and information that are important to you at home and at work.

Make travel reservations at any time of the day or night. Access the facts you need to make key decisions. Pursue business opportunities on the AT&T Business Network. Explore new investment options. Play games. Research academic subjects. Stay abreast of current events. Participate in online newsgroups. Purchase merchandise from leading retailers. Send e-mail.

All you need are a computer with a mouse, a modem, a phone line, and the software enclosed with this mailing. We've taken care of the rest.

If You Can Point and Click, You're There

Finding the information you want on the Internet with AT&T WorldNet Service is easier than you ever imagined it could be. That's because AT&T WorldNet Service integrates a specially customized version of popular Web browser software with advanced Internet directories and search engines. The result is an Internet service that sets a new standard for ease of use — virtually everywhere you want to go is a point and click away.

We're with You Every Step of the Way,
24 Hours a Day, 7 Days a Week.

Nothing is more important to us than making sure that your Internet experience is a truly enriching and satisfying one. That's why our highly trained customer service representatives are available to answer your questions and offer assistance whenever you need — 24 hours a day, 7 days a week. To reach AT&T WorldNet Customer Care, call **1-800-400-1447**.

Safeguard Your Online Purchases

By registering and continuing to charge your AT&T WorldNet Service to your AT&T Universal Card, you'll enjoy peace of mind whenever you shop the Internet. Should your account number be compromised on the Net, you won't be liable for any online transactions charged to your AT&T Universal Card by a person who is not an authorized user.*

Today cardmembers may be liable for the first $50 of charges made by a person who is not an authorized user, which will not be imposed under this program as long as the cardmember notifies AT&T Universal Card of the loss within 24 hours and otherwise complies with the Cardmember Agreement. Refer to Cardmember Agreement for definition of authorized user.

Minimum System Requirements

To run AT&T WorldNet Service on an IBM-compatible personal computer, you need

- An IBM-compatible personal computer with a 386 processor or better
- Microsoft Windows 3.1*x* or Windows 95
- 8MB RAM (16MB or more recommended)
- 11MB of free hard disk space
- 14.4 Kbps (or faster) modem (28.8 Kbps is recommended)
- A standard phone line

Macintosh useres with 68030 processors or higher, and Non-PCI equipped Power Macs need

- System software version 7.1 or higher (System 7.5 recommended for Power Mac users)
- 8MB of RAM
- 12MB of free hard disk space
- 14.4 Kpbs (or faster) modem (28.8 Kbps is recommended)
- A standard phone line

Users of PCI-equipped Power Macintosh and compatibles, users of PowerBook 5300 models, and users of DOS-compatibility software or Connectix Ram Doubler need

- System 7.5.5 or higher
- Open Transport 1.1 or higher
- 8MB of RAM (16MB recommended for better performance)
- 12MB of free hard disk space
- 14.4 Kbps (or faster) modem (28.8 Kbps is recommended)
- A standard phone line

To upgrade to System 7.5.5, obtain System 7.5 Update 2.0 package and System 7.5.5 Update package, both from Apple Computer. You need to install System 7.5 Update 2.0 before installing System 7.5.5 Update.

System software updates can be obtained from Apple Computer by phone at 1-800-294-6617 (Canada 1-800-361-6075) or via Apple's download FTP site at: ftp://ftp.support.apple.com/pub/apple_sw_updates/US/Macintosh/System.

Installation Tips and Instructions

- If you have other Web browsers or online software, please consider uninstalling them according to vendor's instructions.
- At the end of installation, you may be asked to restart your computer. Don't attempt the registration process until you have done so.
- If you are experiencing modem problems trying to dial out, try different modem selections, such as Hayes Compatible. If you still have problems, please call Customer Care at **1-800-400-1447**.
- If you are installing AT&T WorldNet Service on a computer with Local Area Networking, please contact your LAN administrator for setup instructions.
- Follow the initial start-up instructions given to you by the vendor product you purchased. (See Appendix C of *Great Software For Kids & Parents*.) These instructions will tell you how to start the installation of AT&T WorldNet Service Software.
- Follow the on-screen instructions to install AT&T WorldNet Service Software on your computer.

When you have finished installing the software, you may be prompted to restart your computer. Do so when prompted.

Setting Up Your WorldNet Account

The AT&T WorldNet Service Program group/folder will appear on your Windows desktop or Mac's hard disk.

- Double click on the WorldNet Registration icon. (Mac users, double-click the Account Setup icon.)
- Follow the on-screen instructions and complete all the stages of registration.

After all the stages have been completed, you'll be prompted to dial into the network to complete the registration process. Make sure your modem and phone line are not in use.

Registering with AT&T WorldNet Service

Once you have connected with AT&T WorldNet online registration service, you will be presented with a series of screens that confirm billing information and prompt you for additional account set-up data.

The following is a list of registration tips and comments that will help you during the registration process.

I. Use one of the following registration codes, which can also be found in Appendix C of *Great Software For Kids & Parents*: L5SQIM631 if you are an AT&T long-distance residential customer or L5SQIM632 if you use another long-distance phone company.

II. We advise that you use all lowercase letters when assigning an e-mail ID and security code, since they are easier to remember.

III. Choose a special "security code" that you will use to verify who you are when you call Customer Care.

IV. If you make a mistake and exit the registration process prematurely, all you need to do is click on "Create New Account". Do not click on "Edit Existing Account".

V. When choosing your local access telephone number, you will be given several options. Please choose the one nearest to you. Please note that calling a number within your area does not guarantee that the call is free.

Connecting to AT&T WorldNet Service

When you have finished registering with AT&T WorldNet Service, you are ready to make online connections.

- Make sure your modem and phone line are available.
- Double click on the AT&T WorldNet Service icon.

Follow these steps whenever you wish to connect to AT&T WorldNet Service.

Choose the Plan That's Right for You

If you're an AT&T Long Distance residential customer signing up until March 31, 1997, you can experience this exciting new servic for 5 free hours a month for one full year. Beyond your 5 free hours, you'll be charged only $2.50 for each additional hour. Just us the service for a minimum of one hour per month. If you intend to use AT&T WorldNet Service for more than 5 hours a month, consider choosing the plan with unlimited hours for $19.95 per month.*

If you're not an AT&T Long Distance residential customer, you can still benefit from AT&T quality and reliability by starting with th plan that offers 3 hours each month and a low monthly fee of $4.95. Under this plan, you'll be charged $2.50 for each additional hour, or AT&T WorldNet Service can provide you with unlimited online access for $24.95 per month. It's entirely up to you.

AT&T

Davidson Products Age-Grade Chart

Program	Grade: Pre-K (2)	(3)	(4)	(5)	1 (6)	2 (7)	3 (8)	4 (9)	5 (10)	6 (11)	7 (12)	8 (13)	9 (14)	10 (15)	11 (16)	12 (17)	College (18)	Adult
Fisher-Price Ready for Preschool	█	█																
Sleeping Cub's Test of Courage		█	█	█	█	█	█	█										
Liam Finds a Story		█	█	█	█	█	█	█										
The Princess and the Crab		█	█	█	█	█	█	█										
Baba Yaga and the Magic Geese		█	█	█	█	█	█	█										
Imo and the King		█	█	█	█	█	█	█										
The Little Samurai		█	█	█	█	█	█	█										
Fisher-Price Read & Play Library		█	█															
Fisher-Price Ready for School Kindergarten Edition			█	█	█	█												
Kid Phonics 1			█	█	█	█	█											
Math Blaster Jr.			█	█	█	█	█											
Reading Blaster Jr.			█	█	█	█	█											
Science Blaster Jr.			█	█	█	█	█											
Kid Works 2			█	█	█	█	█	█										
Kid Works Deluxe			█	█	█	█	█	█										
Kid Phonics 2					█	█	█	█										
Reading Blaster 2000					█	█	█	█										
Math Blaster 1 – In Search of Spot					█	█	█	█	█	█	█							
Mega Math Blaster					█	█	█	█	█	█	█							
Spell It Deluxe					█	█	█	█	█	█	█	█	█	█	█	█	█	█
Kid CAD					█	█	█	█	█	█	█	█	█	█	█	█	█	█
Stay Tooned!							█	█	█	█	█	█	█	█	█	█	█	█
Eat My Dust							█	█	█	█	█	█	█	█	█	█	█	█
Math Blaster 2 – Secret of The Lost City							█	█	█	█	█	█	█	█	█	█	█	█
The Cruncher							█	█	█	█	█	█	█	█	█	█	█	█
The Multimedia Workshop							█	█	█	█	█	█	█	█	█	█	█	█
Grammar Games									█	█	█	█	█	█	█	█	█	█
Geometry Blaster									█	█	█	█	█	█	█	█	█	█
Math Blaster Mystery: The Great Brain Robbery									█	█	█	█	█	█	█	█	█	█
Word Blaster									█	█	█	█	█	█	█	█	█	█
Alge-Blaster 3									█	█	█	█	█	█	█	█	█	█
Your Personal Trainer for the SAT												█	█	█	█	█	█	█
Your Personal Trainer for the ACT												█	█	█	█	█	█	█

To receive your $5 rebate, just mail this completed coupon, along with a **photocopy** of your original dated sales receipt and one **completed product registration card**, to:

Davidson's IDG $5 Rebate Offer
P.O. Box 52993, Dept. 9067 • Phoenix, AZ 85072-2993
(Allow 4–6 weeks for processing.)

Please print clearly:

Name _____

Address _____

City _____ State _____ Zip _____

Age _____ Phone _____ Date _____

What was the product purchased? _____

Where was the product purchased? _____

Rebate offer good on products purchased between 1/1/97 and 12/31/97. Multi-product packages count as one product. **Limit one $5 coupon per product**. Requests must be postmarked by January 15, 1998. Not valid with any other promotional or rebate offer. All rebate checks will be remitted in U.S. currency. **Offer good on all Davidson brand titles** as well as Fisher-Price Ready for Preschool, Fisher-Price Ready for School, and Fisher-Price Read & Play Library. **All Simon & Schuster and all other Fisher-Price titles excluded.**

IDG BOOKS WORLDWIDE, INC. END-USER LICENSE AGREEMENT

4. **<u>Restrictions on Use of Individual Programs</u>.** You must follow the individual requirements and restrictions detailed for each individual program in the "About the CD" appendix in this Book. These limitations are contained in the individual license agreements recorded on the disk(s)/CD-ROM. These restrictions may include a requirement that after using the program for the period of time specified in its text, the user must pay a registration fee or discontinue use. By opening the Software packet(s), you will be agreeing to abide by the licenses and restrictions for these individual programs. None of the material on this disk(s)/CD-ROM or listed in this Book may ever be distributed, in original or modified form, for commercial purposes.

5. **<u>Limited Warranty</u>.**

   (a) IDGB warrants that the Software and disk(s)/CD-ROM are free from defects in materials and workmanship under normal use for a period of sixty (60) days from the date of purchase of this Book. If IDGB receives notification within the warranty period of defects in materials or workmanship, IDGB will replace the defective disk(s)/CD-ROM.

   (b) IDGB AND THE AUTHORS OF THE BOOK DISCLAIM ALL OTHER WARRANTIES, EXPRESS OR IMPLIED, INCLUDING WITHOUT LIMITATION IMPLIED WARRANTIES OF MERCHANT- ABILITY AND FITNESS FOR A PARTICULAR PURPOSE, WITH RESPECT TO THE SOFTWARE, THE PROGRAMS, THE SOURCE CODE CONTAINED THEREIN, AND/OR THE TECHNIQUES DESCRIBED IN THIS BOOK. IDGB DOES NOT WARRANT THAT THE FUNCTIONS CONTAINED IN THE SOFTWARE WILL MEET YOUR REQUIREMENTS OR THAT THE OPERATION OF THE SOFTWARE WILL BE ERROR FREE.

   (c) This limited warranty gives you specific legal rights, and you may have other rights which vary from jurisdiction to jurisdiction.

6. **<u>Remedies</u>.**

   (a) IDGB's entire liability and your exclusive remedy for defects in materials and workmanship shall be limited to replacement of the Software, which may be returned to IDGB with a copy of your receipt at the following address: Disk Fulfillment Department, Attn: *Great Software For Kids & Parents,* IDG Books Worldwide, Inc., 7260 Shadeland Station, Ste. 100, Indianapolis, IN 46256, or call 1-800-762-2974. Please allow 3–4 weeks for delivery. This Limited Warranty is void if failure of the Software has resulted from accident, abuse, or misapplication. Any replacement Software will be warranted for the remainder of the original warranty period or thirty (30) days, whichever is longer.

(b) In no event shall IDGB or the author be liable for any damages whatsoever (including without limitation damages for loss of business profits, business interruption, loss of business information, or any other pecuniary loss) arising from the use of or inability to use the Book or the Software, even if IDGB has been advised of the possibility of such damages.

(c) Because some jurisdictions do not allow the exclusion or limitation of liability for consequential or incidental damages, the above limitation or exclusion may not apply to you.

7. **U.S. Government Restricted Rights.** Use, duplication, or disclosure of the Software by the U.S. Government is subject to restrictions stated in paragraph (c) (1) (ii) of the Rights in Technical Data and Computer Software clause of DFARS 252.227-7013, and in subparagraphs (a) through (d) of the Commercial Computer—Restricted Rights clause at FAR 52.227-19, and in similar clauses in the NASA FAR supplement, when applicable.

8. **General.** This Agreement constitutes the entire understanding of the parties and revokes and supersedes all prior agreements, oral or written, between them and may not be modified or amended except in a writing signed by both parties hereto which specifically refers to this Agreement. This Agreement shall take precedence over any other documents that may be in conflict herewith. If any one or more provisions contained in this Agreement are held by any court or tribunal to be invalid, illegal, or otherwise unenforceable, each and every other provision shall remain in full force and effect.

Installation Instructions

For Windows 95

1. **Insert the CD in your computer's CD-ROM drive.**

2. **Wait a minute or two to see if the CD starts up automatically.**

   If so, the first thing you see is the IDG license agreement. To use the CD, you need to Accept the terms of this agreement.

   If you then see a picture of a happy Dummies family, the interface is up and running, and you can begin using the software on the CD.

   If nothing appears after a minute or two, you need to move on to the next step.

3. **Click the Start button, and choose <u>R</u>un.**

4. **In the Run dialog box, type** `D:\INSTALL.EXE`.

   Substitute your actual CD-ROM drive letter if it is something other than D.

5. **Click OK.**

   The *Great Software For Kids & Parents* icon is installed in a program group named IDG Books Worldwide, which is located in the Start menu. To run the CD, click Start and choose <u>P</u>rograms⇨IDG Books Worldwide⇨Great Software For Kids & Parents.

   Note: For installation instructions for Windows 3.1 and Macintosh users, please see Appendix C of this book.

(Re)Starting the CD in Windows

Windows 3.1 users can start the CD interface by opening the IDG Books Worldwide program group and double-clicking the *Great Software For Kids & Parents* icon.

Windows 95 users without the IDG Books Worldwide group in their Start⇨<u>P</u>rograms menu can double-click the My Computer icon, and then double-click the CD-ROM icon to restart the interface.

Windows 95 users who have the IDG Books Worldwide group in their Start⇨<u>P</u>rograms menu can open that group and select the *Great Software For Kids & Parents* icon to run the interface.

IDG BOOKS WORLDWIDE REGISTRATION CARD

RETURN THIS REGISTRATION CARD FOR FREE CATALOG

Title of this book: Great Software For Kids & Parents™

My overall rating of this book: ❑ Very good [1]   ❑ Good [2]   ❑ Satisfactory [3]   ❑ Fair [4]   ❑ Poor [5]

How I first heard about this book:

❑ Found in bookstore; name: [6]   ❑ Book review: [7]

❑ Advertisement: [8]   ❑ Catalog: [9]

❑ Word of mouth; heard about book from friend, co-worker, etc.: [10]   ❑ Other: [11]

What I liked most about this book:

What I would change, add, delete, etc., in future editions of this book:

Other comments:

Number of computer books I purchase in a year: ❑ I [12]   ❑ 2-5 [13]   ❑ 6-10 [14]   ❑ More than 10 [15]

I would characterize my computer skills as: ❑ Beginner [16] ❑ Intermediate [17] ❑ Advanced [18] ❑ Professional [19]

I use ❑ DOS [20]   ❑ Windows [21]   ❑ OS/2 [22]   ❑ Unix [23]   ❑ Macintosh [24]   ❑ Other: [25]_____
                                                                                                    (please specify)

I would be interested in new books on the following subjects:
(please check all that apply, and use the spaces provided to identify specific software)

❑ Word processing: [26]   ❑ Spreadsheets: [27]

❑ Data bases: [28]   ❑ Desktop publishing: [29]

❑ File Utilities: [30]   ❑ Money management: [31]

❑ Networking: [32]   ❑ Programming languages: [33]

❑ Other: [34]

I use a PC at (please check all that apply): ❑ home [35]   ❑ work [36]   ❑ school [37]   ❑ other: [38] _____

The disks I prefer to use are ❑ 5.25 [39]   ❑ 3.5 [40]   ❑ other: [41]_____

I have a CD ROM: ❑ yes [42]   ❑ no [43]

I plan to buy or upgrade computer hardware this year: ❑ yes [44]   ❑ no [45]

I plan to buy or upgrade computer software this year: ❑ yes [46]   ❑ no [47]

Name: _____ Business title: [48] _____ Type of Business: [49] _____

Address (❑ home [50] ❑ work [51]/Company name: _____)

Street/Suite# _____

City [52]/State [53]/Zipcode [54]: _____ Country [55] _____

❑ **I liked this book!** You may quote me by name in future
IDG Books Worldwide promotional materials.

My daytime phone number is _____

IDG BOOKS

THE WORLD OF
COMPUTER
KNOWLEDGE

❏ YES!

Please keep me informed about IDG's World of Computer Knowledge.
Send me the latest IDG Books catalog.